SIMON SPURRIER × MATÍAS BERGARA

CODA™

VOLUME TWO

BOOM!™
STUDIOS

CODA Volume Two, June 2019.
Published by BOOM! Studios, a division of
Boom Entertainment, Inc. Coda is ™ &
© 2019 Simon Spurrier, Ltd. & Matías
Bergara. Originally published in single
magazine form as CODA No. 5-8. ™ &
© 2018 Simon Spurrier, Ltd. & Matías Bergara. All rights reserved. BOOM!
Studios™ and the BOOM! Studios logo are trademarks of Boom Entertainment,
Inc., registered in various countries and categories. All characters, events, and
institutions depicted herein are fictional. Any similarity between any of the
names, characters, persons, events, and/or institutions in this publication to
actual names, characters, persons, events, and/or institutions, whether living or dead, events, and/
or institutions is unintended and purely coincidental. BOOM! Studios does not
read or accept unsolicited submissions of ideas, stories, or artwork.

BOOM! Studios, 5670 Wilshire Boulevard, Suite 400, Los Angeles, CA 90036-
5679. Printed in China. First Printing.

ISBN: 978-1-68415-369-5, eISBN: 978-1-64144-352-4

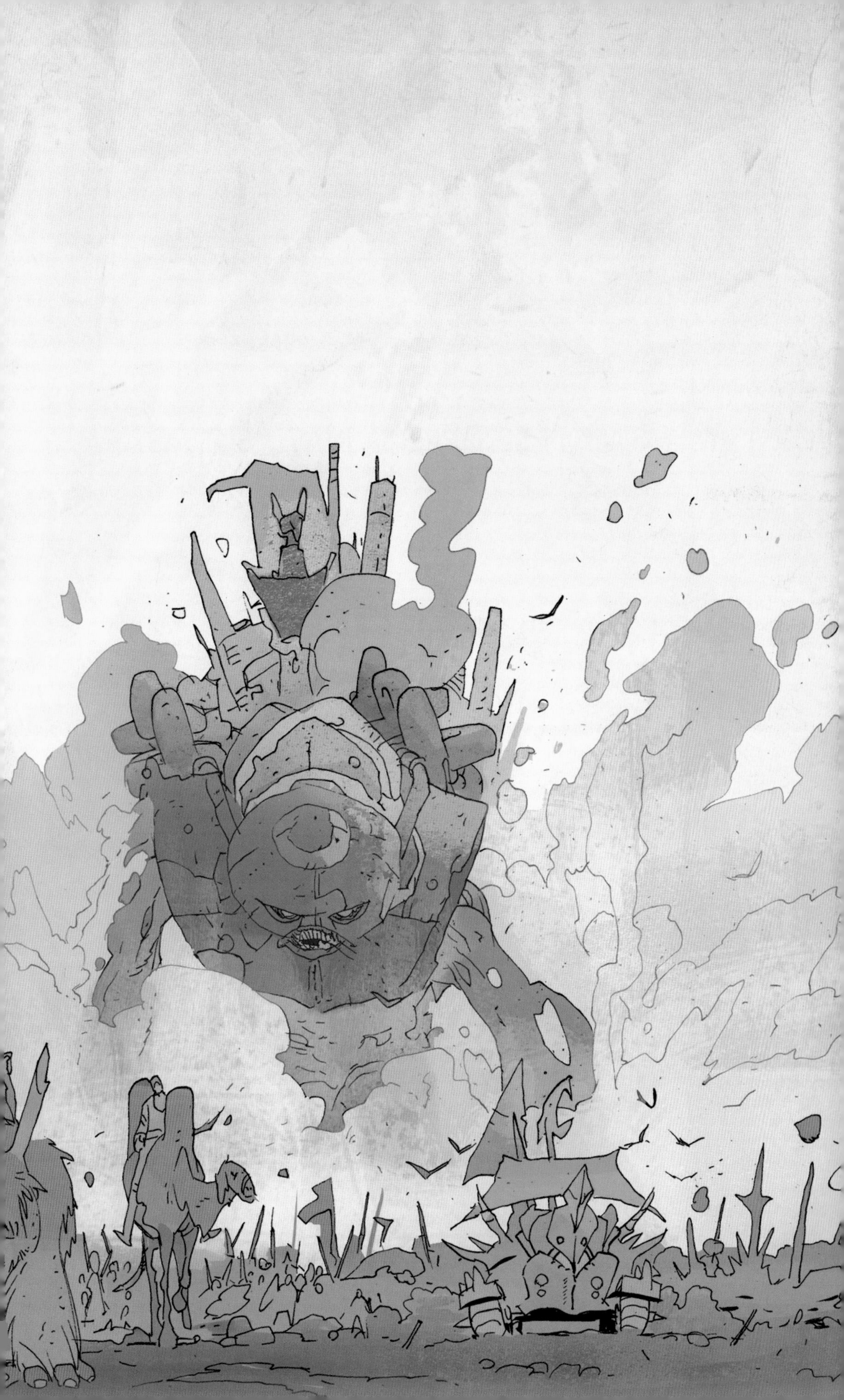

CODA™

CREATED BY **SIMON SPURRIER & MATÍAS BERGARA**

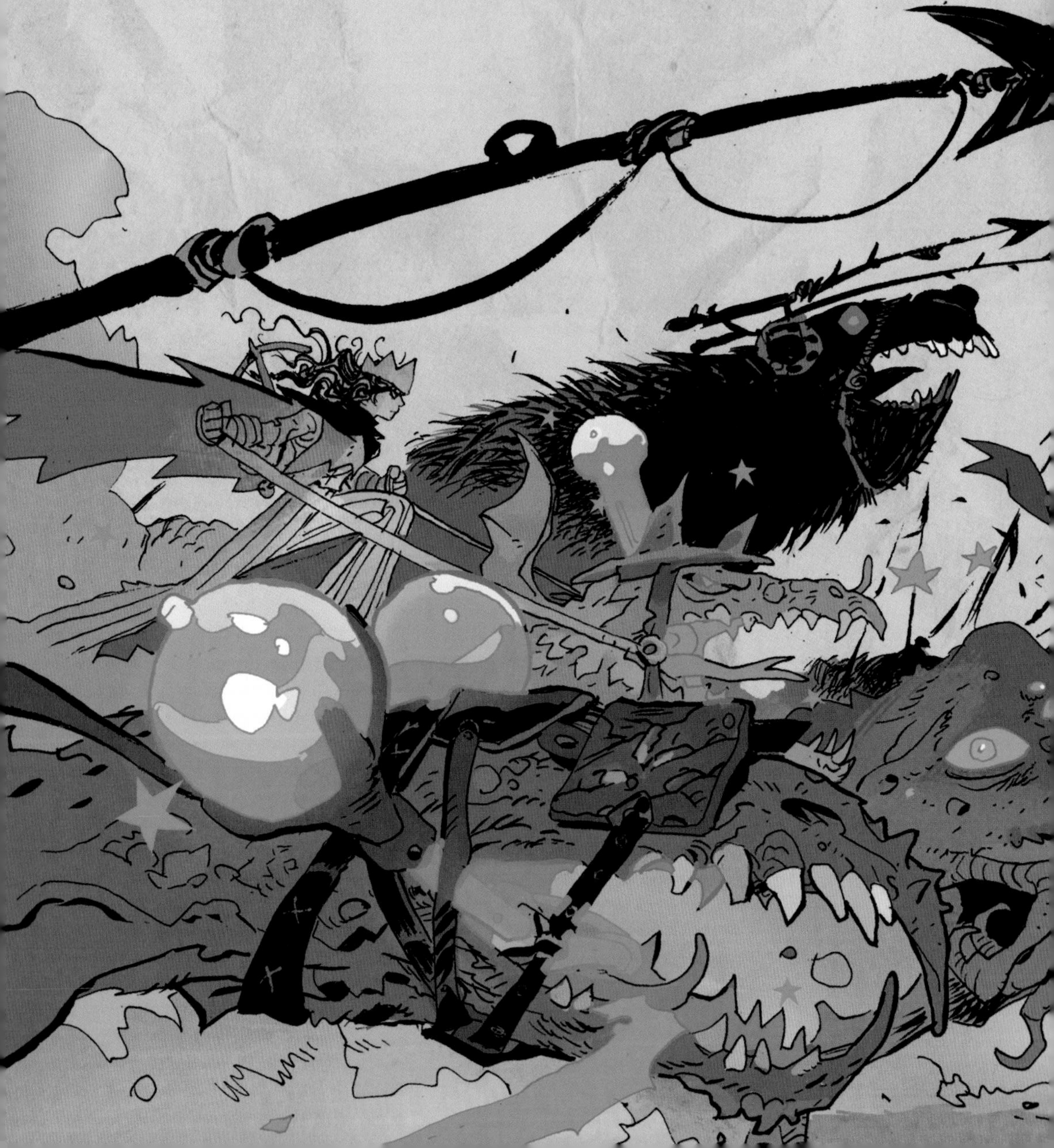

WRITTEN BY **SIMON SPURRIER**
ILLUSTRATED BY **MATÍAS BERGARA**
WITH COLOR ASSISTS BY **MICHAEL DOIG**
LETTERED BY **JIM CAMPBELL**

COVER BY **MATÍAS BERGARA**

SERIES DESIGNER **MARIE KRUPINA**
COLLECTION DESIGNER **CHELSEA ROBERTS**
ASSISTANT EDITOR **GAVIN GRONENTHAL**
EDITOR **ERIC HARBURN**

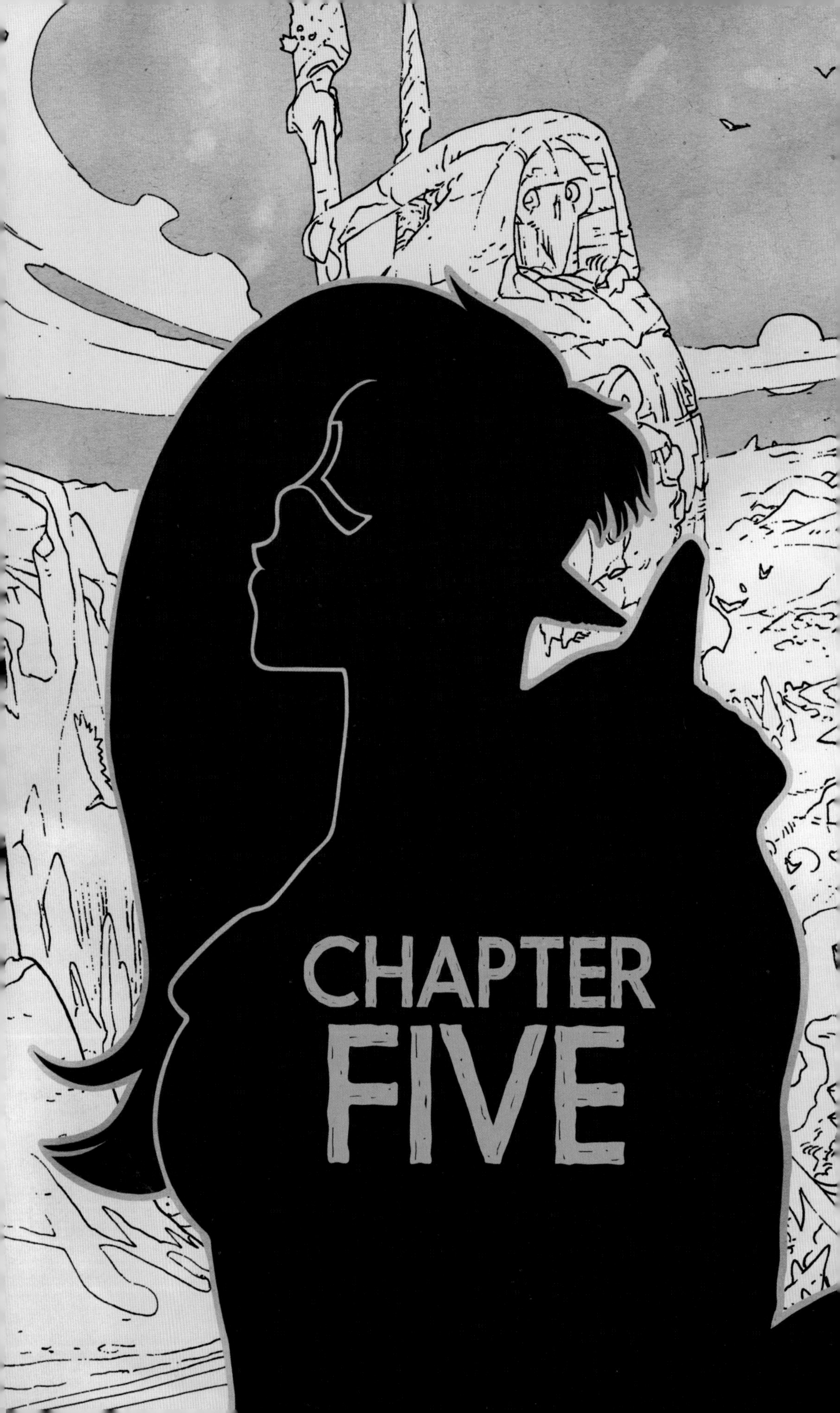
CHAPTER
FIVE

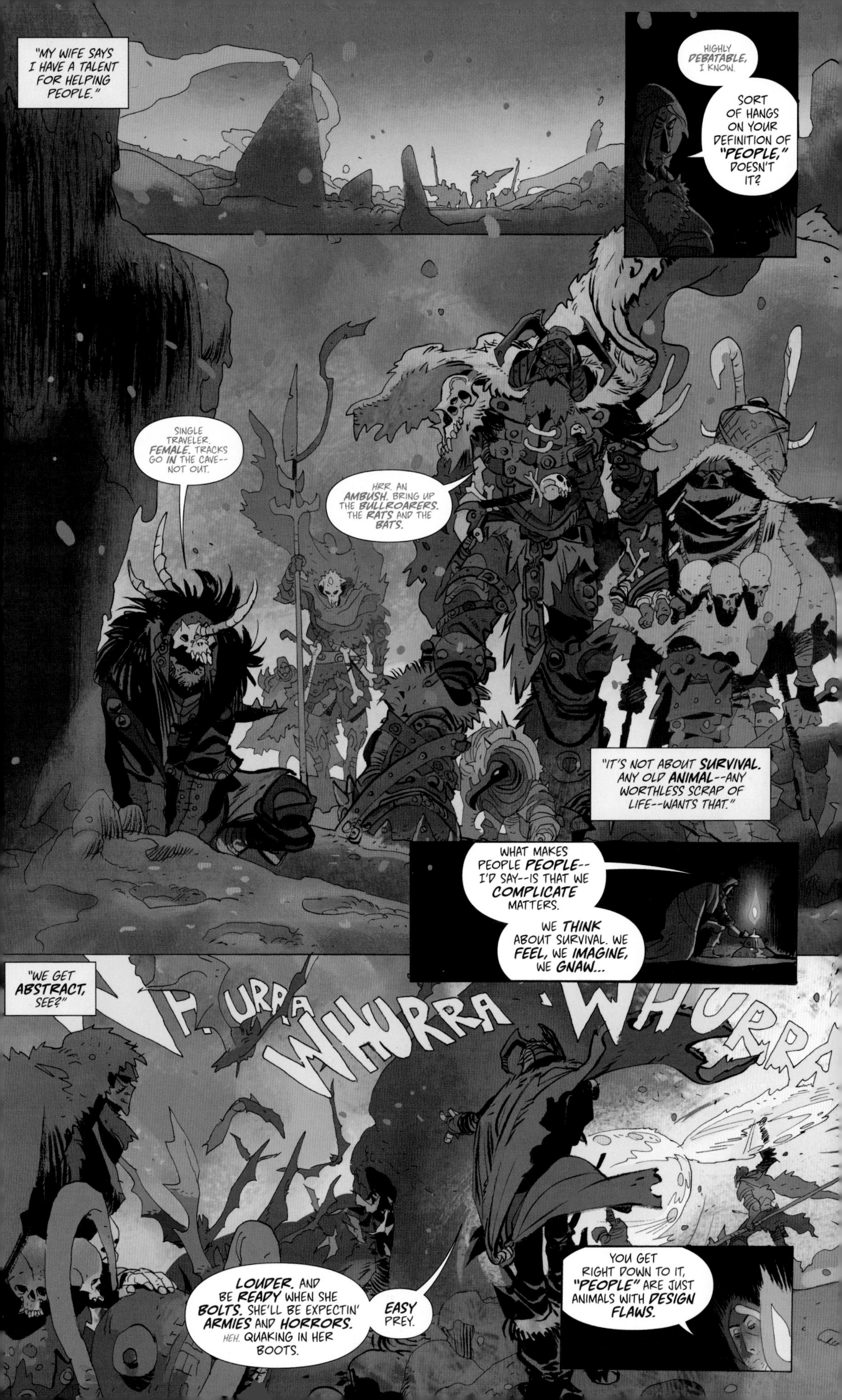
"MY WIFE SAYS I HAVE A TALENT FOR HELPING PEOPLE."
HIGHLY DEBATABLE, I KNOW.
SORT OF HANGS ON YOUR DEFINITION OF "PEOPLE," DOESN'T IT?
SINGLE TRAVELER. FEMALE. TRACKS GO IN THE CAVE--NOT OUT.
HRR. AN AMBUSH. BRING UP THE BULLROARERS. THE RATS AND THE BATS.
"IT'S NOT ABOUT SURVIVAL. ANY OLD ANIMAL--ANY WORTHLESS SCRAP OF LIFE--WANTS THAT."
WHAT MAKES PEOPLE PEOPLE--I'D SAY--IS THAT WE COMPLICATE MATTERS.
WE THINK ABOUT SURVIVAL. WE FEEL, WE IMAGINE, WE GNAW...
"WE GET ABSTRACT, SEE?"
WHURRA WHURRA
LOUDER. AND BE READY WHEN SHE BOLTS. SHE'LL BE EXPECTIN' ARMIES AND HORRORS. HEH. QUAKING IN HER BOOTS.
EASY PREY.
YOU GET RIGHT DOWN TO IT, "PEOPLE" ARE JUST ANIMALS WITH DESIGN FLAWS.

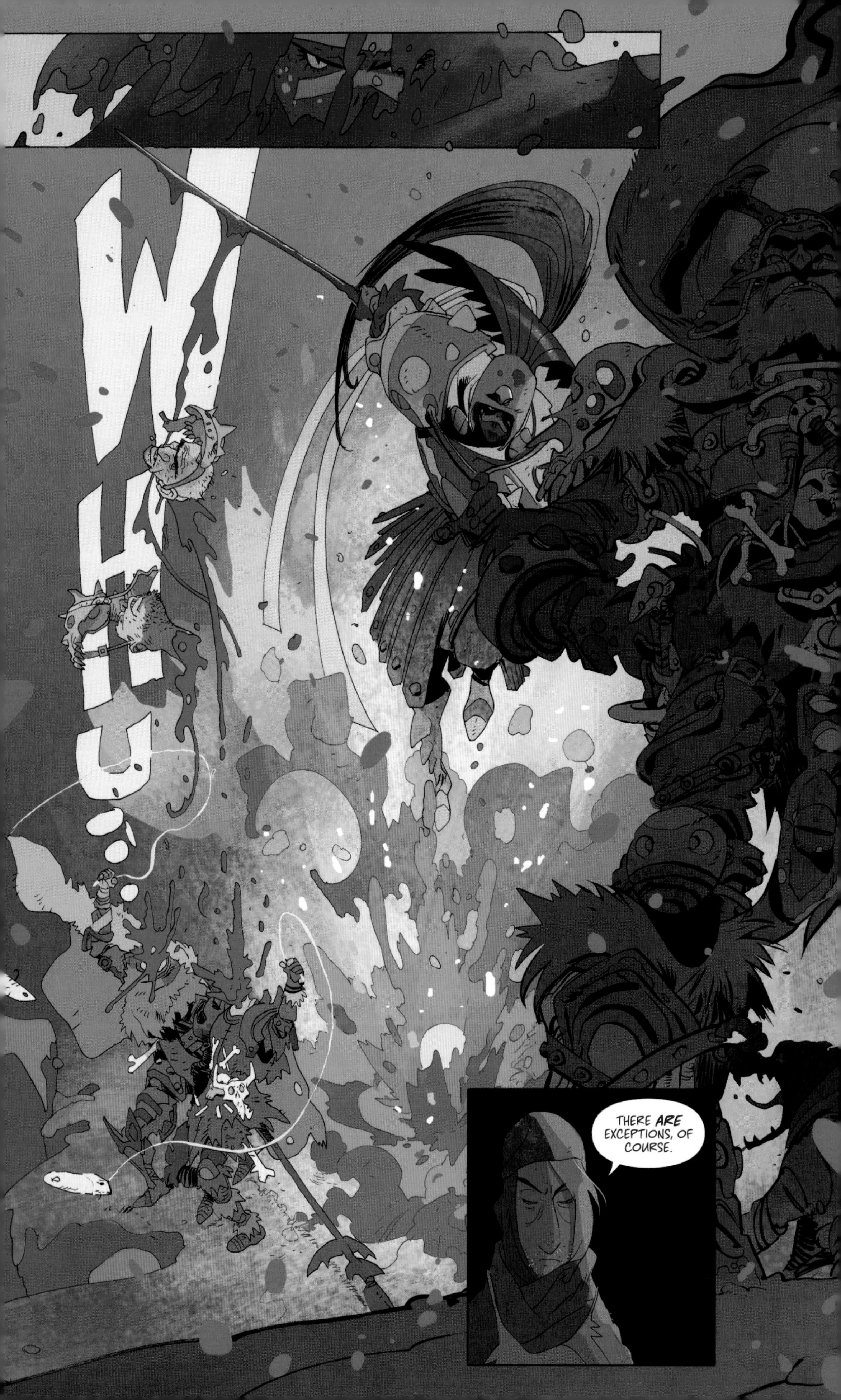
THERE ARE EXCEPTIONS, OF COURSE.

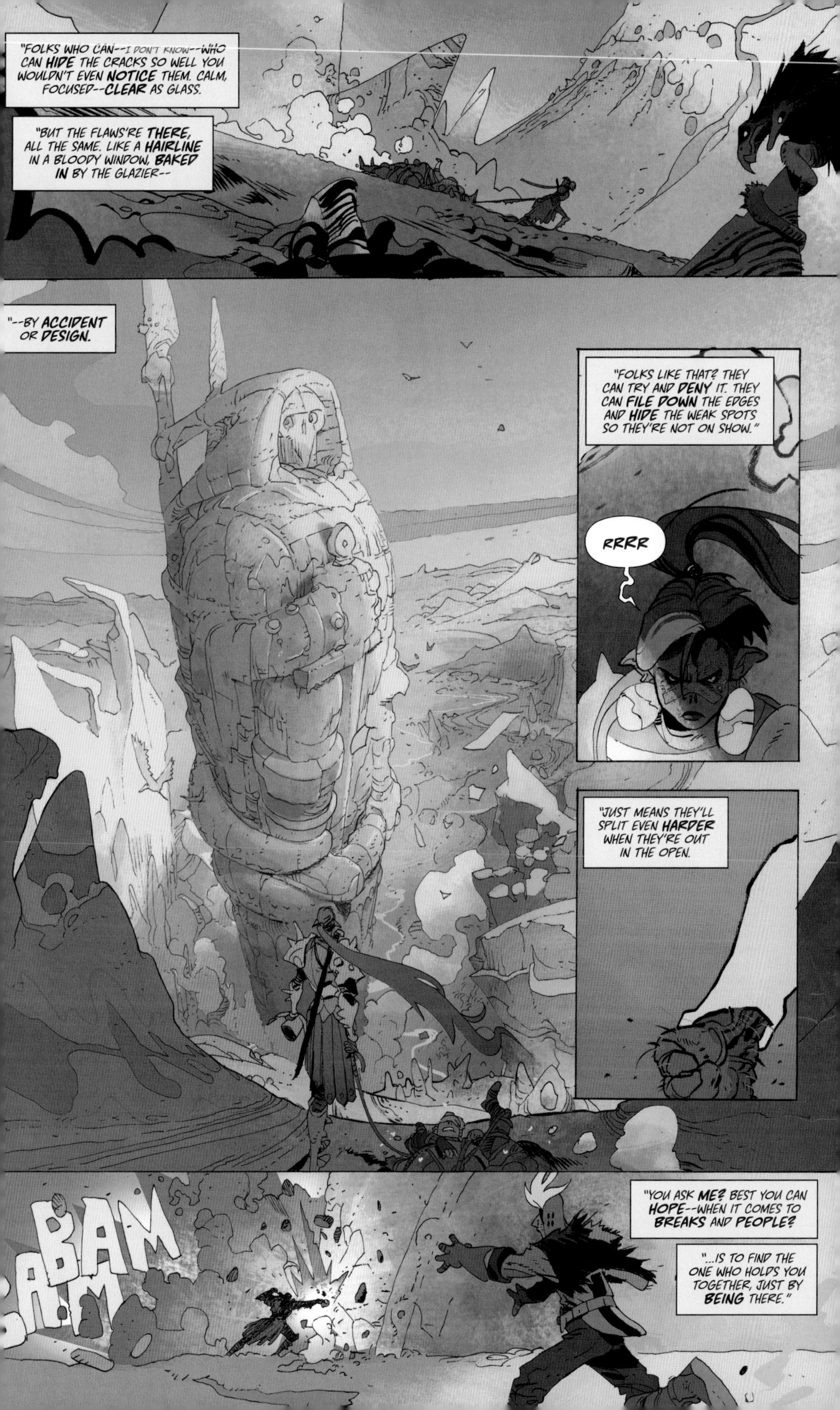
"FOLKS WHO CAN--I DON'T KNOW--WHO CAN HIDE THE CRACKS SO WELL YOU WOULDN'T EVEN NOTICE THEM. CALM, FOCUSED--CLEAR AS GLASS.
"BUT THE FLAWS'RE THERE, ALL THE SAME. LIKE A HAIRLINE IN A BLOODY WINDOW, BAKED IN BY THE GLAZIER--
"--BY ACCIDENT OR DESIGN.
"FOLKS LIKE THAT? THEY CAN TRY AND DENY IT. THEY CAN FILE DOWN THE EDGES AND HIDE THE WEAK SPOTS SO THEY'RE NOT ON SHOW."
RRRR
"JUST MEANS THEY'LL SPLIT EVEN HARDER WHEN THEY'RE OUT IN THE OPEN.
BAM
"YOU ASK ME? BEST YOU CAN HOPE--WHEN IT COMES TO BREAKS AND PEOPLE?
"...IS TO FIND THE ONE WHO HOLDS YOU TOGETHER, JUST BY BEING THERE."

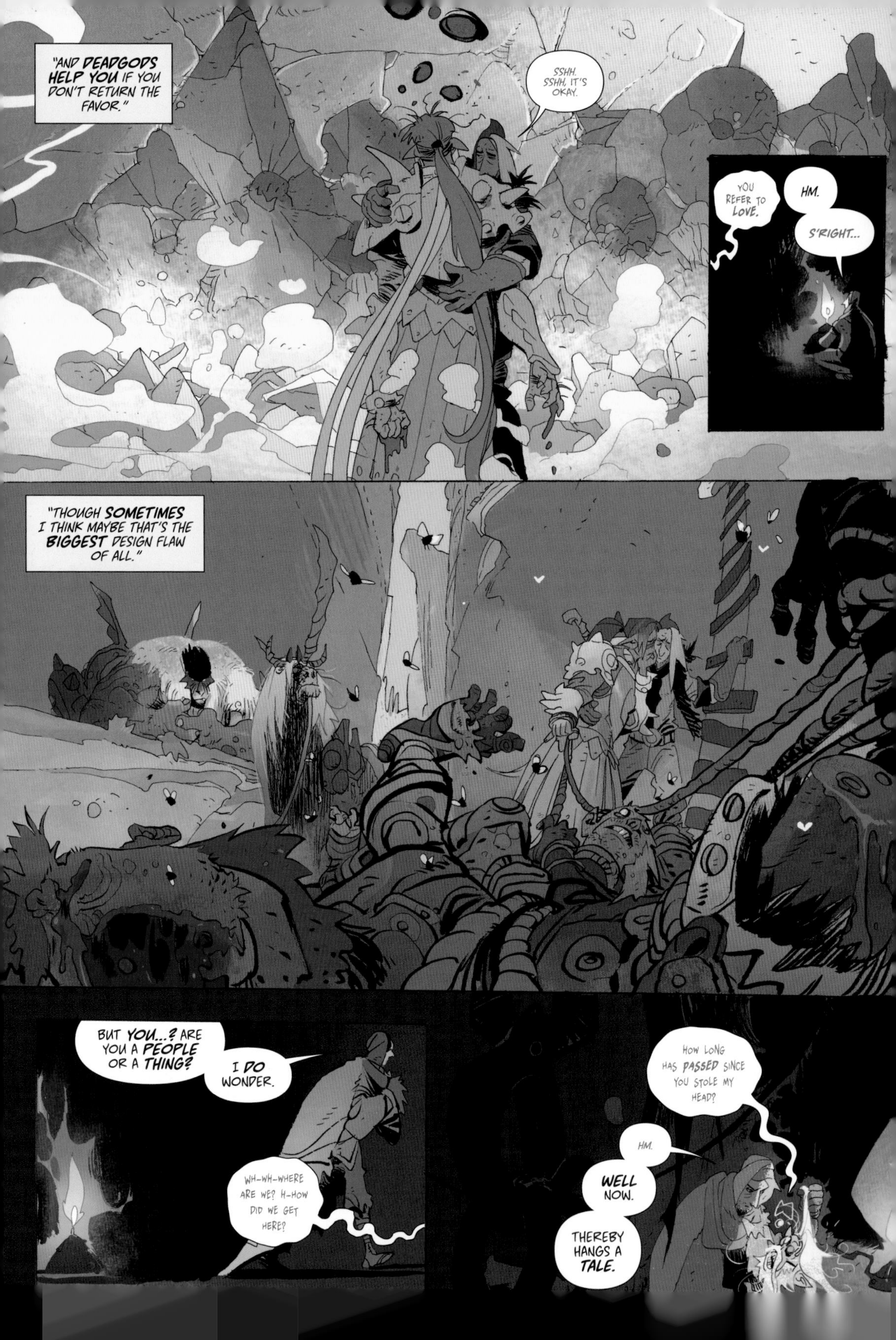
"AND DEADGODS HELP YOU IF YOU DON'T RETURN THE FAVOR."
SSHH. SSHH, IT'S OKAY.
YOU REFER TO LOVE.
HM.
S'RIGHT...
"THOUGH SOMETIMES I THINK MAYBE THAT'S THE BIGGEST DESIGN FLAW OF ALL."
BUT YOU...? ARE YOU A PEOPLE OR A THING?
I DO WONDER.
WH-WH-WHERE ARE WE? H-HOW DID WE GET HERE?
HOW LONG HAS PASSED SINCE YOU STOLE MY HEAD?
HM.
WELL NOW.
THEREBY HANGS A TALE.

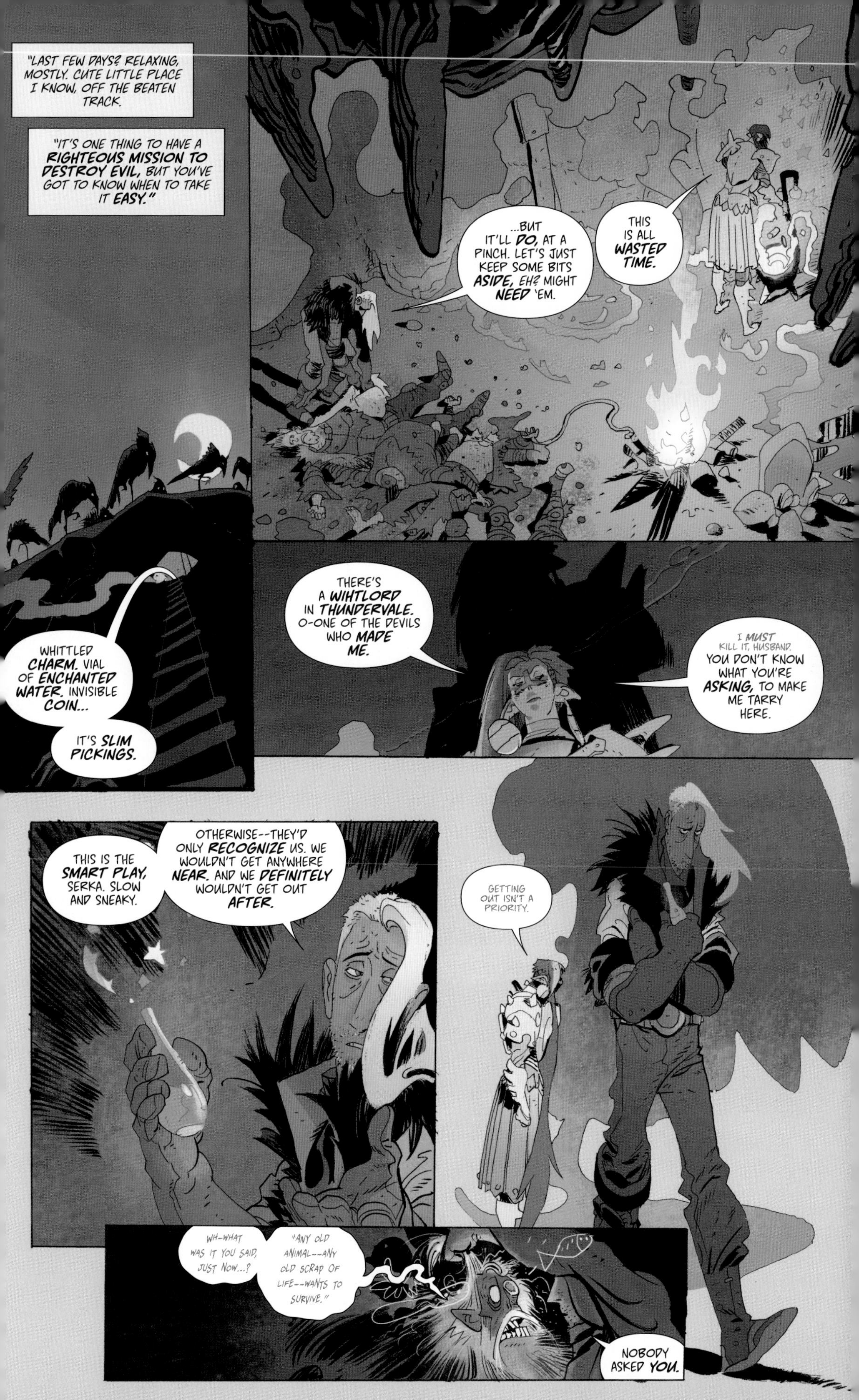
"LAST FEW DAYS? RELAXING, MOSTLY. CUTE LITTLE PLACE I KNOW, OFF THE BEATEN TRACK.
"IT'S ONE THING TO HAVE A RIGHTEOUS MISSION TO DESTROY EVIL, BUT YOU'VE GOT TO KNOW WHEN TO TAKE IT EASY."
THIS IS ALL WASTED TIME.
...BUT IT'LL DO, AT A PINCH. LET'S JUST KEEP SOME BITS ASIDE, EH? MIGHT NEED 'EM.
WHITTLED CHARM. VIAL OF ENCHANTED WATER. INVISIBLE COIN...
IT'S SLIM PICKINGS.
THERE'S A WIHTLORD IN THUNDERVALE. O-ONE OF THE DEVILS WHO MADE ME.
I MUST KILL IT, HUSBAND. YOU DON'T KNOW WHAT YOU'RE ASKING, TO MAKE ME TARRY HERE.
THIS IS THE SMART PLAY, SERKA. SLOW AND SNEAKY.
OTHERWISE--THEY'D ONLY RECOGNIZE US. WE WOULDN'T GET ANYWHERE NEAR. AND WE DEFINITELY WOULDN'T GET OUT AFTER.
GETTING OUT ISN'T A PRIORITY.
WH-WHAT WAS IT YOU SAID, JUST NOW...?
"ANY OLD ANIMAL--ANY OLD SCRAP OF LIFE--WANTS TO SURVIVE."
NOBODY ASKED YOU.

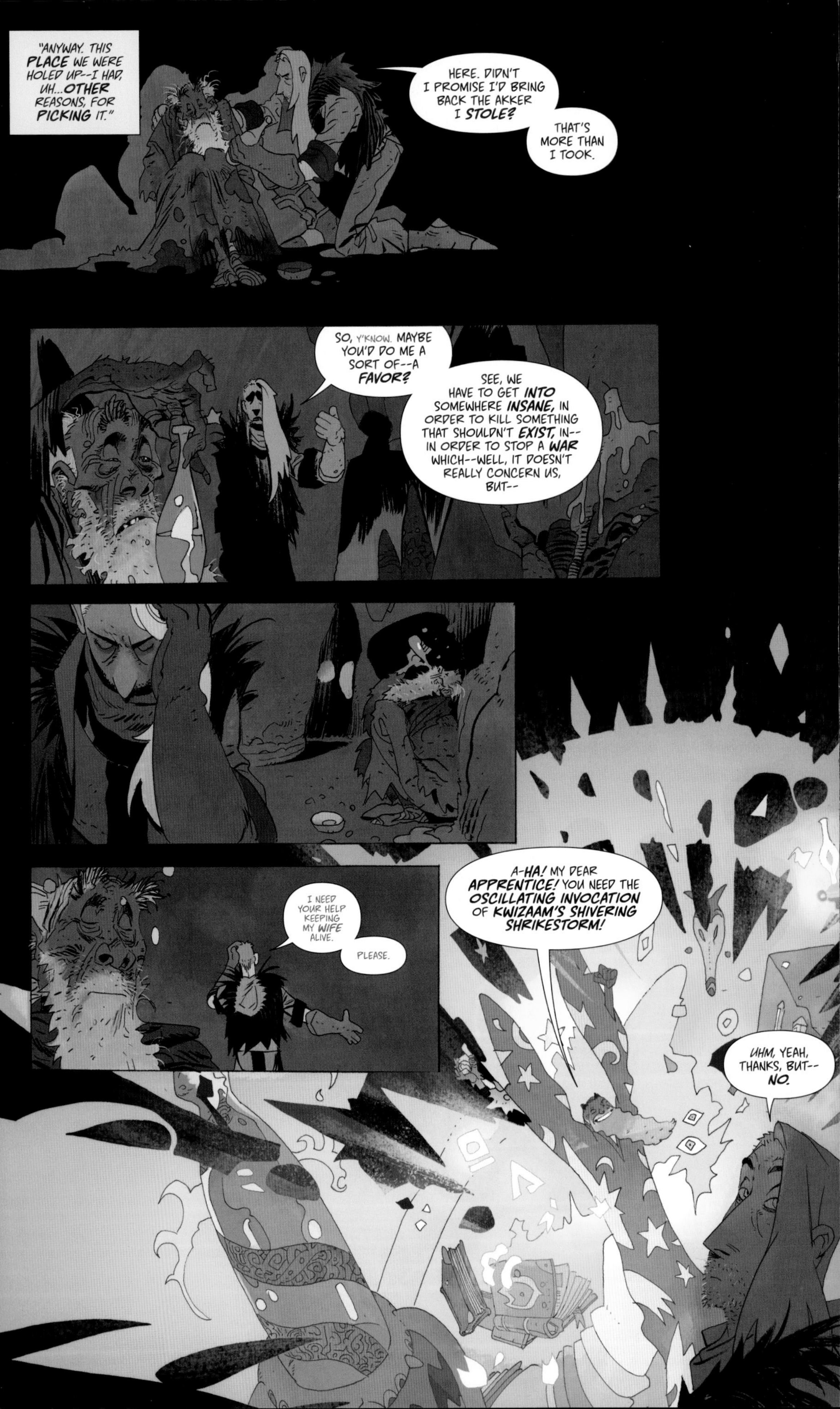
"ANYWAY. THIS PLACE WE WERE HOLED UP--I HAD, UH...OTHER REASONS, FOR PICKING IT."
HERE. DIDN'T I PROMISE I'D BRING BACK THE AKKER I STOLE?
THAT'S MORE THAN I TOOK.
SO, Y'KNOW. MAYBE YOU'D DO ME A SORT OF--A FAVOR?
SEE, WE HAVE TO GET INTO SOMEWHERE INSANE, IN ORDER TO KILL SOMETHING THAT SHOULDN'T EXIST, IN--IN ORDER TO STOP A WAR WHICH--WELL, IT DOESN'T REALLY CONCERN US, BUT--
I NEED YOUR HELP KEEPING MY WIFE ALIVE.
PLEASE.
A-HA! MY DEAR APPRENTICE! YOU NEED THE OSCILLATING INVOCATION OF KWIZAAM'S SHIVERING SHRIKESTORM!
UHM, YEAH, THANKS, BUT--NO.

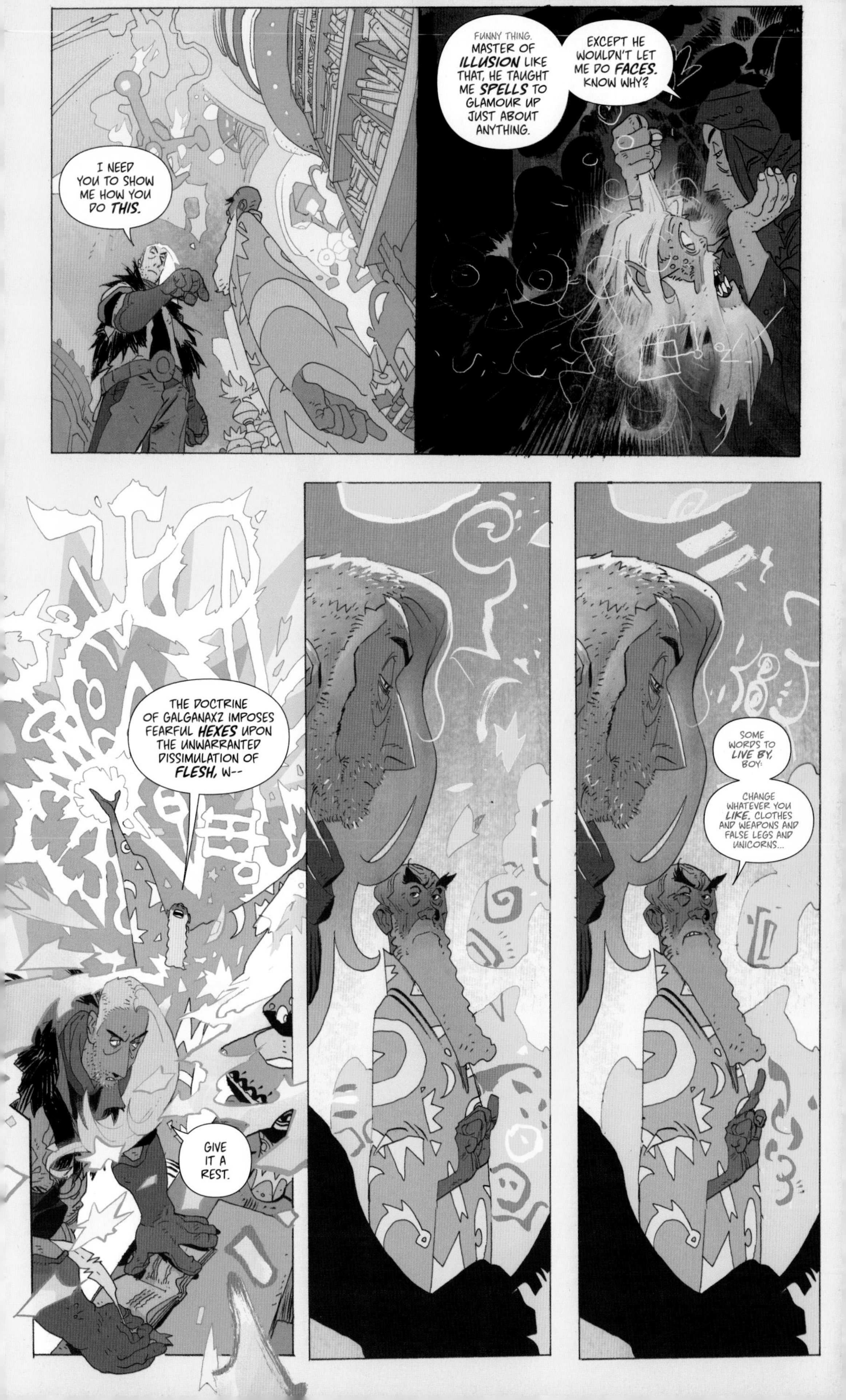
I NEED YOU TO SHOW ME HOW YOU DO THIS.
FUNNY THING. MASTER OF ILLUSION LIKE THAT, HE TAUGHT ME SPELLS TO GLAMOUR UP JUST ABOUT ANYTHING.
EXCEPT HE WOULDN'T LET ME DO FACES. KNOW WHY?
THE DOCTRINE OF GALGANAXZ IMPOSES FEARFUL HEXES UPON THE UNWARRANTED DISSIMULATION OF FLESH, W--
GIVE IT A REST.
SOME WORDS TO LIVE BY, BOY:
CHANGE WHATEVER YOU LIKE. CLOTHES AND WEAPONS AND FALSE LEGS AND UNICORNS...

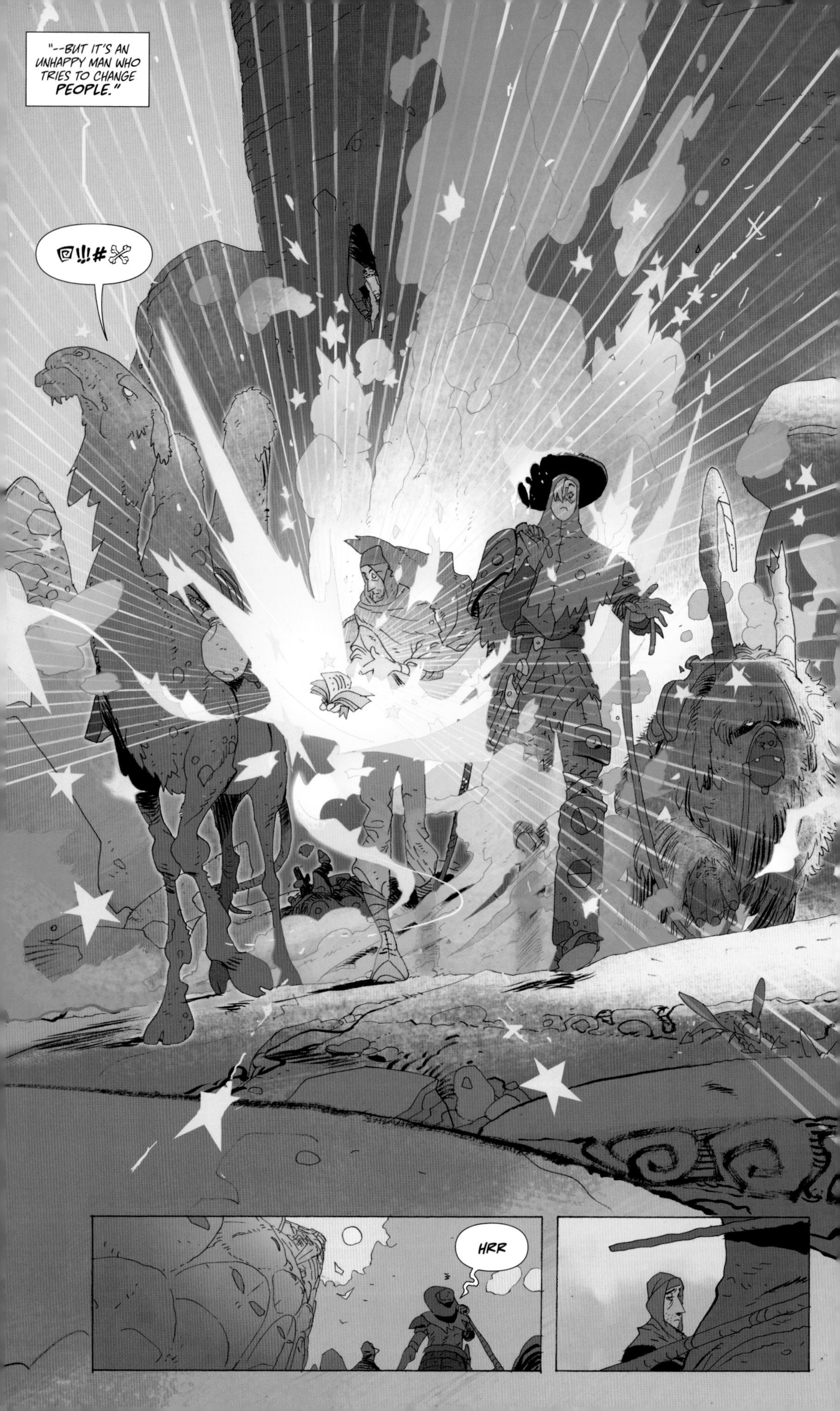
"--BUT IT'S AN UNHAPPY MAN WHO TRIES TO CHANGE PEOPLE."
HRR

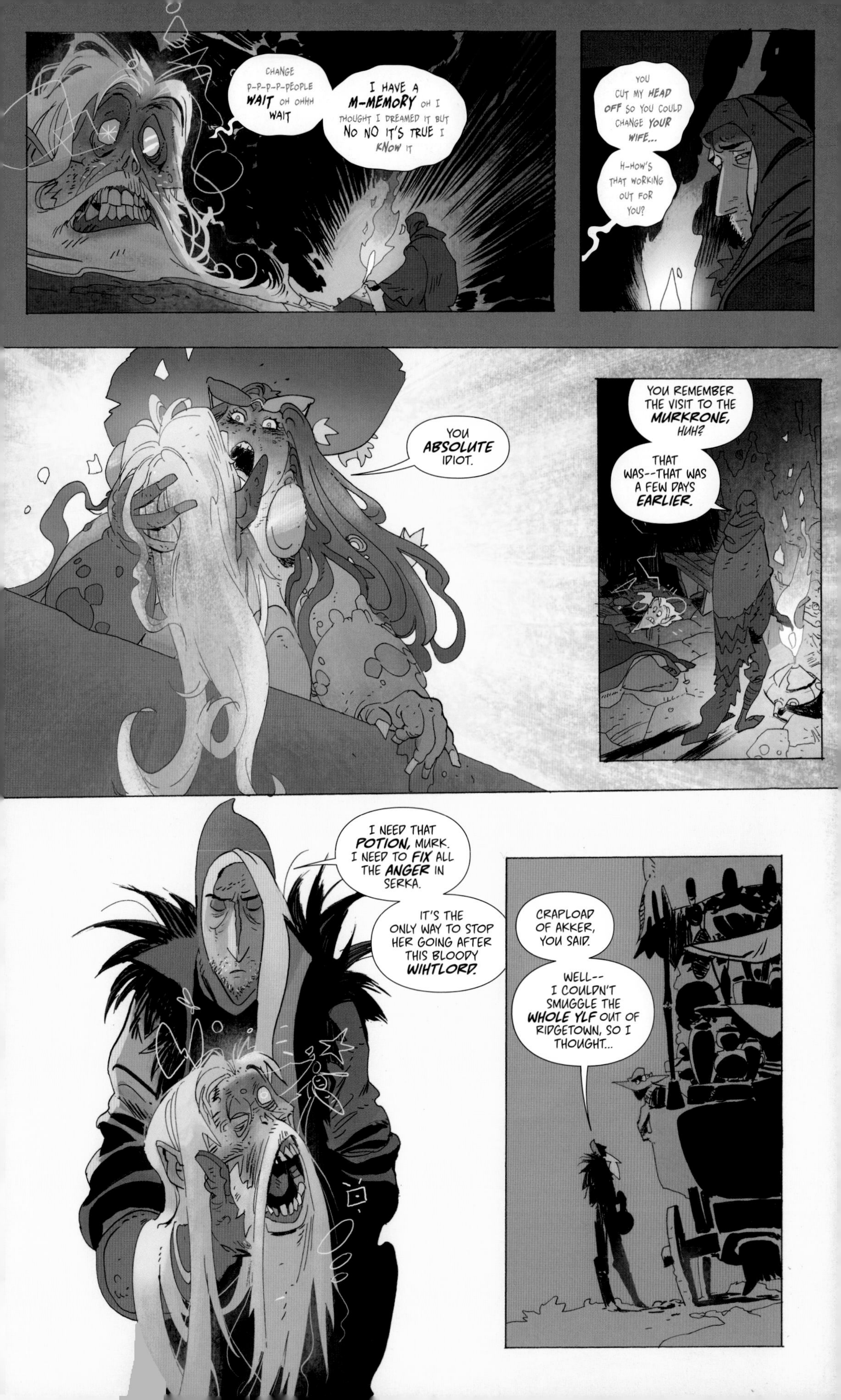
CHANGE P-P-P-P-PEOPLE WAIT OH OHHH WAIT
I HAVE A M-MEMORY OH I THOUGHT I DREAMED IT BUT NO NO IT'S TRUE I KNOW IT
YOU CUT MY HEAD OFF SO YOU COULD CHANGE YOUR WIFE...
H-HOW'S THAT WORKING OUT FOR YOU?
YOU ABSOLUTE IDIOT.
YOU REMEMBER THE VISIT TO THE MURKRONE, HUH?
THAT WAS--THAT WAS A FEW DAYS EARLIER.
I NEED THAT POTION, MURK. I NEED TO FIX ALL THE ANGER IN SERKA.
IT'S THE ONLY WAY TO STOP HER GOING AFTER THIS BLOODY WIHTLORD.
CRAPLOAD OF AKKER, YOU SAID.
WELL-- I COULDN'T SMUGGLE THE WHOLE YLF OUT OF RIDGETOWN, SO I THOUGHT...

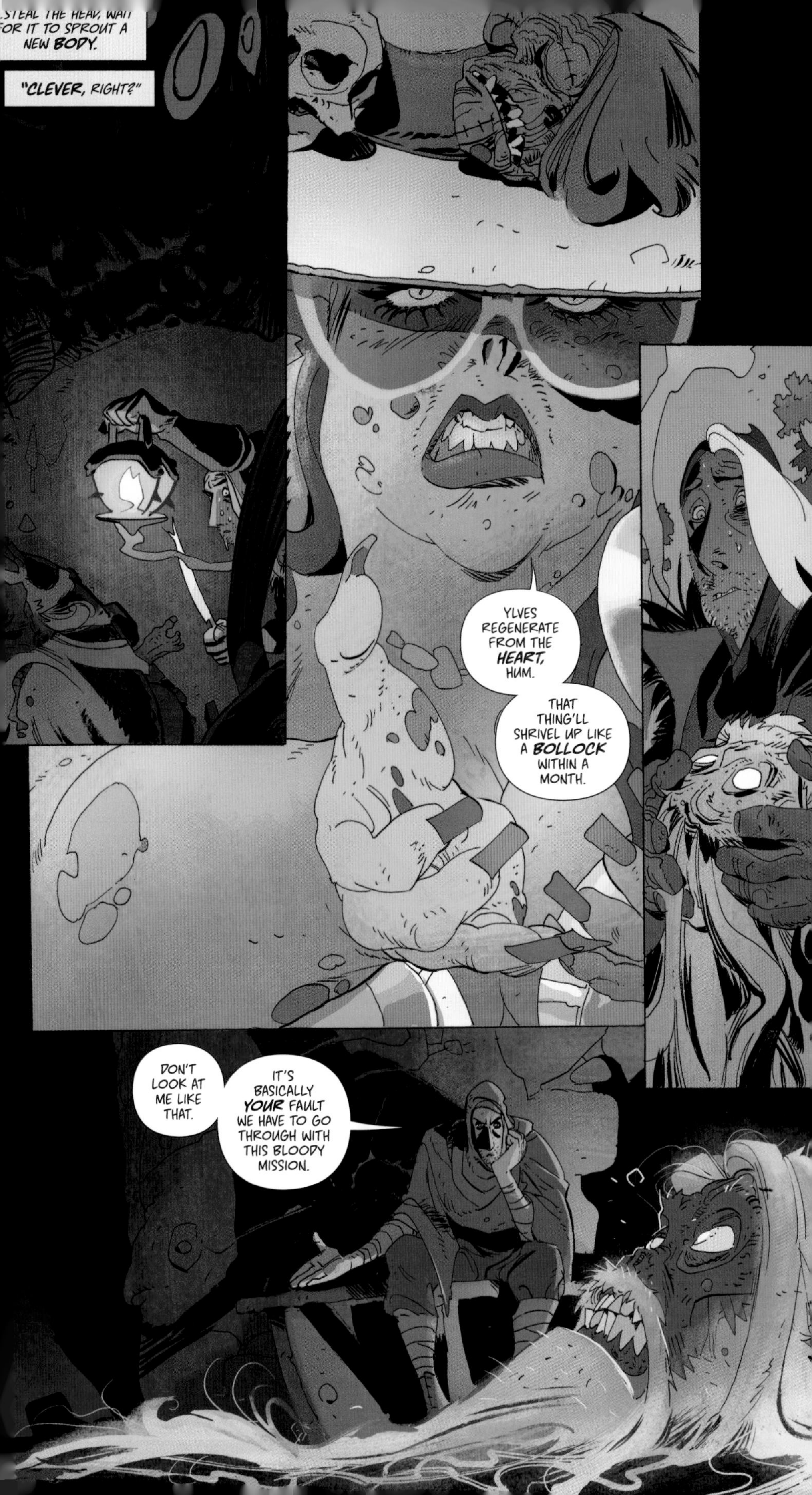

...STEAL THE HEAD, WAIT FOR IT TO SPROUT A NEW BODY.
"CLEVER, RIGHT?"
YLVES REGENERATE FROM THE HEART, HUM.
THAT THING'LL SHRIVEL UP LIKE A BOLLOCK WITHIN A MONTH.
DON'T LOOK AT ME LIKE THAT.
IT'S BASICALLY YOUR FAULT WE HAVE TO GO THROUGH WITH THIS BLOODY MISSION.

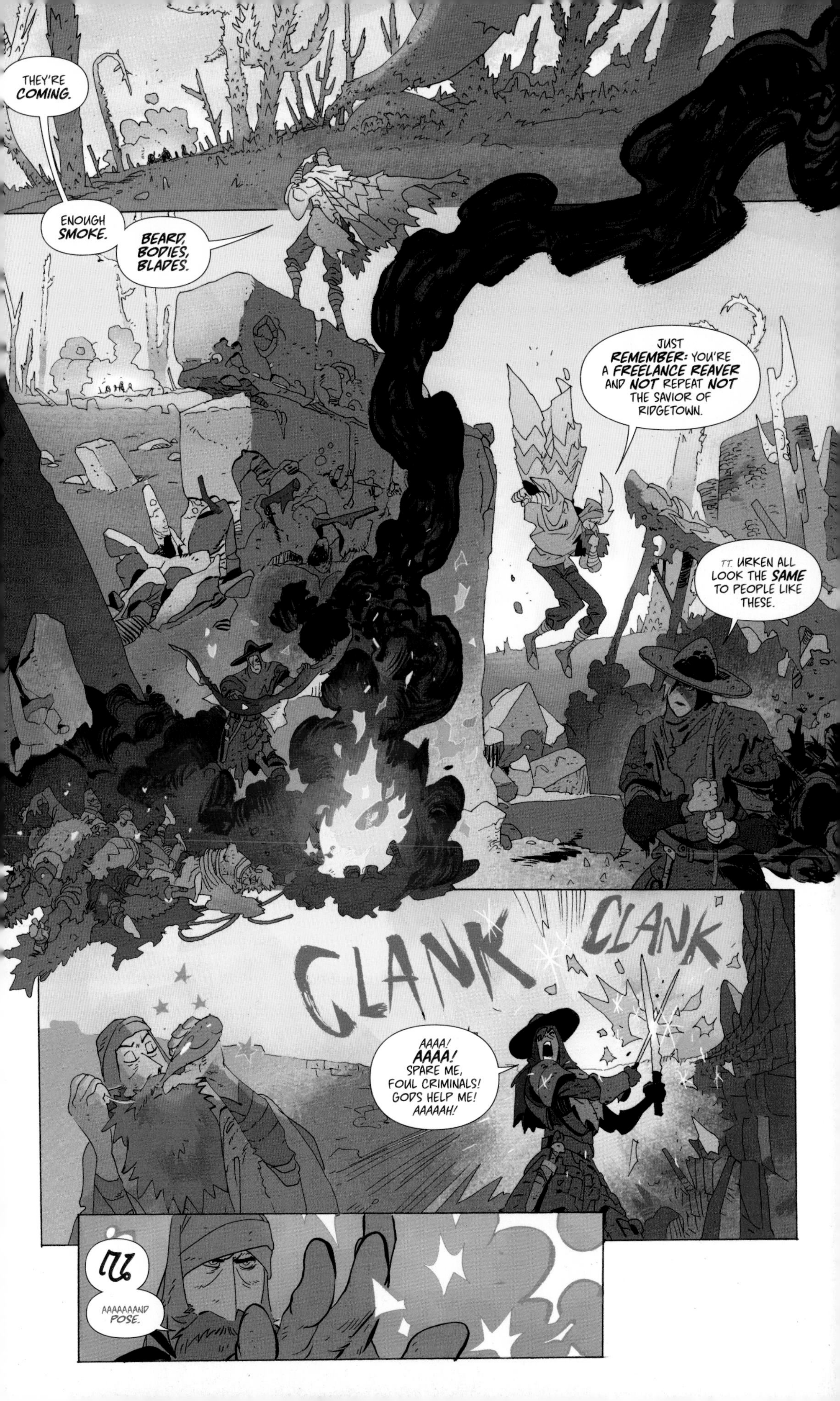

THEY'RE COMING.
ENOUGH SMOKE.
BEARD, BODIES, BLADES.
JUST REMEMBER: YOU'RE A FREELANCE REAVER AND NOT REPEAT NOT THE SAVIOR OF RIDGETOWN.
TT. URKEN ALL LOOK THE SAME TO PEOPLE LIKE THESE.
CLANK
CLANK
AAAA! AAAA! SPARE ME, FOUL CRIMINALS! GODS HELP ME! AAAAAH!
AAAAAAAND POSE.

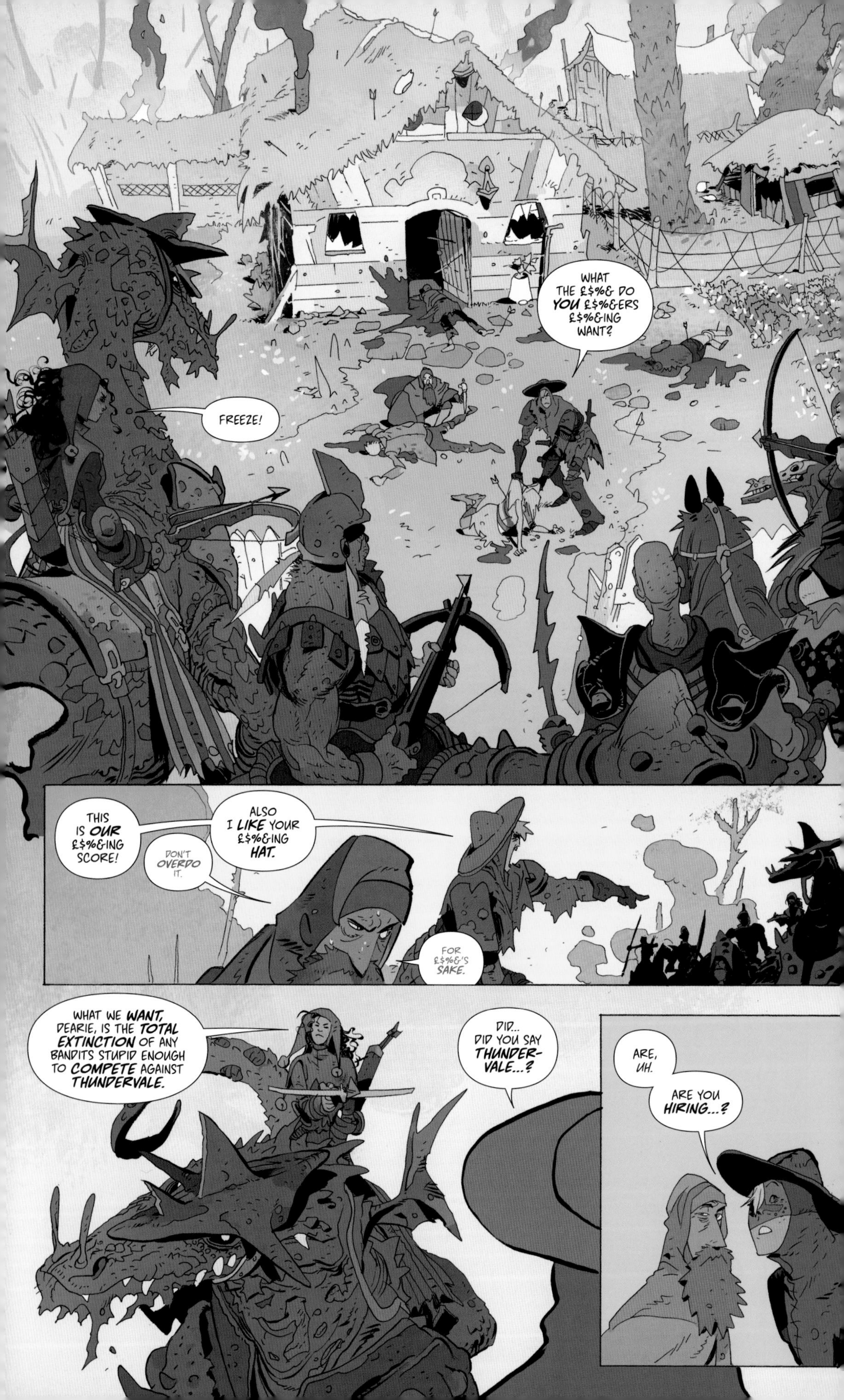
WHAT THE £$%& DO YOU £$%&ERS £$%&ING WANT?
FREEZE!
THIS IS OUR £$%&ING SCORE!
ALSO I LIKE YOUR £$%&ING HAT.
DON'T OVERDO IT.
FOR £$%&'S SAKE.
WHAT WE WANT, DEARIE, IS THE TOTAL EXTINCTION OF ANY BANDITS STUPID ENOUGH TO COMPETE AGAINST THUNDERVALE.
DID... DID YOU SAY THUNDER-VALE...?
ARE, UH.
ARE YOU HIRING...?

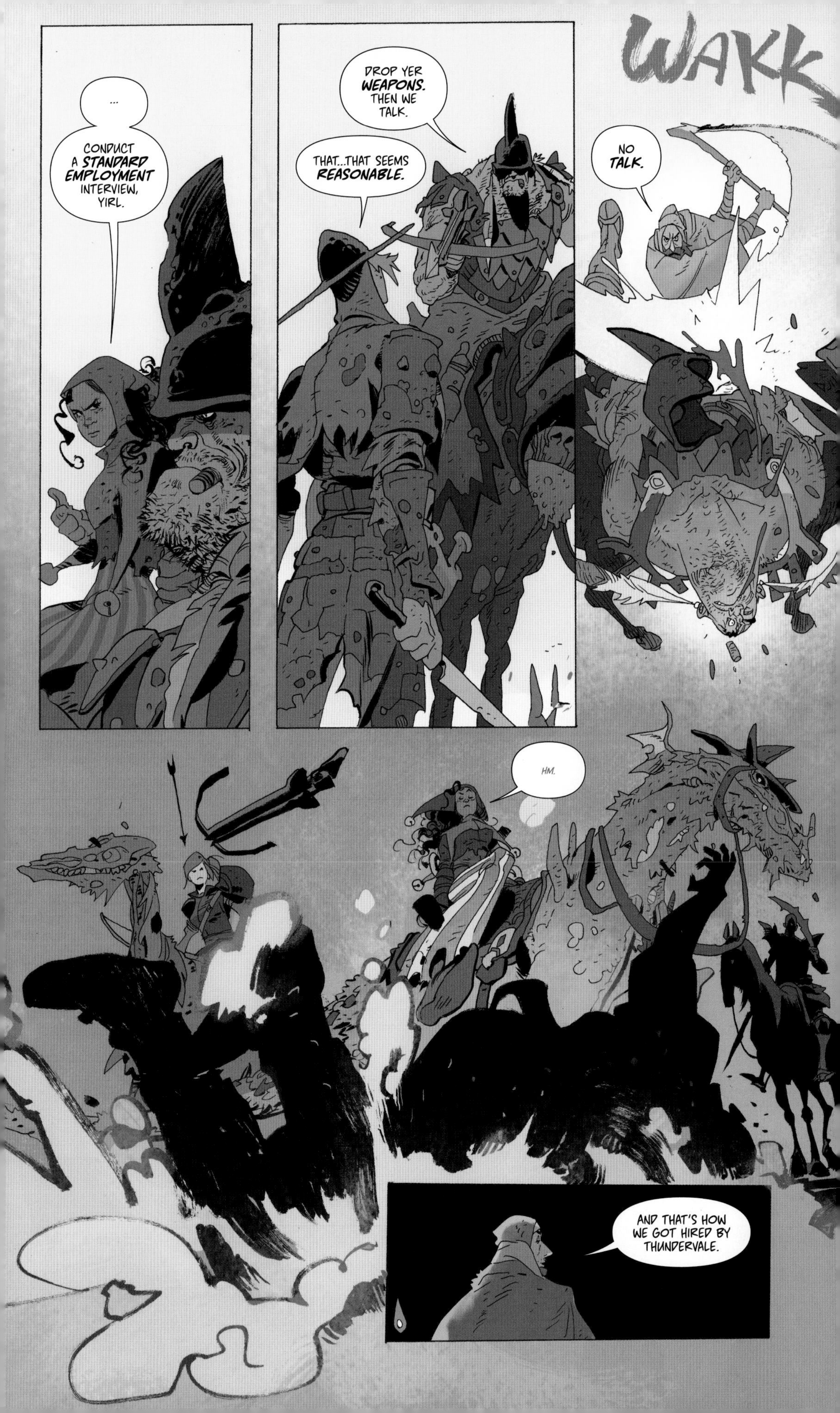
...
CONDUCT A STANDARD EMPLOYMENT INTERVIEW, YIRL.
DROP YER WEAPONS. THEN WE TALK.
THAT...THAT SEEMS REASONABLE.
WAKK
NO TALK.
HM.
AND THAT'S HOW WE GOT HIRED BY THUNDERVALE.

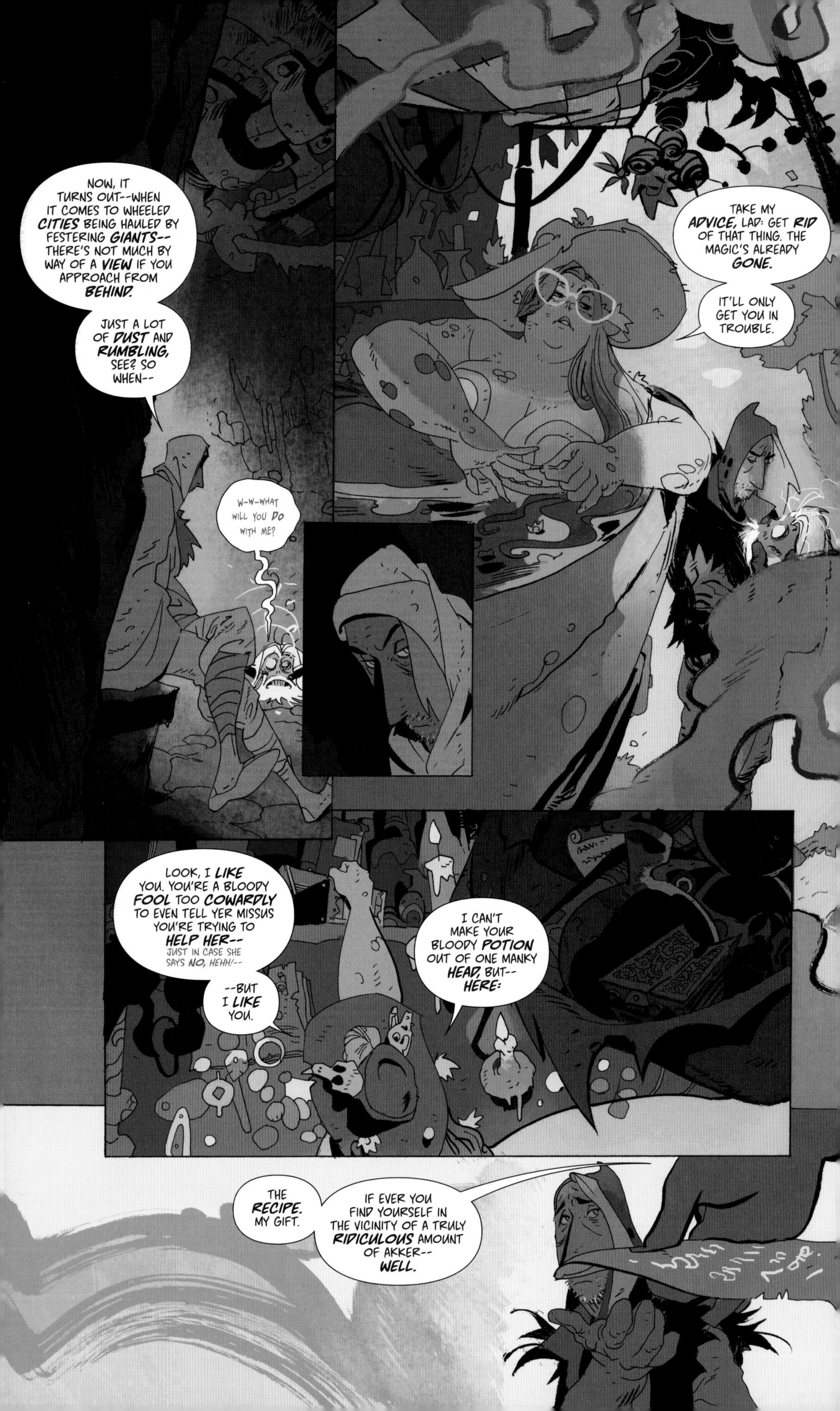

NOW, IT TURNS OUT--WHEN IT COMES TO WHEELED CITIES BEING HAULED BY FESTERING GIANTS--THERE'S NOT MUCH BY WAY OF A VIEW IF YOU APPROACH FROM BEHIND.
JUST A LOT OF DUST AND RUMBLING, SEE? SO WHEN--
TAKE MY ADVICE, LAD: GET RID OF THAT THING. THE MAGIC'S ALREADY GONE.
IT'LL ONLY GET YOU IN TROUBLE.
W-W-WHAT WILL YOU DO WITH ME?
LOOK, I LIKE YOU. YOU'RE A BLOODY FOOL TOO COWARDLY TO EVEN TELL YER MISSUS YOU'RE TRYING TO HELP HER-- JUST IN CASE SHE SAYS NO, HEHH!--
--BUT I LIKE YOU.
I CAN'T MAKE YOUR BLOODY POTION OUT OF ONE MANKY HEAD, BUT-- HERE:
THE RECIPE. MY GIFT.
IF EVER YOU FIND YOURSELF IN THE VICINITY OF A TRULY RIDICULOUS AMOUNT OF AKKER-- WELL.

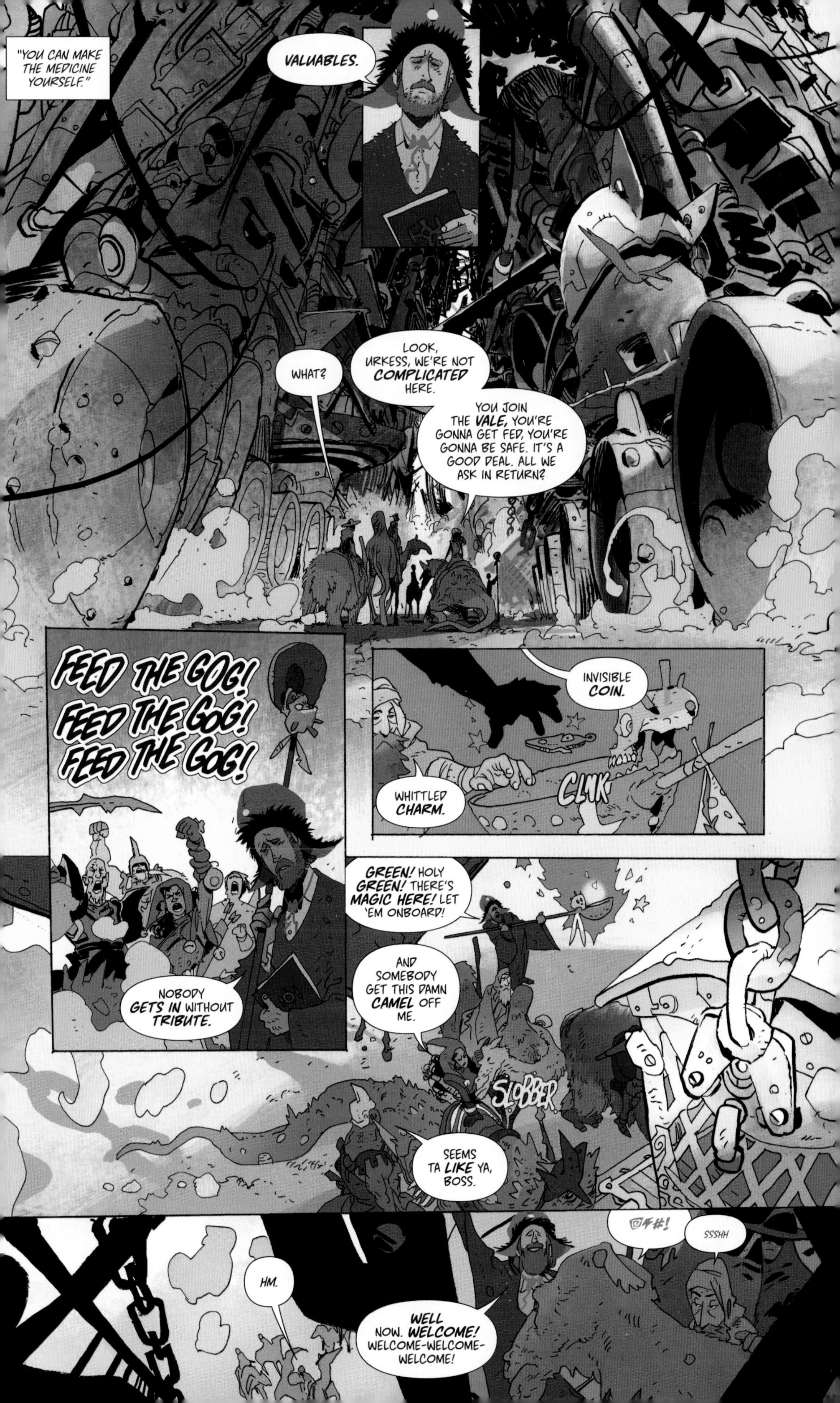
"YOU CAN MAKE THE MEDICINE YOURSELF."
VALUABLES.
WHAT?
LOOK, URKESS, WE'RE NOT COMPLICATED HERE.
YOU JOIN THE VALE, YOU'RE GONNA GET FED, YOU'RE GONNA BE SAFE. IT'S A GOOD DEAL. ALL WE ASK IN RETURN?
FEED THE GOG! FEED THE GOG! FEED THE GOG!
NOBODY GETS IN WITHOUT TRIBUTE.
INVISIBLE COIN.
WHITTLED CHARM.
CLNK
GREEN! HOLY GREEN! THERE'S MAGIC HERE! LET 'EM ONBOARD!
AND SOMEBODY GET THIS DAMN CAMEL OFF ME.
SLOBBER
SEEMS TA LIKE YA, BOSS.
@#!
SSSHH
HM.
WELL NOW. WELCOME! WELCOME-WELCOME-WELCOME!

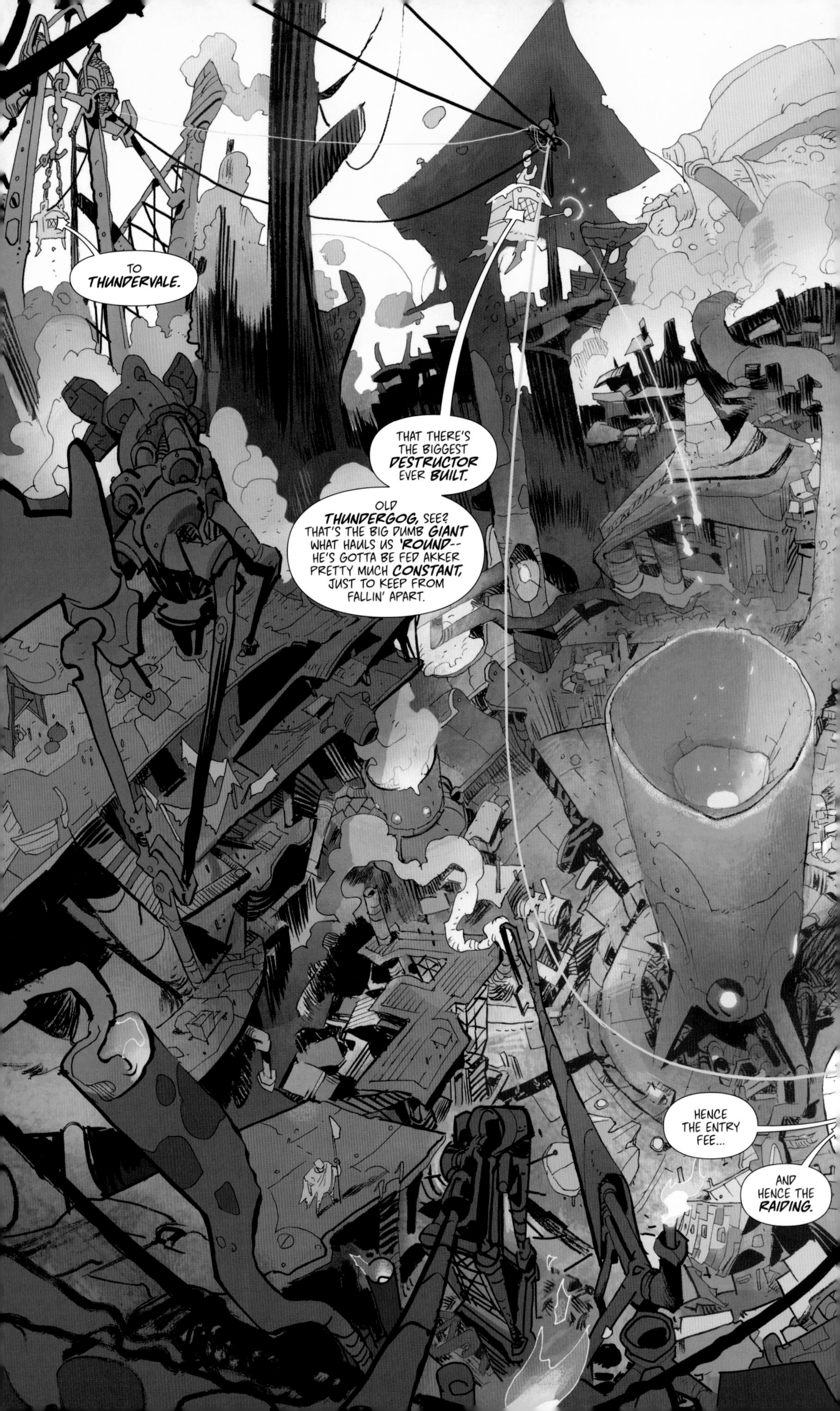
TO THUNDERVALE.
THAT THERE'S THE BIGGEST DESTRUCTOR EVER BUILT.
OLD THUNDERGOG, SEE? THAT'S THE BIG DUMB GIANT WHAT HAULS US 'ROUND-- HE'S GOTTA BE FED AKKER PRETTY MUCH CONSTANT, JUST TO KEEP FROM FALLIN' APART.
HENCE THE ENTRY FEE...
AND HENCE THE RAIDING.

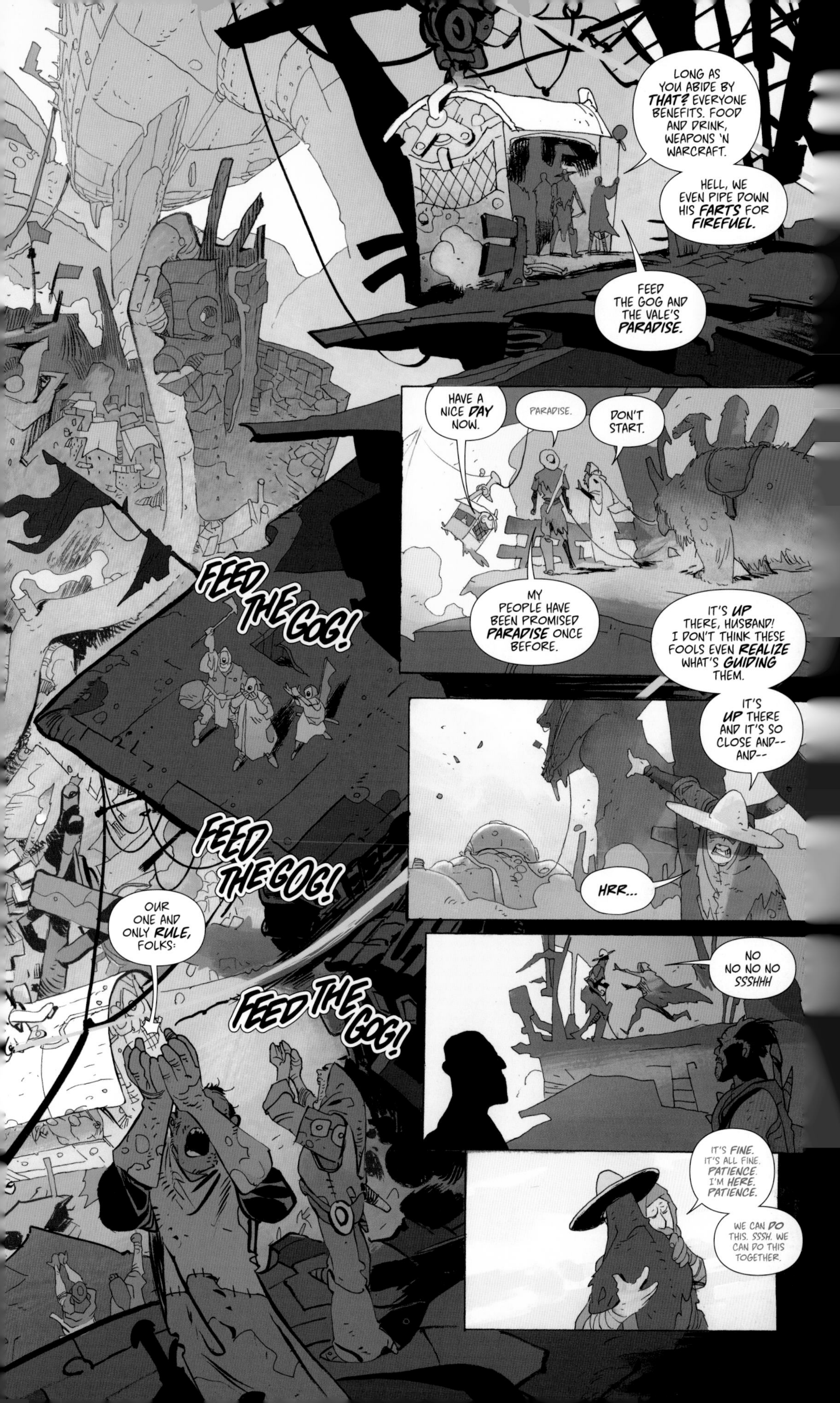

LONG AS YOU ABIDE BY THAT? EVERYONE BENEFITS. FOOD AND DRINK, WEAPONS 'N WARCRAFT.
HELL, WE EVEN PIPE DOWN HIS FARTS FOR FIREFUEL.
FEED THE GOG AND THE VALE'S PARADISE.
FEED THE GOG!
FEED THE GOG!
OUR ONE AND ONLY RULE, FOLKS:
FEED THE GOG!
HAVE A NICE DAY NOW.
PARADISE.
DON'T START.
MY PEOPLE HAVE BEEN PROMISED PARADISE ONCE BEFORE.
IT'S UP THERE, HUSBAND! I DON'T THINK THESE FOOLS EVEN REALIZE WHAT'S GUIDING THEM.
IT'S UP THERE AND IT'S SO CLOSE AND-- AND--
HRR...
NO NO NO NO SSSHHH
IT'S FINE. IT'S ALL FINE. PATIENCE. I'M HERE. PATIENCE.
WE CAN DO THIS. SSSH. WE CAN DO THIS TOGETHER.

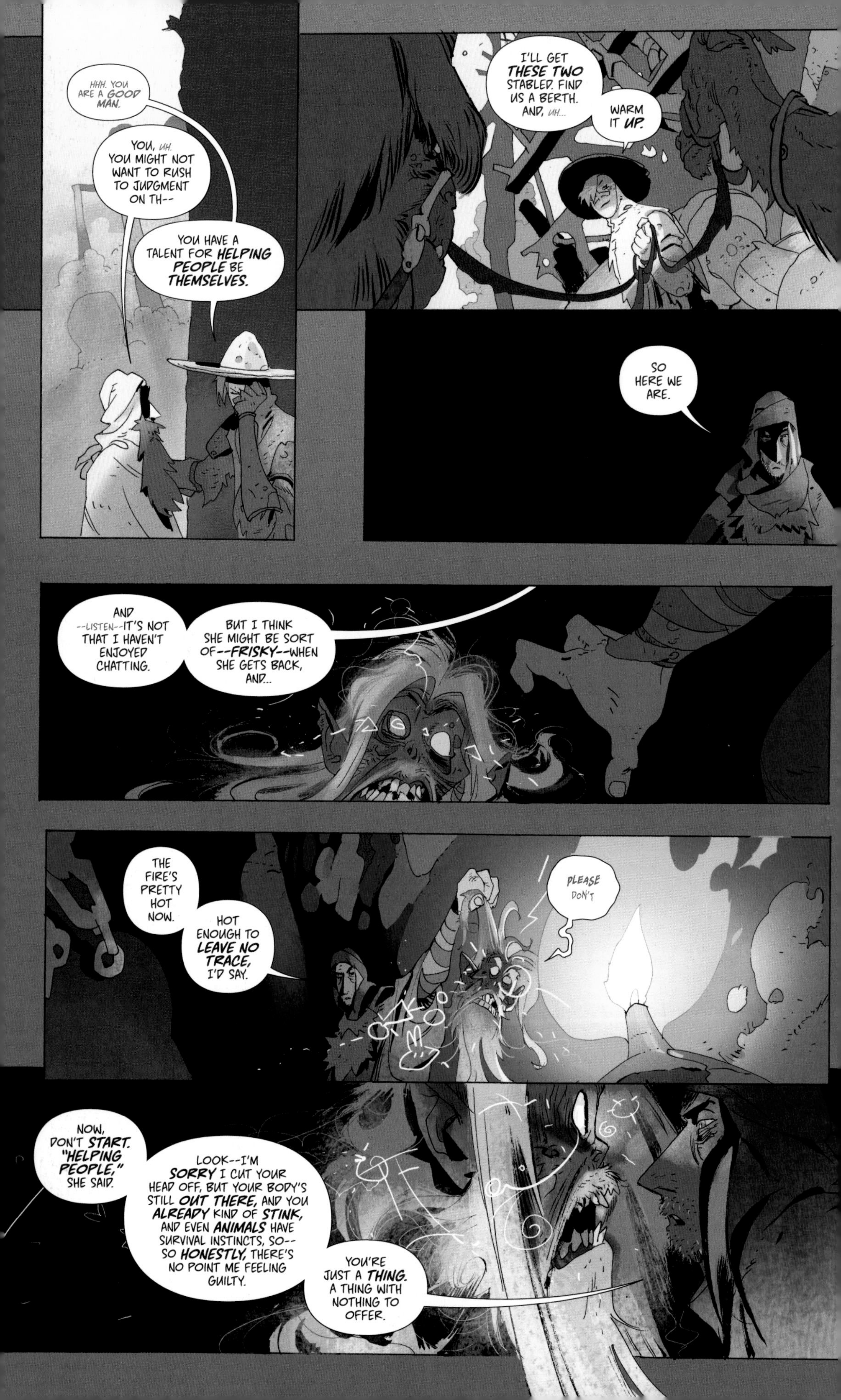
HHH. YOU ARE A GOOD MAN.
YOU, UH. YOU MIGHT NOT WANT TO RUSH TO JUDGMENT ON TH--
YOU HAVE A TALENT FOR HELPING PEOPLE BE THEMSELVES.
I'LL GET THESE TWO STABLED. FIND US A BERTH. AND, UH...
WARM IT UP.
SO HERE WE ARE.
AND --LISTEN-- IT'S NOT THAT I HAVEN'T ENJOYED CHATTING.
BUT I THINK SHE MIGHT BE SORT OF --FRISKY-- WHEN SHE GETS BACK, AND...
THE FIRE'S PRETTY HOT NOW.
HOT ENOUGH TO LEAVE NO TRACE, I'D SAY.
PLEASE DON'T
NOW, DON'T START. "HELPING PEOPLE," SHE SAID.
LOOK--I'M SORRY I CUT YOUR HEAD OFF, BUT YOUR BODY'S STILL OUT THERE, AND YOU ALREADY KIND OF STINK, AND EVEN ANIMALS HAVE SURVIVAL INSTINCTS, SO-- SO HONESTLY, THERE'S NO POINT ME FEELING GUILTY.
YOU'RE JUST A THING. A THING WITH NOTHING TO OFFER.

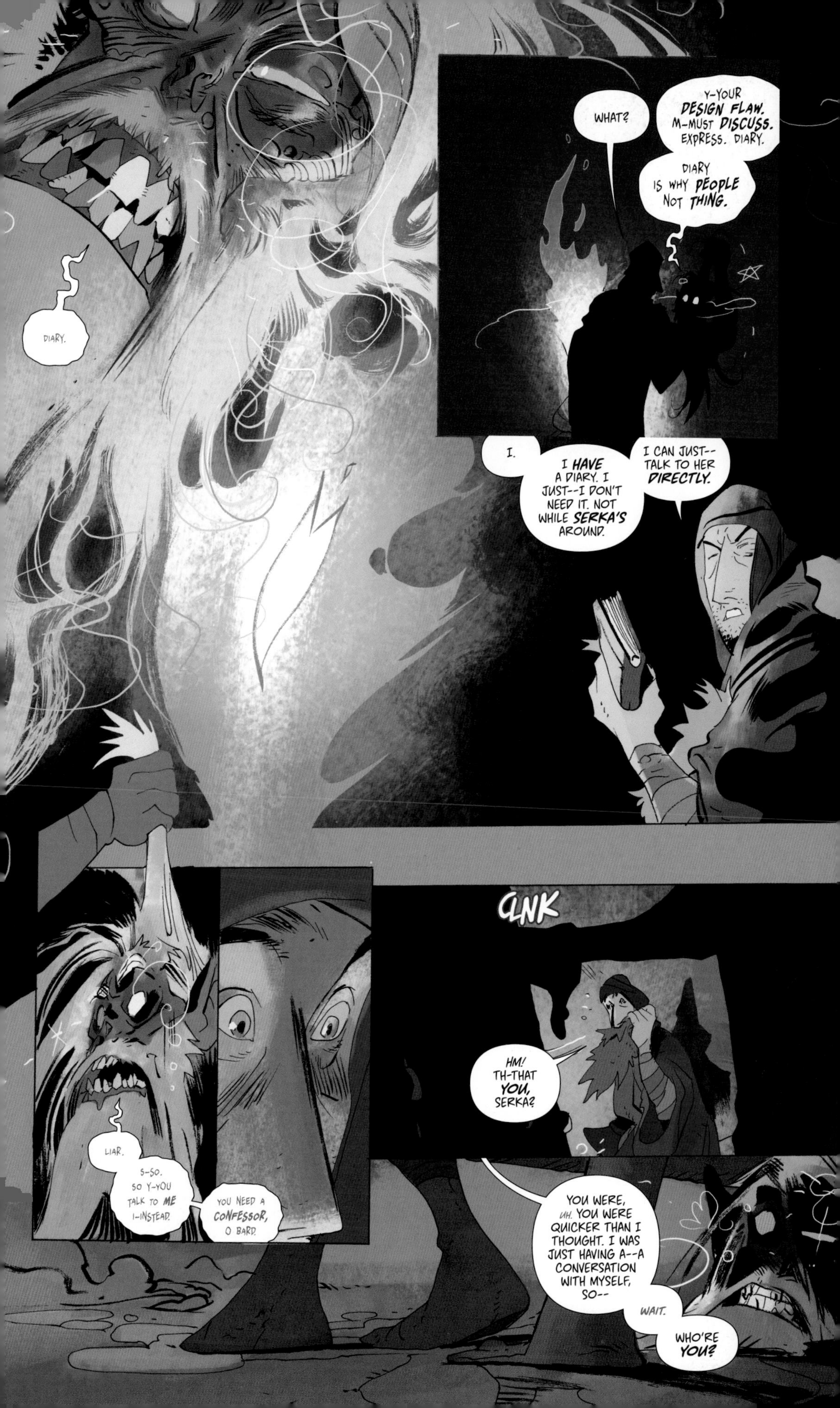
DIARY.
WHAT?
Y-YOUR DESIGN FLAW. M-MUST DISCUSS. EXPRESS. DIARY.
DIARY IS WHY PEOPLE NOT THING.
I.
I HAVE A DIARY. I JUST--I DON'T NEED IT. NOT WHILE SERKA'S AROUND.
I CAN JUST-- TALK TO HER DIRECTLY.
LIAR.
S-SO. SO Y-YOU TALK TO ME I-INSTEAD.
YOU NEED A CONFESSOR, O BARD.
CLNK
HM! TH-THAT YOU, SERKA?
YOU WERE, UH, YOU WERE QUICKER THAN I THOUGHT. I WAS JUST HAVING A--A CONVERSATION WITH MYSELF, SO--
WAIT.
WHO'RE YOU?

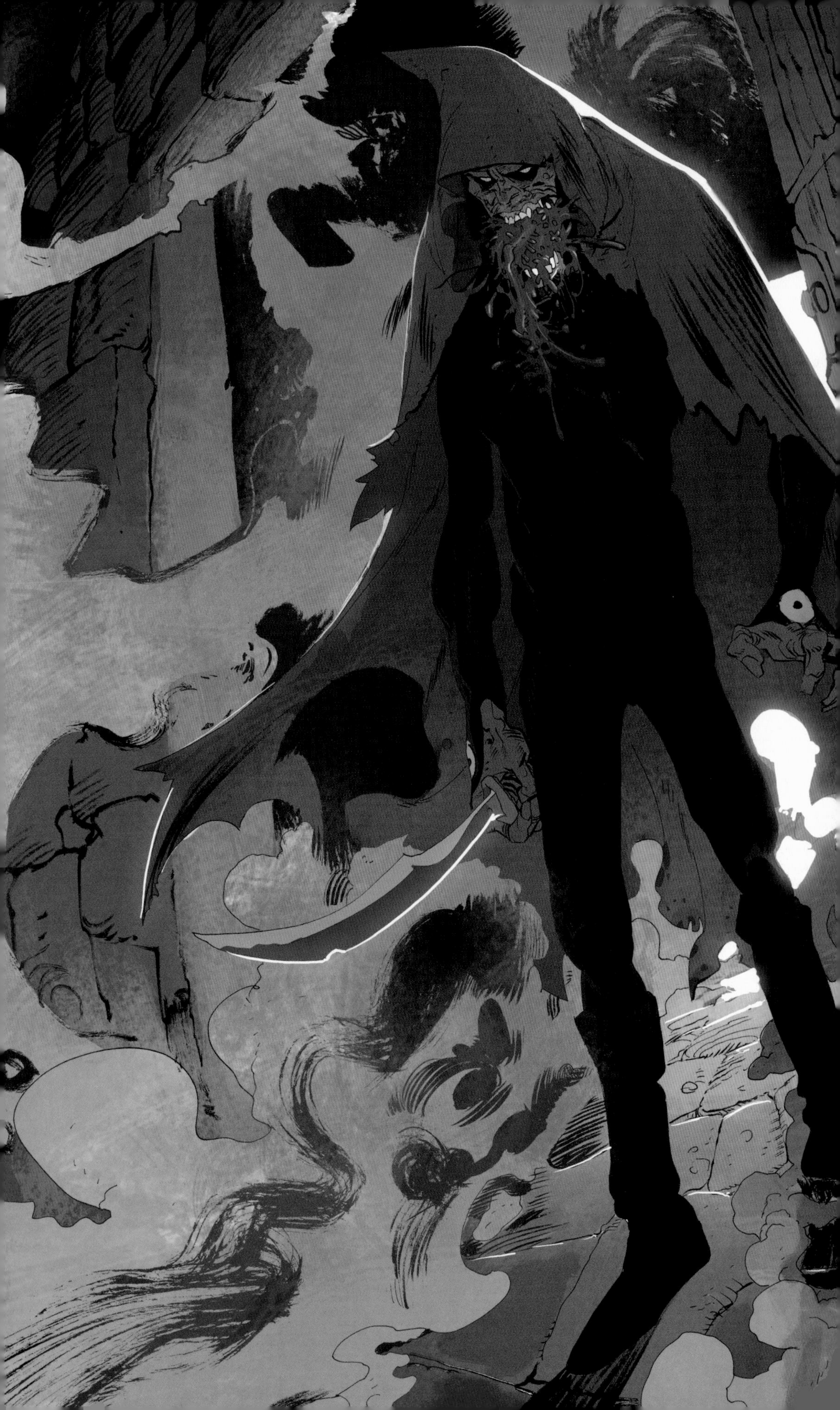

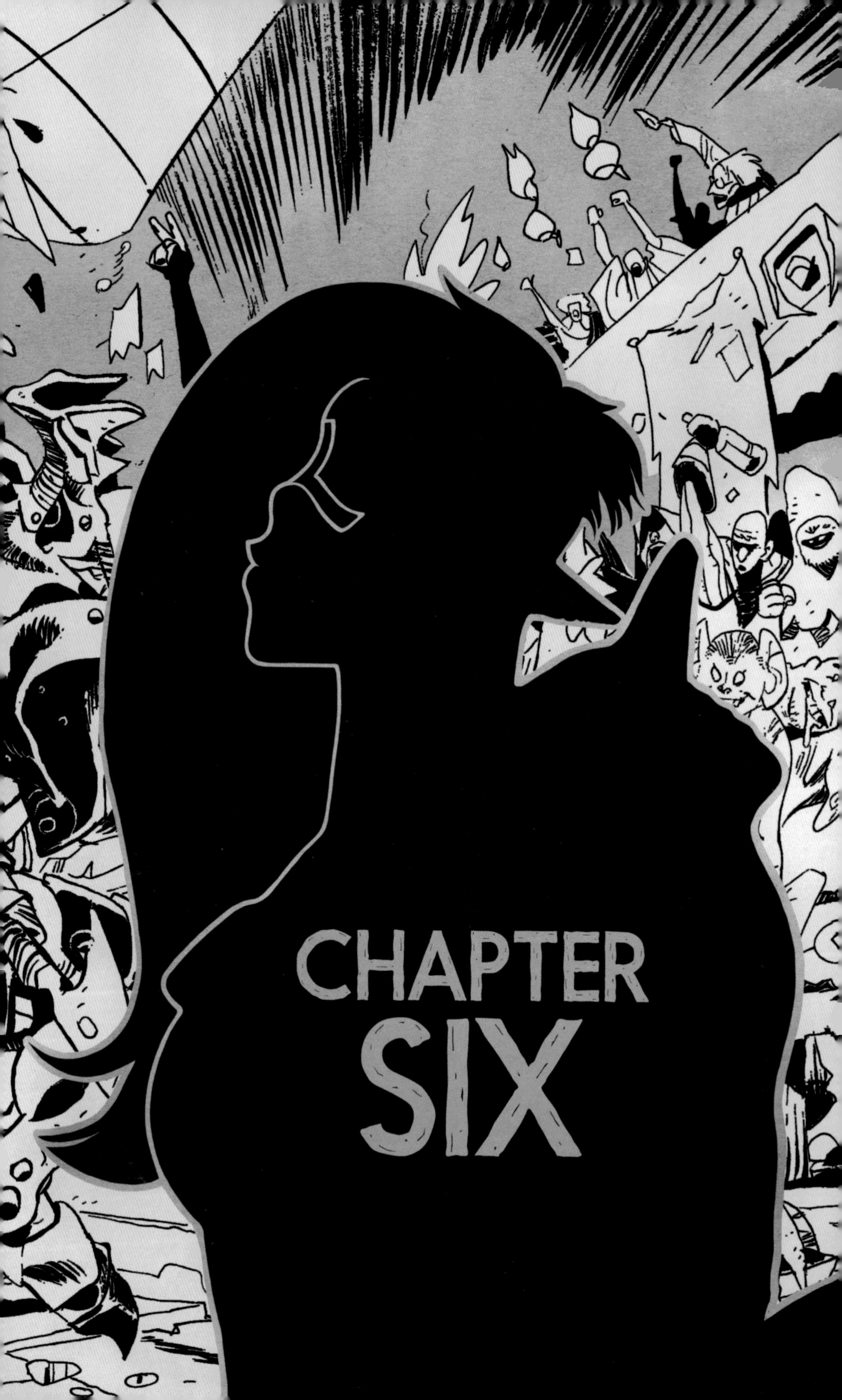
CHAPTER
SIX

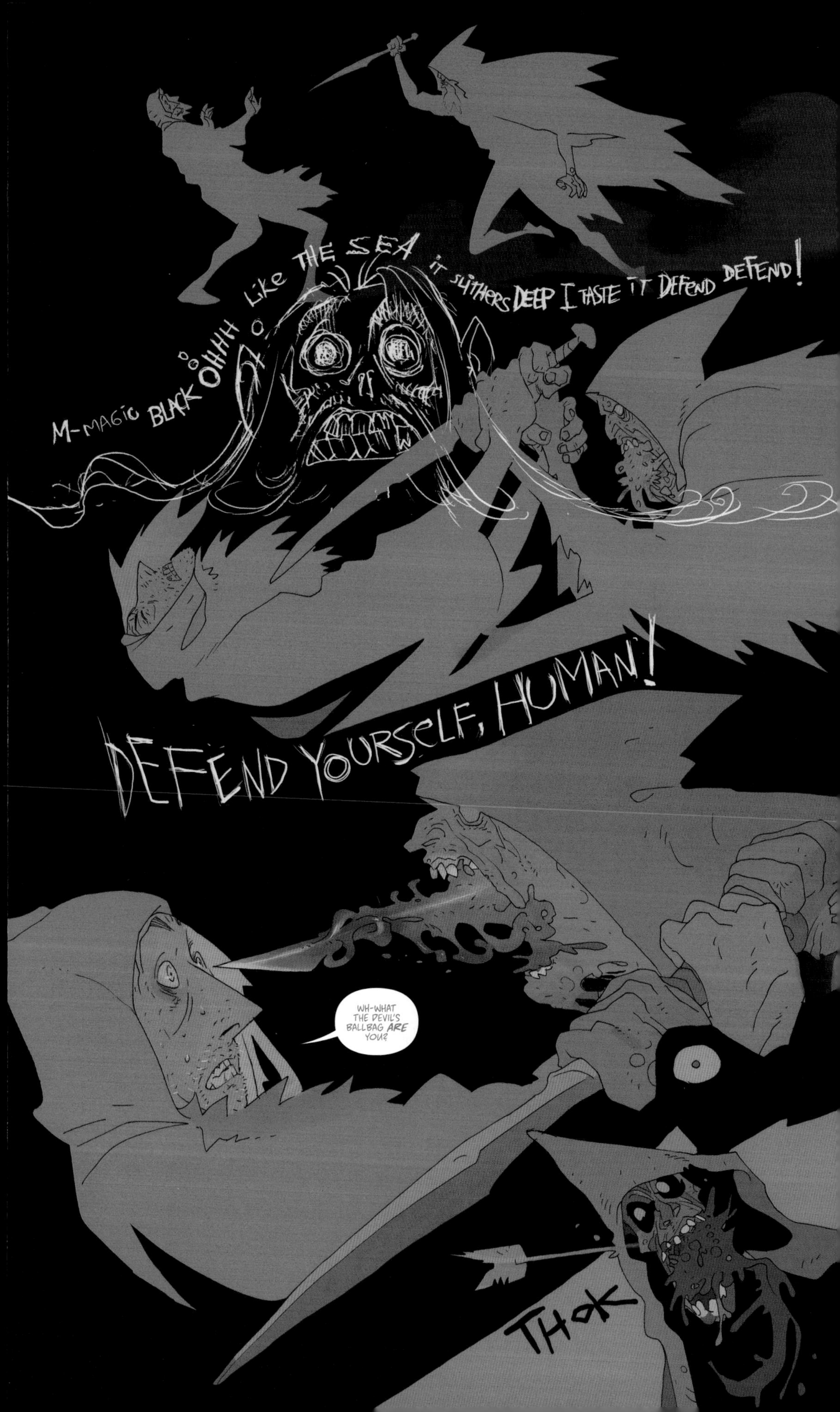
M-MAGIC BLACK OHHH like THE SEA it slithers DEEP I TASTE IT DEFEND DEFEND!
DEFEND YOURSELF, HUMAN!
WH-WHAT THE DEVIL'S BALLBAG ARE YOU?
THOK

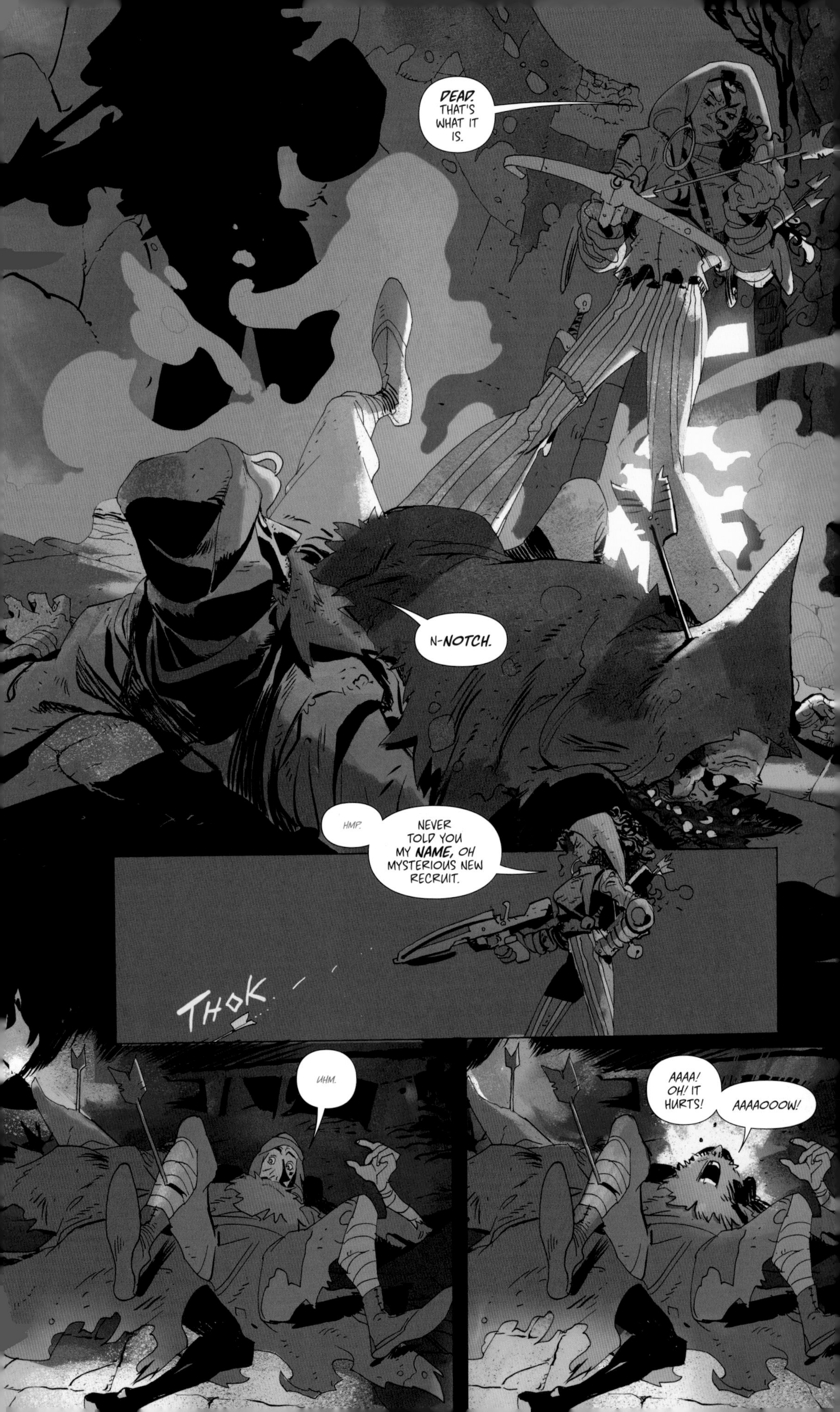
DEAD. THAT'S WHAT IT IS.
N-NOTCH.
HMP.
NEVER TOLD YOU MY NAME, OH MYSTERIOUS NEW RECRUIT.
THOK
UHM.
AAAA! OH! IT HURTS!
AAAAOOOW!

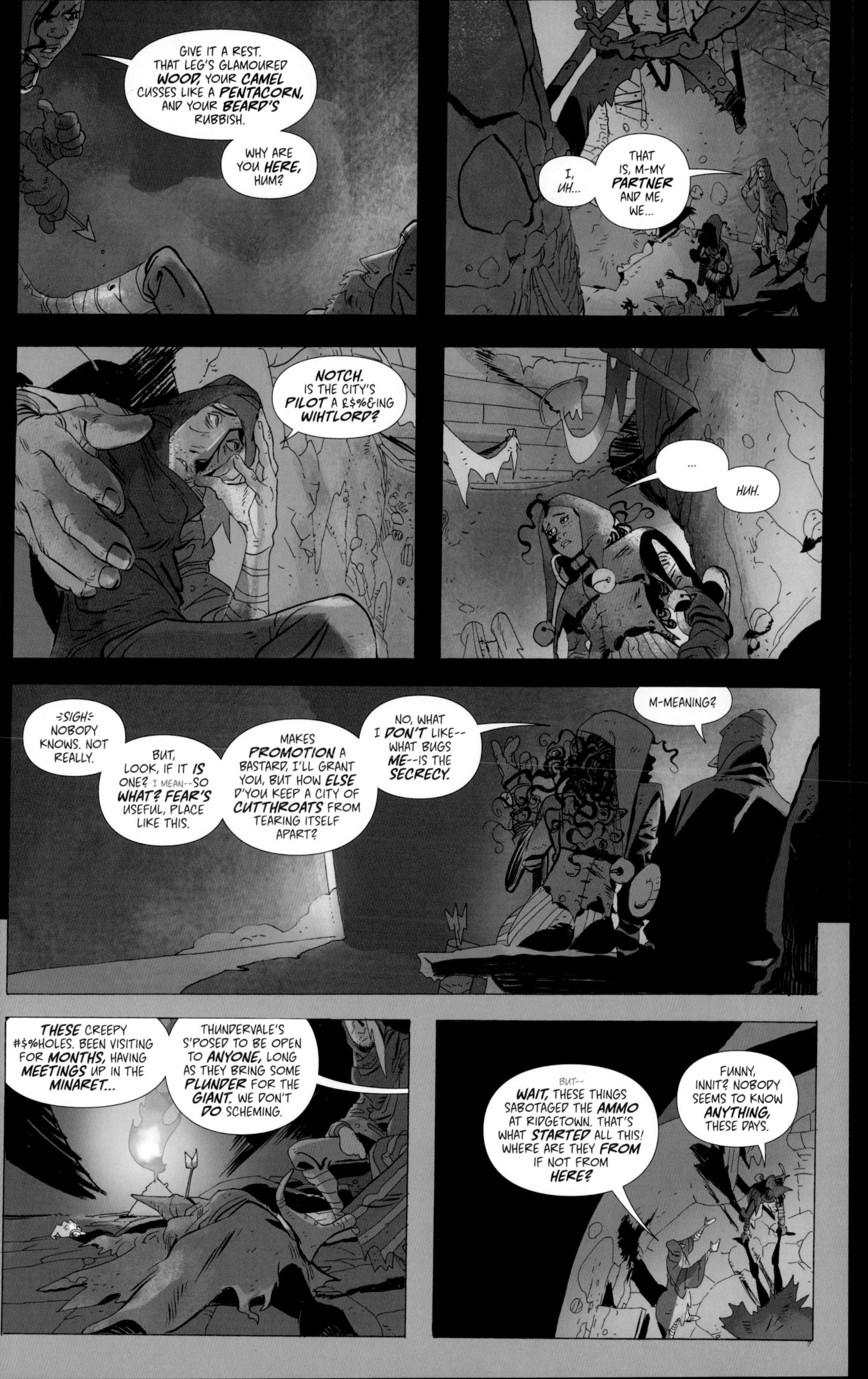
GIVE IT A REST. THAT LEG'S GLAMOURED WOOD, YOUR CAMEL CUSSES LIKE A PENTACORN, AND YOUR BEARD'S RUBBISH.
WHY ARE YOU HERE, HUM?
I, UH...
THAT IS, M-MY PARTNER AND ME, WE...
NOTCH. IS THE CITY'S PILOT A £$%&ING WIHTLORD?
...
HUH.
=SIGH= NOBODY KNOWS. NOT REALLY.
BUT, LOOK, IF IT IS ONE? I MEAN--SO WHAT? FEAR'S USEFUL, PLACE LIKE THIS.
MAKES PROMOTION A BASTARD, I'LL GRANT YOU, BUT HOW ELSE D'YOU KEEP A CITY OF CUTTHROATS FROM TEARING ITSELF APART?
NO, WHAT I DON'T LIKE--WHAT BUGS ME--IS THE SECRECY.
M-MEANING?
THESE CREEPY #$%HOLES. BEEN VISITING FOR MONTHS, HAVING MEETINGS UP IN THE MINARET...
THUNDERVALE'S S'POSED TO BE OPEN TO ANYONE, LONG AS THEY BRING SOME PLUNDER FOR THE GIANT. WE DON'T DO SCHEMING.
BUT--
WAIT, THESE THINGS SABOTAGED THE AMMO AT RIDGETOWN. THAT'S WHAT STARTED ALL THIS! WHERE ARE THEY FROM IF NOT FROM HERE?
FUNNY, INNIT? NOBODY SEEMS TO KNOW ANYTHING, THESE DAYS.

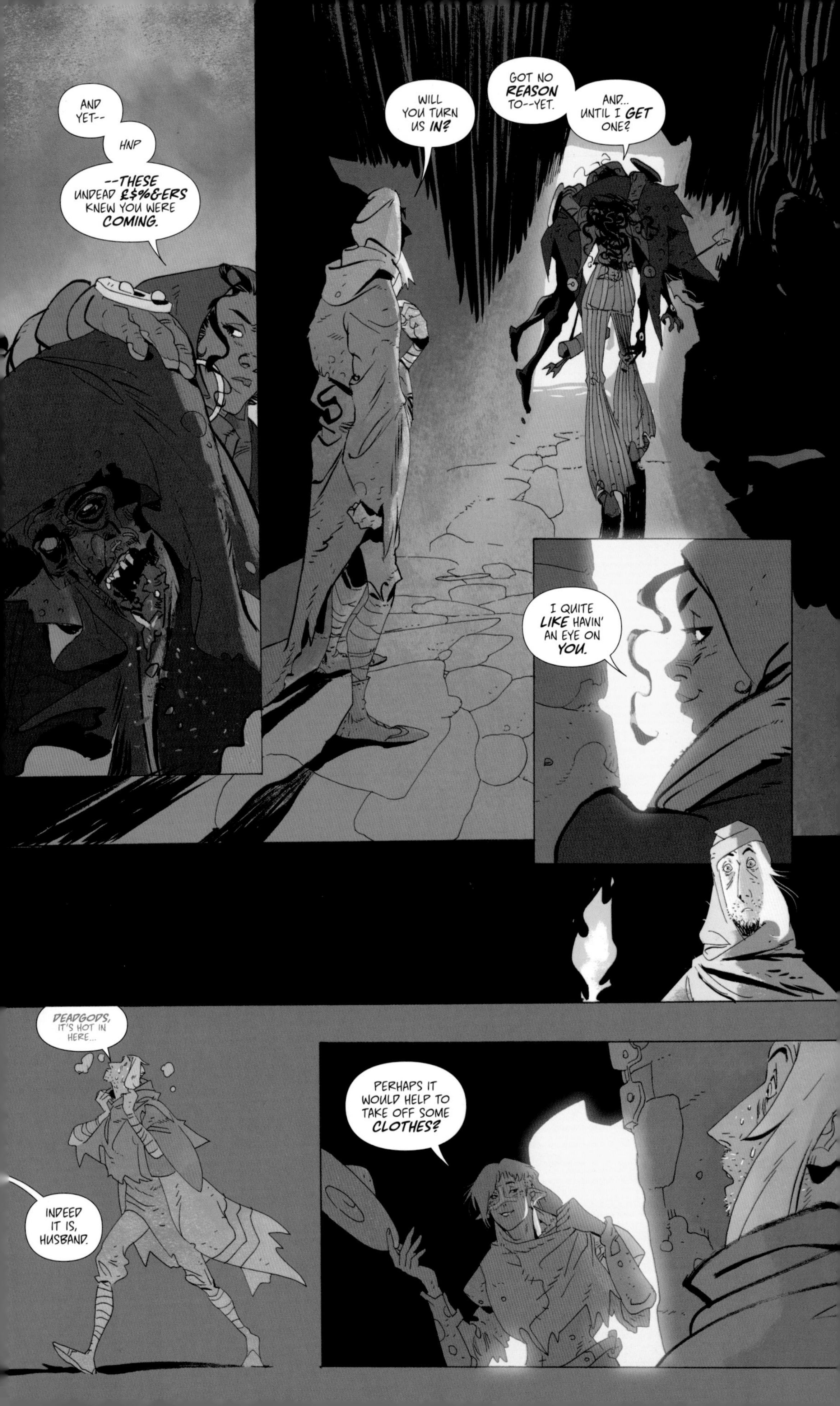
AND YET--
HNP
--THESE UNDEAD £$%&ERS KNEW YOU WERE COMING.
WILL YOU TURN US IN?
GOT NO REASON TO--YET.
AND... UNTIL I GET ONE?
I QUITE LIKE HAVIN' AN EYE ON YOU.
DEADGODS, IT'S HOT IN HERE...
INDEED IT IS, HUSBAND.
PERHAPS IT WOULD HELP TO TAKE OFF SOME CLOTHES?

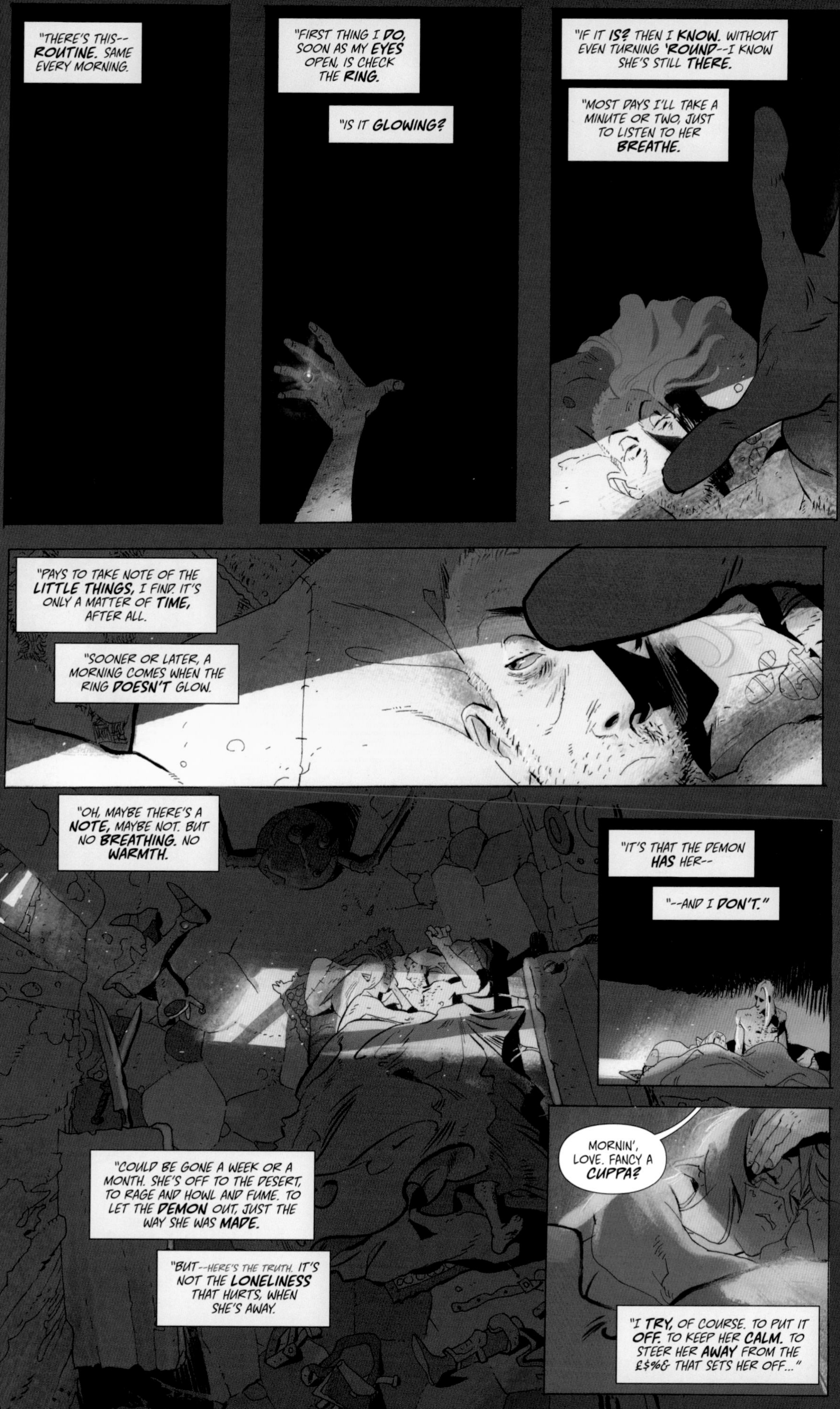
"THERE'S THIS--ROUTINE. SAME EVERY MORNING.
"FIRST THING I DO, SOON AS MY EYES OPEN, IS CHECK THE RING.
"IS IT GLOWING?
"IF IT IS? THEN I KNOW. WITHOUT EVEN TURNING 'ROUND--I KNOW SHE'S STILL THERE.
"MOST DAYS I'LL TAKE A MINUTE OR TWO, JUST TO LISTEN TO HER BREATHE.
"PAYS TO TAKE NOTE OF THE LITTLE THINGS, I FIND. IT'S ONLY A MATTER OF TIME, AFTER ALL.
"SOONER OR LATER, A MORNING COMES WHEN THE RING DOESN'T GLOW.
"OH, MAYBE THERE'S A NOTE, MAYBE NOT. BUT NO BREATHING. NO WARMTH.
"COULD BE GONE A WEEK OR A MONTH. SHE'S OFF TO THE DESERT, TO RAGE AND HOWL AND FUME. TO LET THE DEMON OUT, JUST THE WAY SHE WAS MADE.
"BUT--HERE'S THE TRUTH. IT'S NOT THE LONELINESS THAT HURTS, WHEN SHE'S AWAY.
"IT'S THAT THE DEMON HAS HER--
"--AND I DON'T."
MORNIN', LOVE. FANCY A CUPPA?
"I TRY, OF COURSE. TO PUT IT OFF. TO KEEP HER CALM. TO STEER HER AWAY FROM THE £$%& THAT SETS HER OFF..."

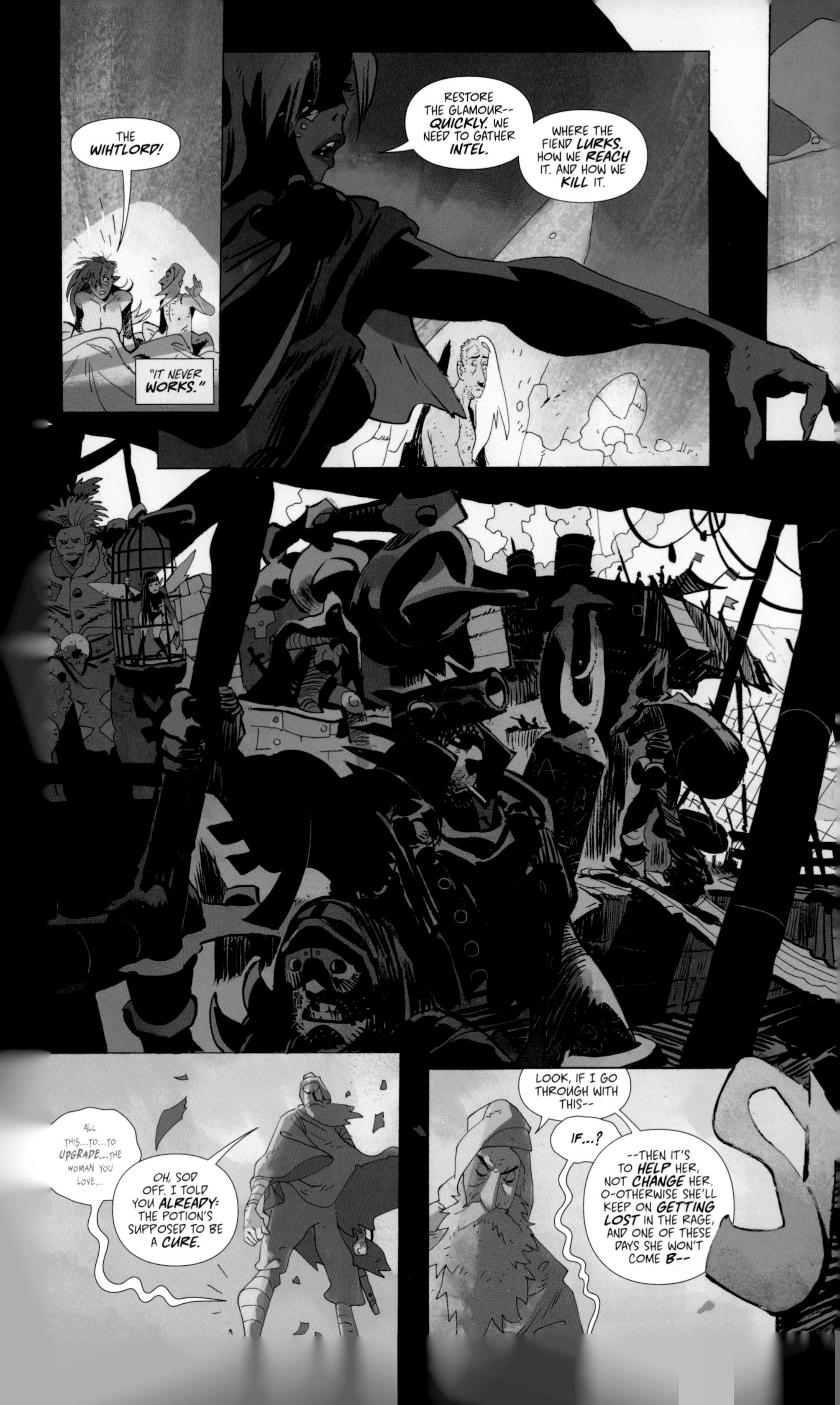
THE WIHTLORD!
"IT NEVER WORKS."
RESTORE THE GLAMOUR--QUICKLY. WE NEED TO GATHER INTEL.
WHERE THE FIEND LURKS. HOW WE REACH IT. AND HOW WE KILL IT.
ALL THIS...TO...TO UPGRADE...THE WOMAN YOU LOVE...
OH, SOD OFF. I TOLD YOU ALREADY: THE POTION'S SUPPOSED TO BE A CURE.
LOOK, IF I GO THROUGH WITH THIS--
IF...?
--THEN IT'S TO HELP HER, NOT CHANGE HER. O-OTHERWISE SHE'LL KEEP ON GETTING LOST IN THE RAGE, AND ONE OF THESE DAYS SHE WON'T COME B--

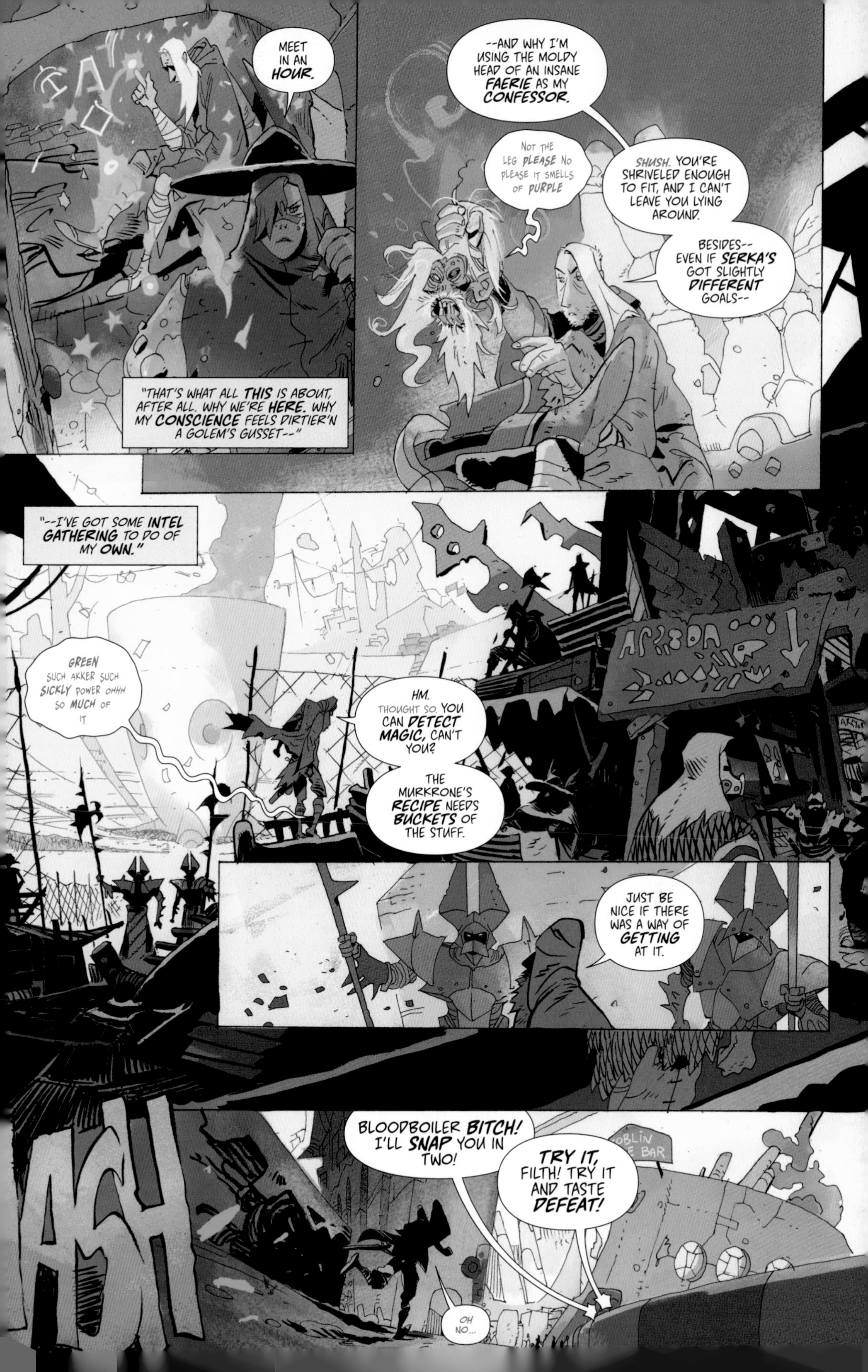
MEET IN AN HOUR.
"THAT'S WHAT ALL THIS IS ABOUT, AFTER ALL. WHY WE'RE HERE. WHY MY CONSCIENCE FEELS DIRTIER'N A GOLEM'S GUSSET--"
--AND WHY I'M USING THE MOLDY HEAD OF AN INSANE FAERIE AS MY CONFESSOR.
NOT THE LEG PLEASE NO PLEASE IT SMELLS OF PURPLE
SHUSH. YOU'RE SHRIVELED ENOUGH TO FIT, AND I CAN'T LEAVE YOU LYING AROUND.
BESIDES-- EVEN IF SERKA'S GOT SLIGHTLY DIFFERENT GOALS--
"--I'VE GOT SOME INTEL GATHERING TO DO OF MY OWN."
GREEN SUCH AKKER SUCH SICKLY POWER OHHH SO MUCH OF IT
HM. THOUGHT SO. YOU CAN DETECT MAGIC, CAN'T YOU?
THE MURKRONE'S RECIPE NEEDS BUCKETS OF THE STUFF.
JUST BE NICE IF THERE WAS A WAY OF GETTING AT IT.
BLOODBOILER BITCH! I'LL SNAP YOU IN TWO!
TRY IT, FILTH! TRY IT AND TASTE DEFEAT!
OH NO...

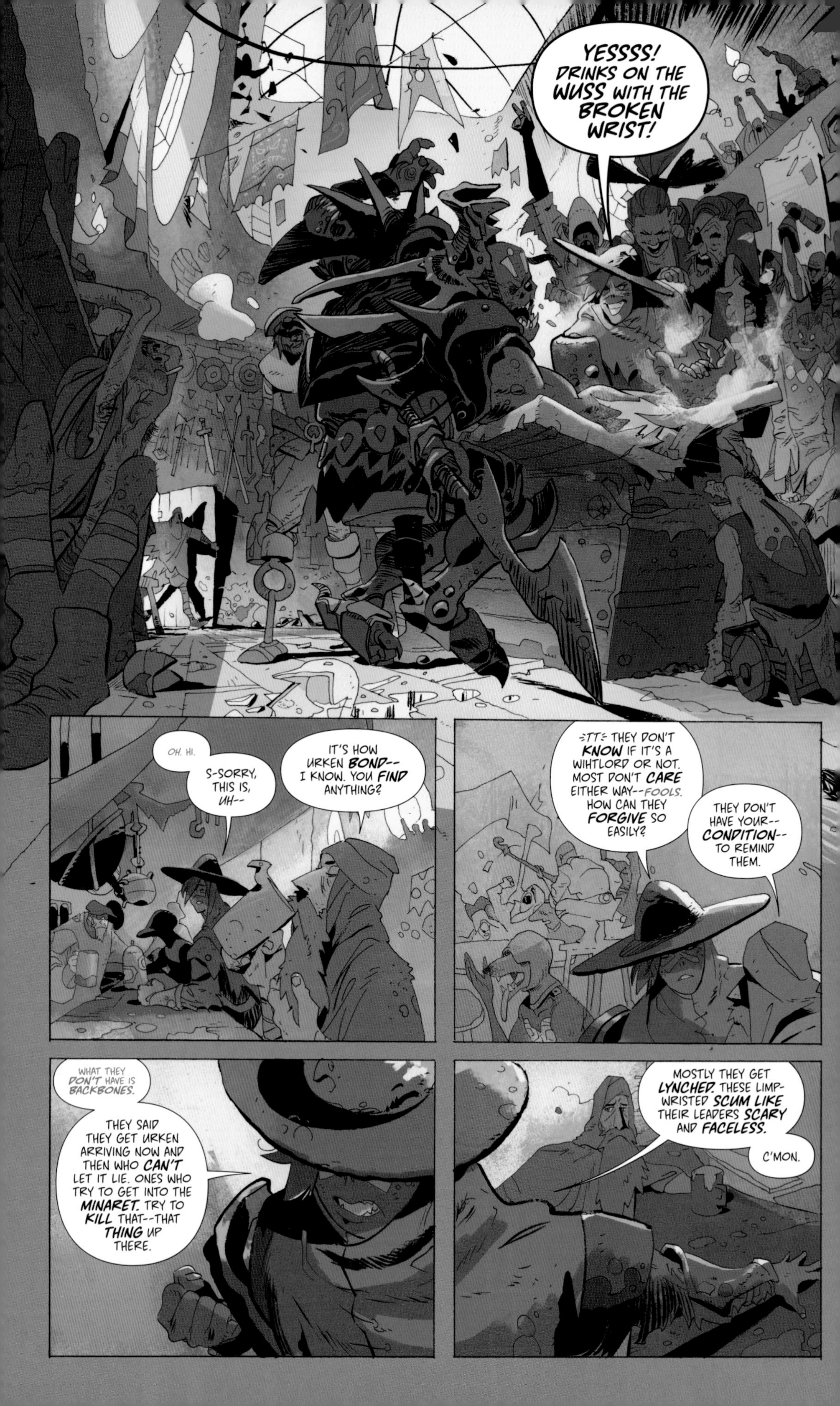

YESSSS! DRINKS ON THE WUSS WITH THE BROKEN WRIST!
OH. HI.
S-SORRY, THIS IS, UH--
IT'S HOW URKEN BOND-- I KNOW. YOU FIND ANYTHING?
=TT= THEY DON'T KNOW IF IT'S A WIHTLORD OR NOT. MOST DON'T CARE EITHER WAY--FOOLS. HOW CAN THEY FORGIVE SO EASILY?
THEY DON'T HAVE YOUR-- CONDITION-- TO REMIND THEM.
WHAT THEY DON'T HAVE IS BACKBONES.
THEY SAID THEY GET URKEN ARRIVING NOW AND THEN WHO CAN'T LET IT LIE. ONES WHO TRY TO GET INTO THE MINARET. TRY TO KILL THAT--THAT THING UP THERE.
MOSTLY THEY GET LYNCHED. THESE LIMP-WRISTED SCUM LIKE THEIR LEADERS SCARY AND FACELESS.
C'MON.

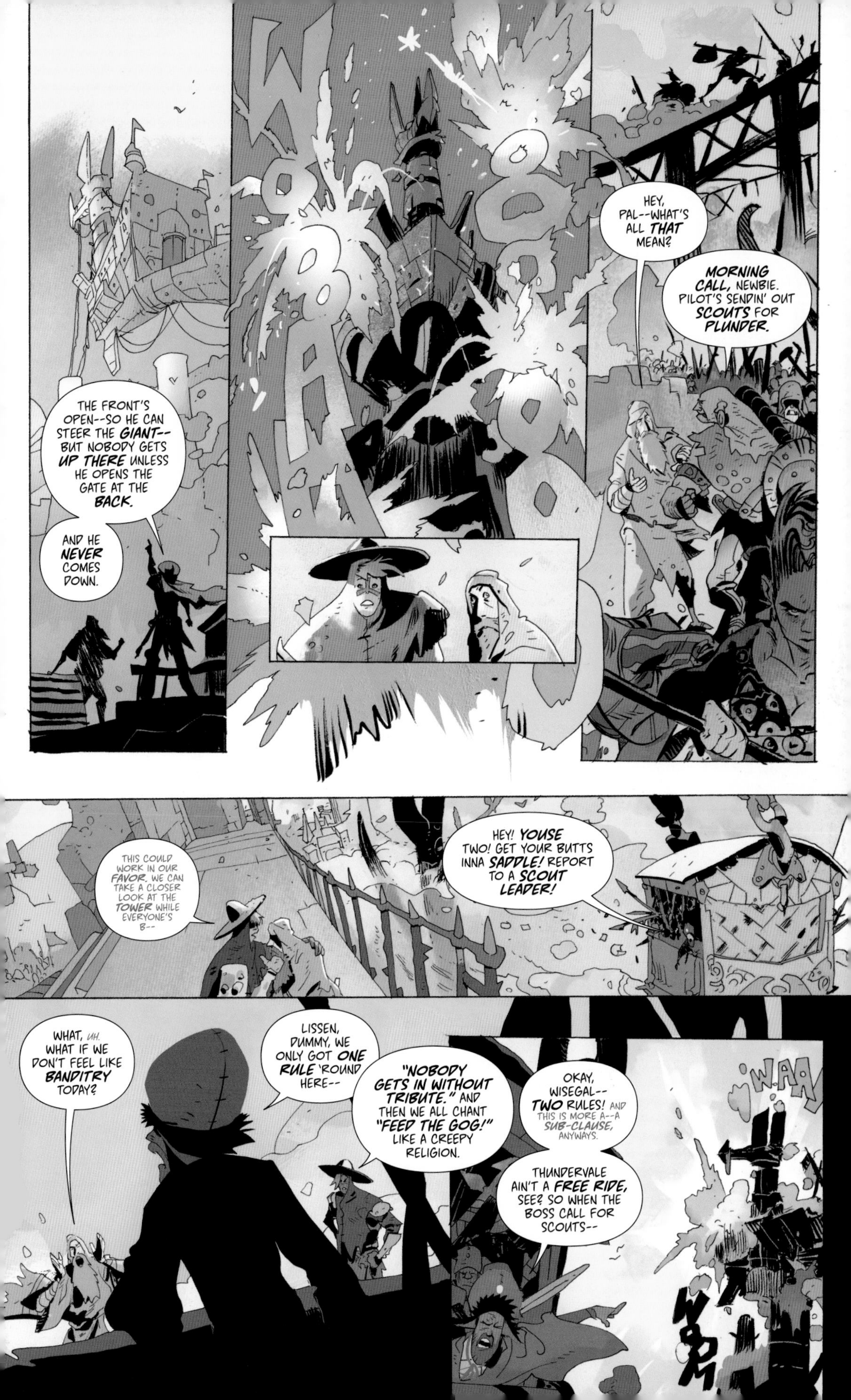
THE FRONT'S OPEN--SO HE CAN STEER THE GIANT--BUT NOBODY GETS UP THERE UNLESS HE OPENS THE GATE AT THE BACK.
AND HE NEVER COMES DOWN.
HEY, PAL--WHAT'S ALL THAT MEAN?
MORNING CALL, NEWBIE. PILOT'S SENDIN' OUT SCOUTS FOR PLUNDER.
THIS COULD WORK IN OUR FAVOR. WE CAN TAKE A CLOSER LOOK AT THE TOWER WHILE EVERYONE'S B--
HEY! YOUSE TWO! GET YOUR BUTTS INNA SADDLE! REPORT TO A SCOUT LEADER!
WHAT, UH. WHAT IF WE DON'T FEEL LIKE BANDITRY TODAY?
LISSEN, DUMMY, WE ONLY GOT ONE RULE 'ROUND HERE--
"NOBODY GETS IN WITHOUT TRIBUTE." AND THEN WE ALL CHANT "FEED THE GOG!" LIKE A CREEPY RELIGION.
OKAY, WISEGAL--TWO RULES! AND THIS IS MORE A--A SUB-CLAUSE, ANYWAYS.
THUNDERVALE AIN'T A FREE RIDE, SEE? SO WHEN THE BOSS CALL FOR SCOUTS--

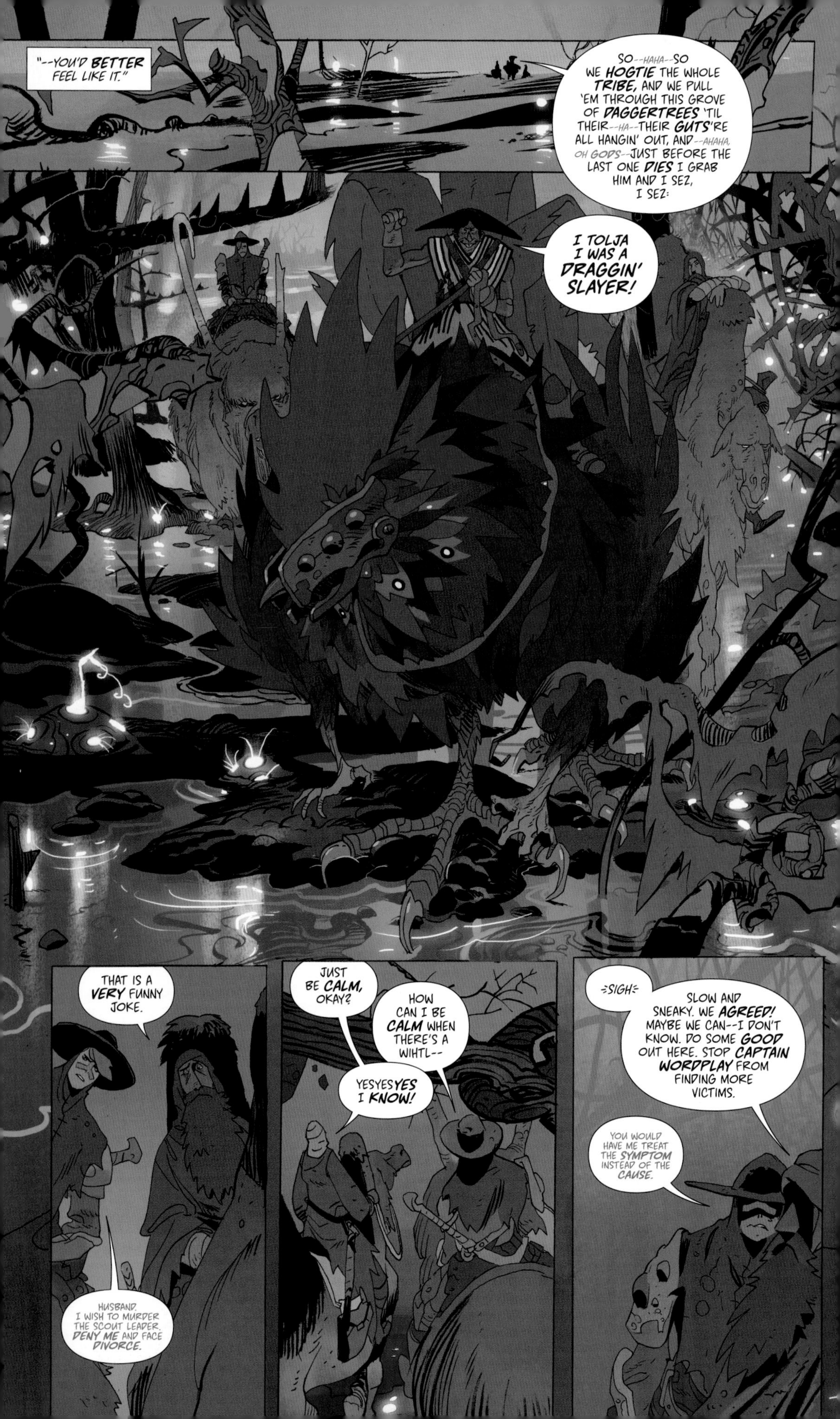
"--YOU'D BETTER FEEL LIKE IT."
SO--HAHA--SO WE HOGTIE THE WHOLE TRIBE, AND WE PULL 'EM THROUGH THIS GROVE OF DAGGERTREES 'TIL THEIR--HA--THEIR GUTS'RE ALL HANGIN' OUT, AND--AHAHA, OH GODS--JUST BEFORE THE LAST ONE DIES I GRAB HIM AND I SEZ, I SEZ:
I TOLJA I WAS A DRAGGIN' SLAYER!
THAT IS A VERY FUNNY JOKE.
HUSBAND. I WISH TO MURDER THE SCOUT LEADER. DENY ME AND FACE DIVORCE.
JUST BE CALM, OKAY?
HOW CAN I BE CALM WHEN THERE'S A WIHTL--
YESYESYES I KNOW!
=SIGH=
SLOW AND SNEAKY. WE AGREED! MAYBE WE CAN--I DON'T KNOW. DO SOME GOOD OUT HERE. STOP CAPTAIN WORDPLAY FROM FINDING MORE VICTIMS.
YOU WOULD HAVE ME TREAT THE SYMPTOM INSTEAD OF THE CAUSE.

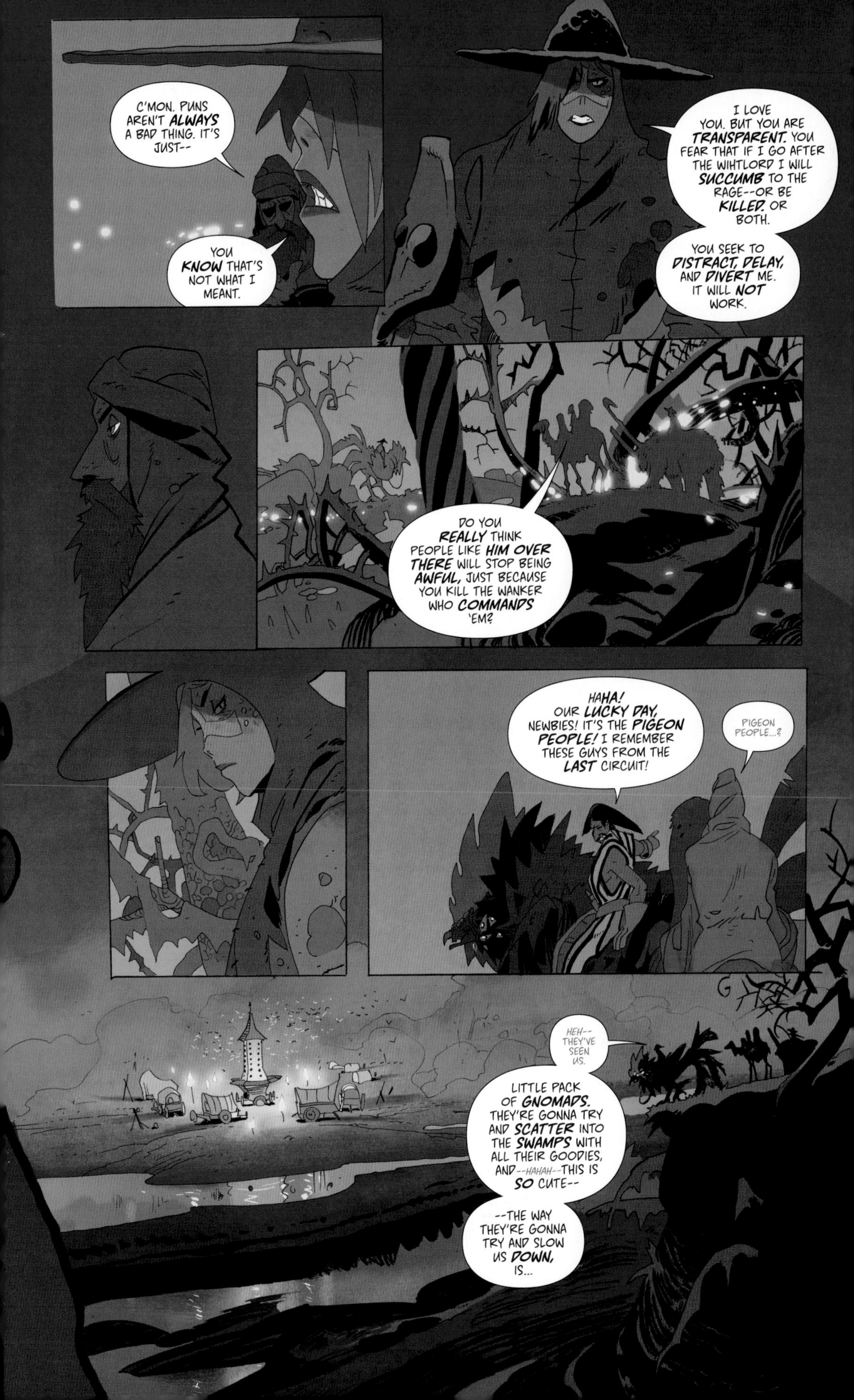
C'MON. PUNS AREN'T ALWAYS A BAD THING. IT'S JUST--
YOU KNOW THAT'S NOT WHAT I MEANT.
I LOVE YOU. BUT YOU ARE TRANSPARENT. YOU FEAR THAT IF I GO AFTER THE WIHTLORD I WILL SUCCUMB TO THE RAGE--OR BE KILLED. OR BOTH.
YOU SEEK TO DISTRACT, DELAY, AND DIVERT ME. IT WILL NOT WORK.
DO YOU REALLY THINK PEOPLE LIKE HIM OVER THERE WILL STOP BEING AWFUL, JUST BECAUSE YOU KILL THE WANKER WHO COMMANDS 'EM?
HAHA! OUR LUCKY DAY, NEWBIES! IT'S THE PIGEON PEOPLE! I REMEMBER THESE GUYS FROM THE LAST CIRCUIT!
PIGEON PEOPLE...?
HEH-- THEY'VE SEEN US.
LITTLE PACK OF GNOMADS. THEY'RE GONNA TRY AND SCATTER INTO THE SWAMPS WITH ALL THEIR GOODIES, AND--HAHAH--THIS IS SO CUTE--
--THE WAY THEY'RE GONNA TRY AND SLOW US DOWN, IS...

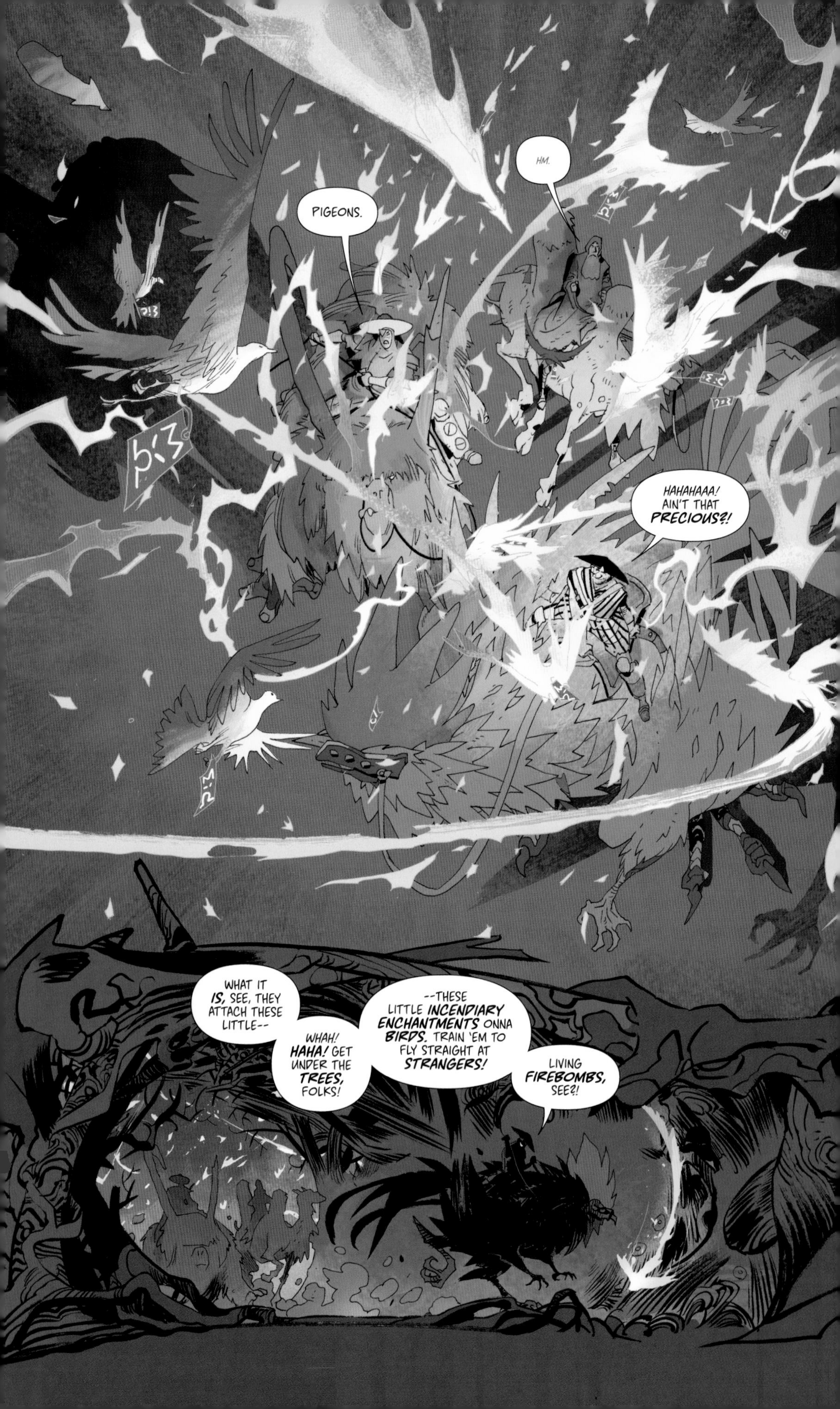
PIGEONS.
HM.
HAHAHAAA! AIN'T THAT PRECIOUS?!
WHAT IT IS, SEE, THEY ATTACH THESE LITTLE--
WHAH! HAHA! GET UNDER THE TREES, FOLKS!
--THESE LITTLE INCENDIARY ENCHANTMENTS ONNA BIRDS. TRAIN 'EM TO FLY STRAIGHT AT STRANGERS!
LIVING FIREBOMBS, SEE?!

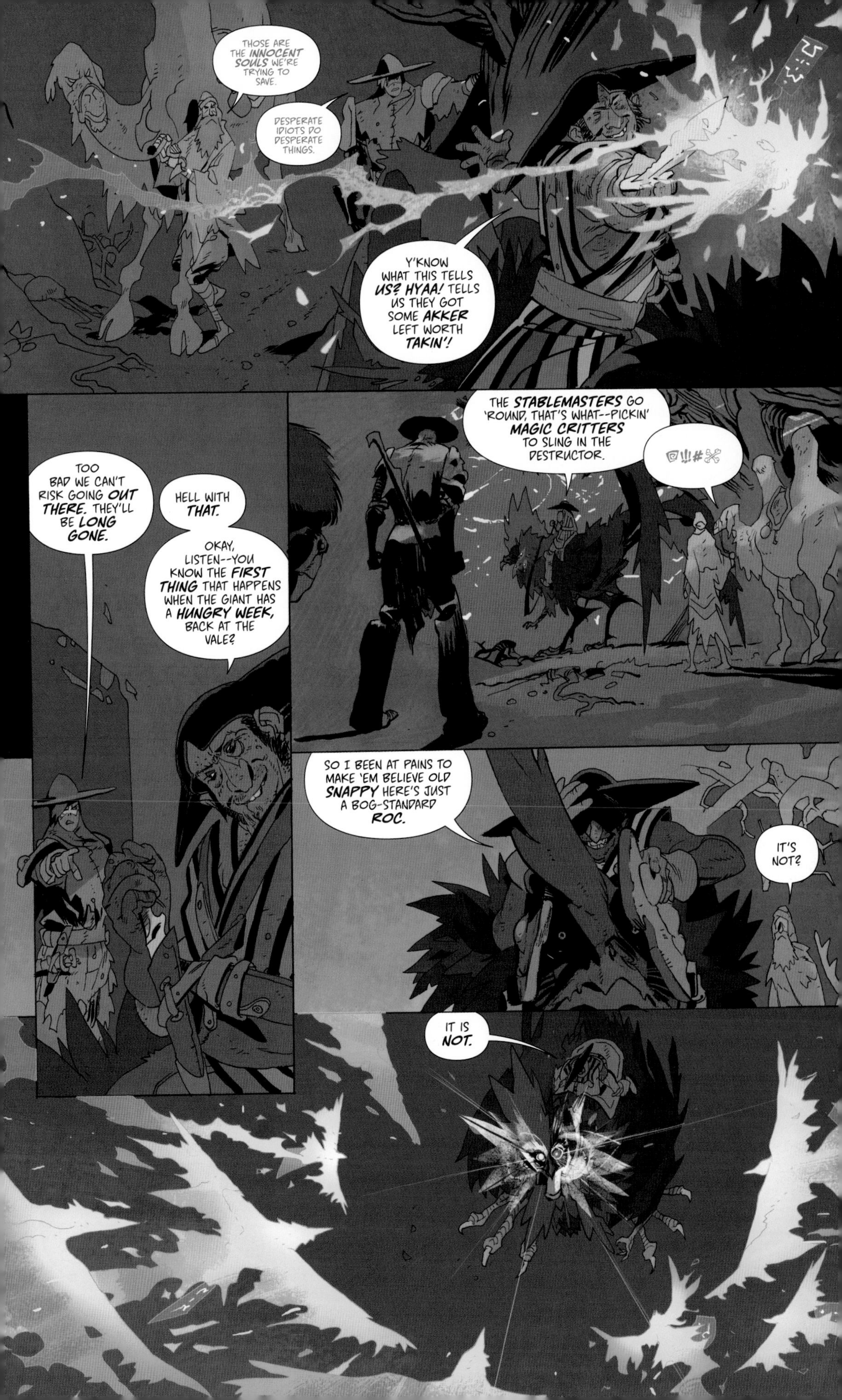
THOSE ARE THE INNOCENT SOULS WE'RE TRYING TO SAVE.
DESPERATE IDIOTS DO DESPERATE THINGS.
Y'KNOW WHAT THIS TELLS US? HYAA! TELLS US THEY GOT SOME AKKER LEFT WORTH TAKIN'!
TOO BAD WE CAN'T RISK GOING OUT THERE. THEY'LL BE LONG GONE.
HELL WITH THAT.
OKAY, LISTEN--YOU KNOW THE FIRST THING THAT HAPPENS WHEN THE GIANT HAS A HUNGRY WEEK, BACK AT THE VALE?
THE STABLEMASTERS GO 'ROUND, THAT'S WHAT--PICKIN' MAGIC CRITTERS TO SLING IN THE DESTRUCTOR.
@!!#
SO I BEEN AT PAINS TO MAKE 'EM BELIEVE OLD SNAPPY HERE'S JUST A BOG-STANDARD ROC.
IT'S NOT?
IT IS NOT.

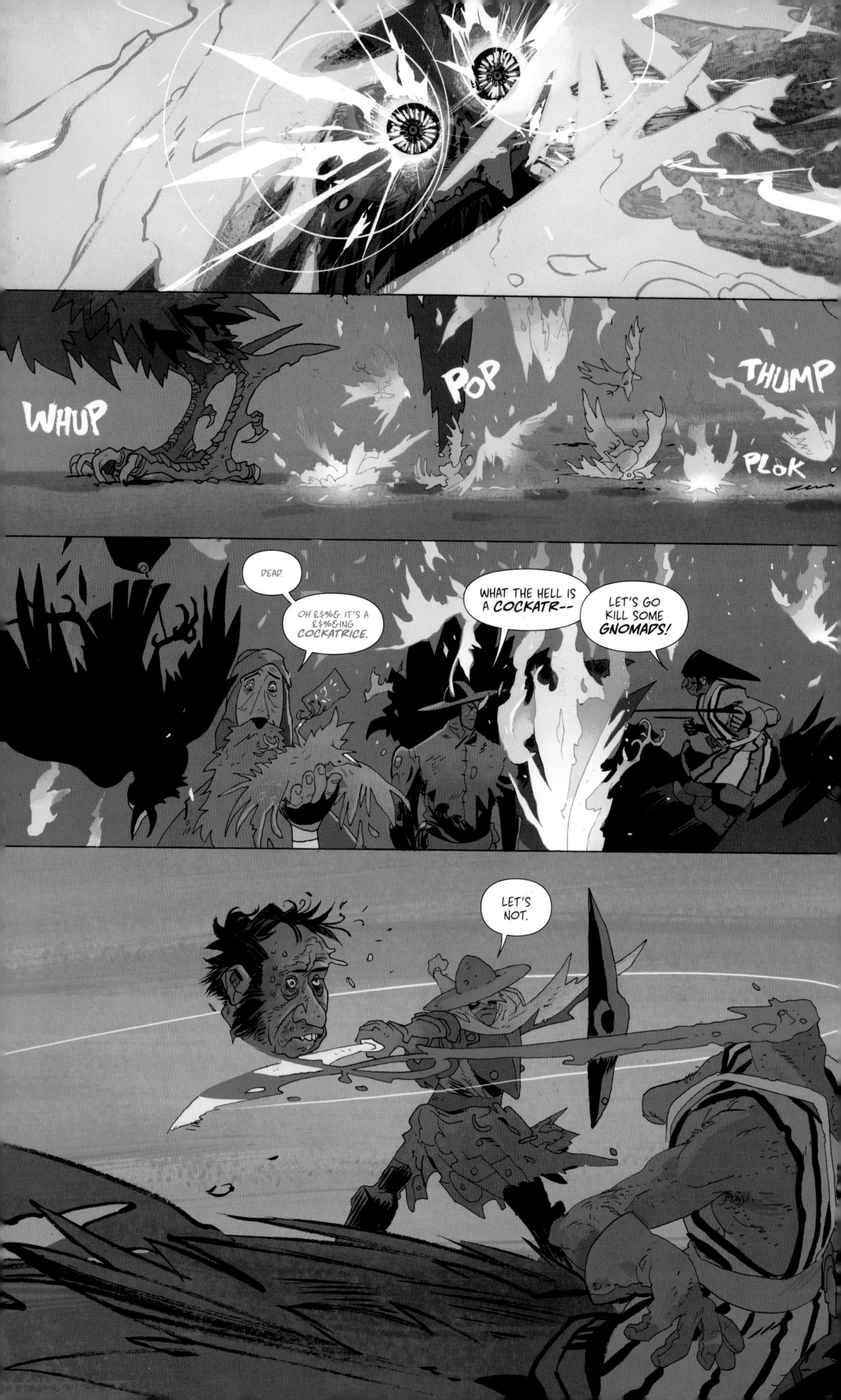
WHUP
POP
THUMP
PLOK
DEAD.
OH £$%& IT'S A £$%&ING COCKATRICE.
WHAT THE HELL IS A COCKATR--
LET'S GO KILL SOME GNOMADS!
LET'S NOT.

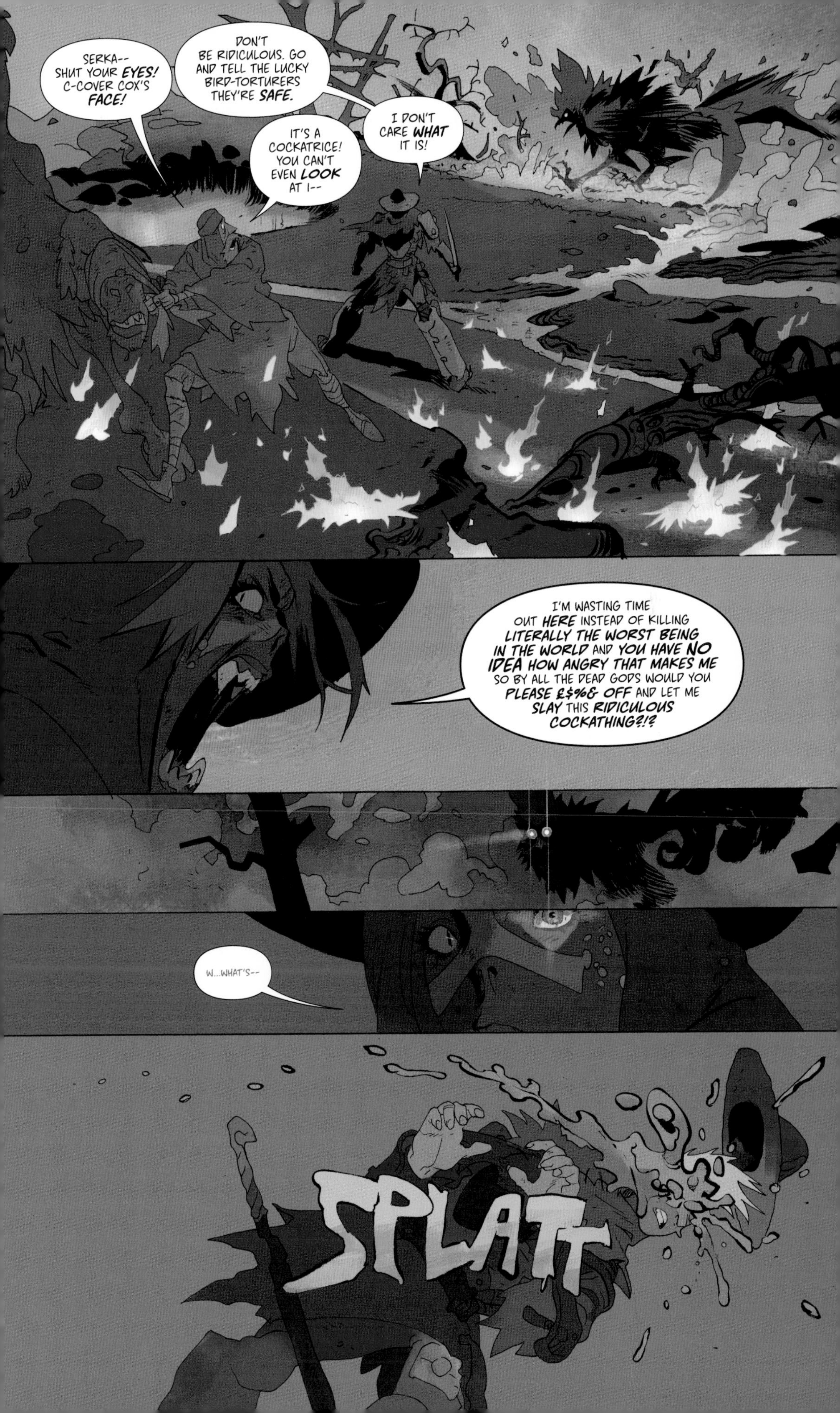
SERKA-- SHUT YOUR EYES! C-COVER COX'S FACE!
DON'T BE RIDICULOUS. GO AND TELL THE LUCKY BIRD-TORTURERS THEY'RE SAFE.
IT'S A COCKATRICE! YOU CAN'T EVEN LOOK AT I--
I DON'T CARE WHAT IT IS!
I'M WASTING TIME OUT HERE INSTEAD OF KILLING LITERALLY THE WORST BEING IN THE WORLD AND YOU HAVE NO IDEA HOW ANGRY THAT MAKES ME SO BY ALL THE DEAD GODS WOULD YOU PLEASE £$%& OFF AND LET ME SLAY THIS RIDICULOUS COCKATHING?!?
W...WHAT'S--
SPLATT

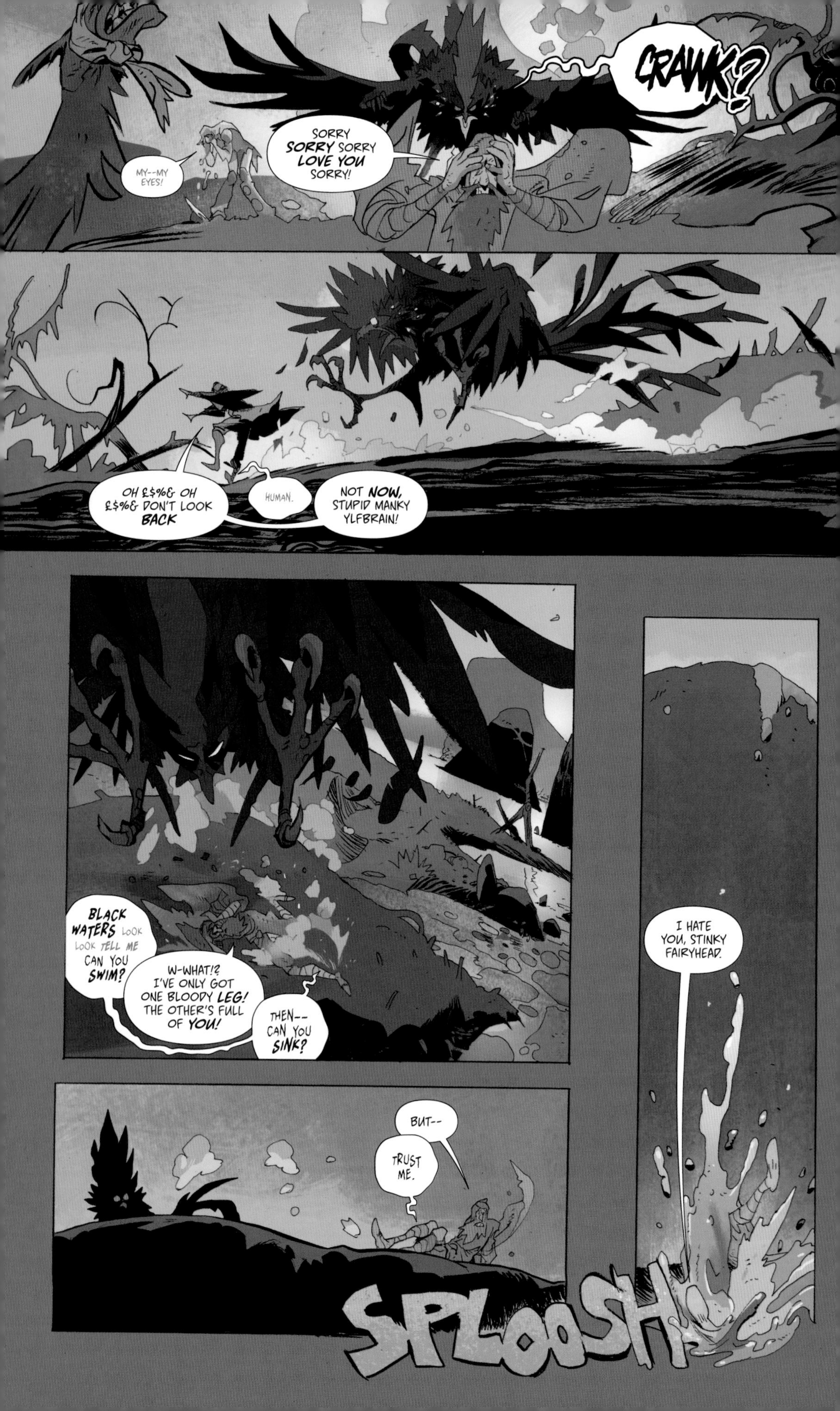
CRAWK?
SORRY SORRY SORRY LOVE YOU SORRY!
MY--MY EYES!
OH £$%& OH £$%& DON'T LOOK BACK
HUMAN.
NOT NOW, STUPID MANKY YLFBRAIN!
BLACK WATERS LOOK LOOK TELL ME CAN YOU SWIM?
W-WHAT!? I'VE ONLY GOT ONE BLOODY LEG! THE OTHER'S FULL OF YOU!
THEN-- CAN YOU SINK?
I HATE YOU, STINKY FAIRYHEAD.
BUT--
TRUST ME.
SPLOOSH

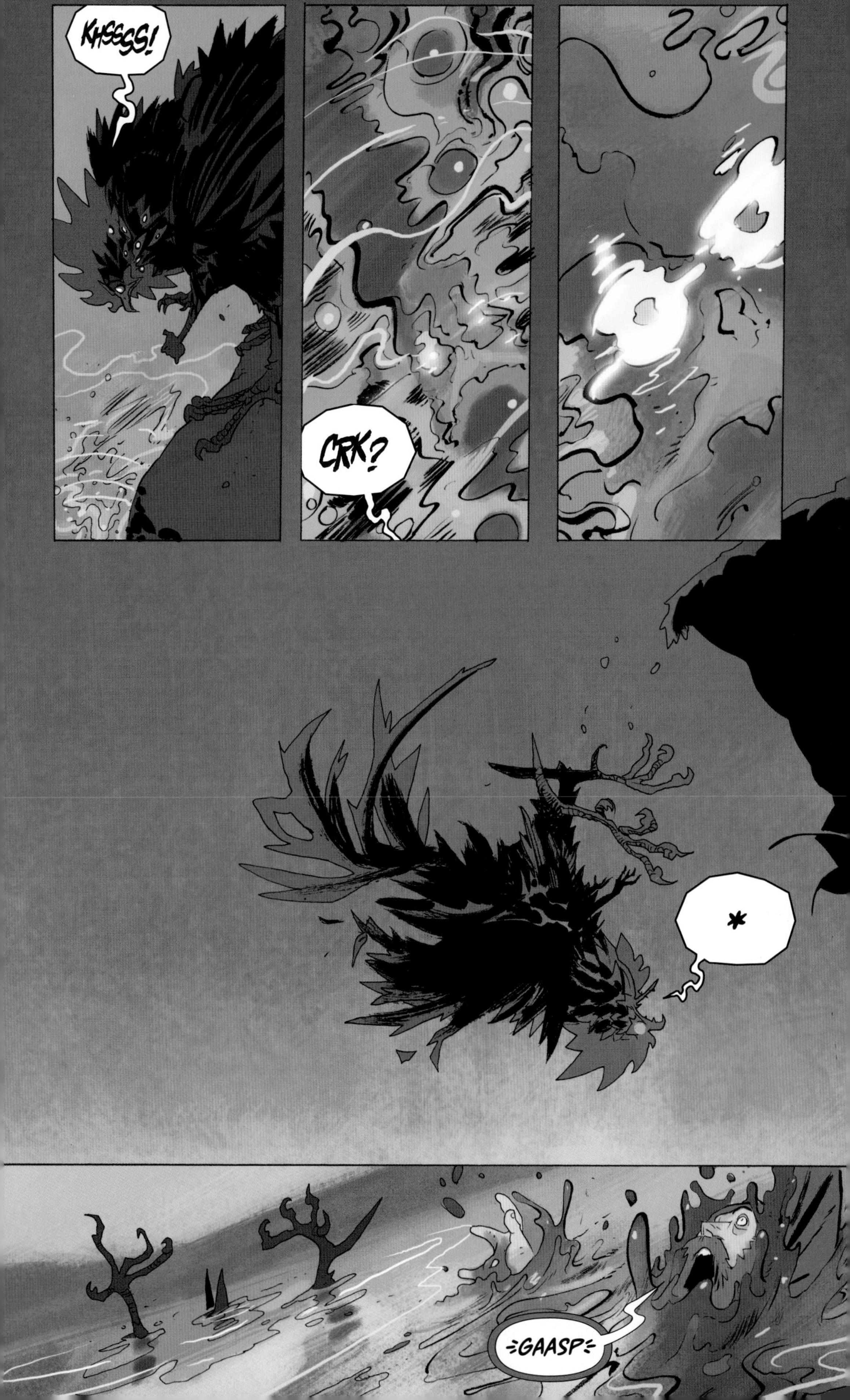
KHSSSS!
CRK?
*
=GAASP=

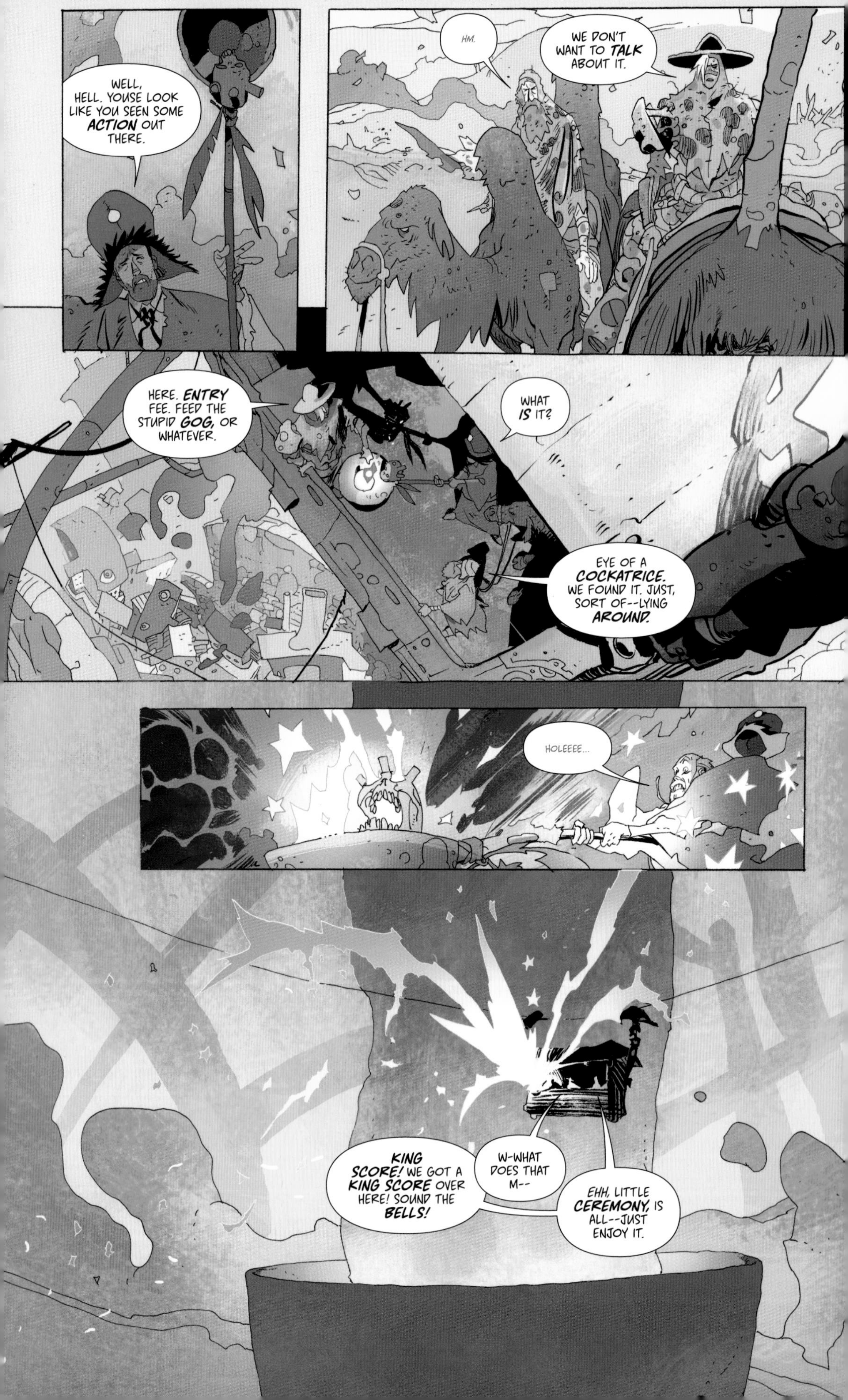
WELL, HELL. YOUSE LOOK LIKE YOU SEEN SOME ACTION OUT THERE.
HM.
WE DON'T WANT TO TALK ABOUT IT.
HERE. ENTRY FEE. FEED THE STUPID GOG, OR WHATEVER.
WHAT IS IT?
EYE OF A COCKATRICE. WE FOUND IT. JUST, SORT OF--LYING AROUND.
HOLEEEE...
KING SCORE! WE GOT A KING SCORE OVER HERE! SOUND THE BELLS!
W-WHAT DOES THAT M--
EHH, LITTLE CEREMONY, IS ALL--JUST ENJOY IT.

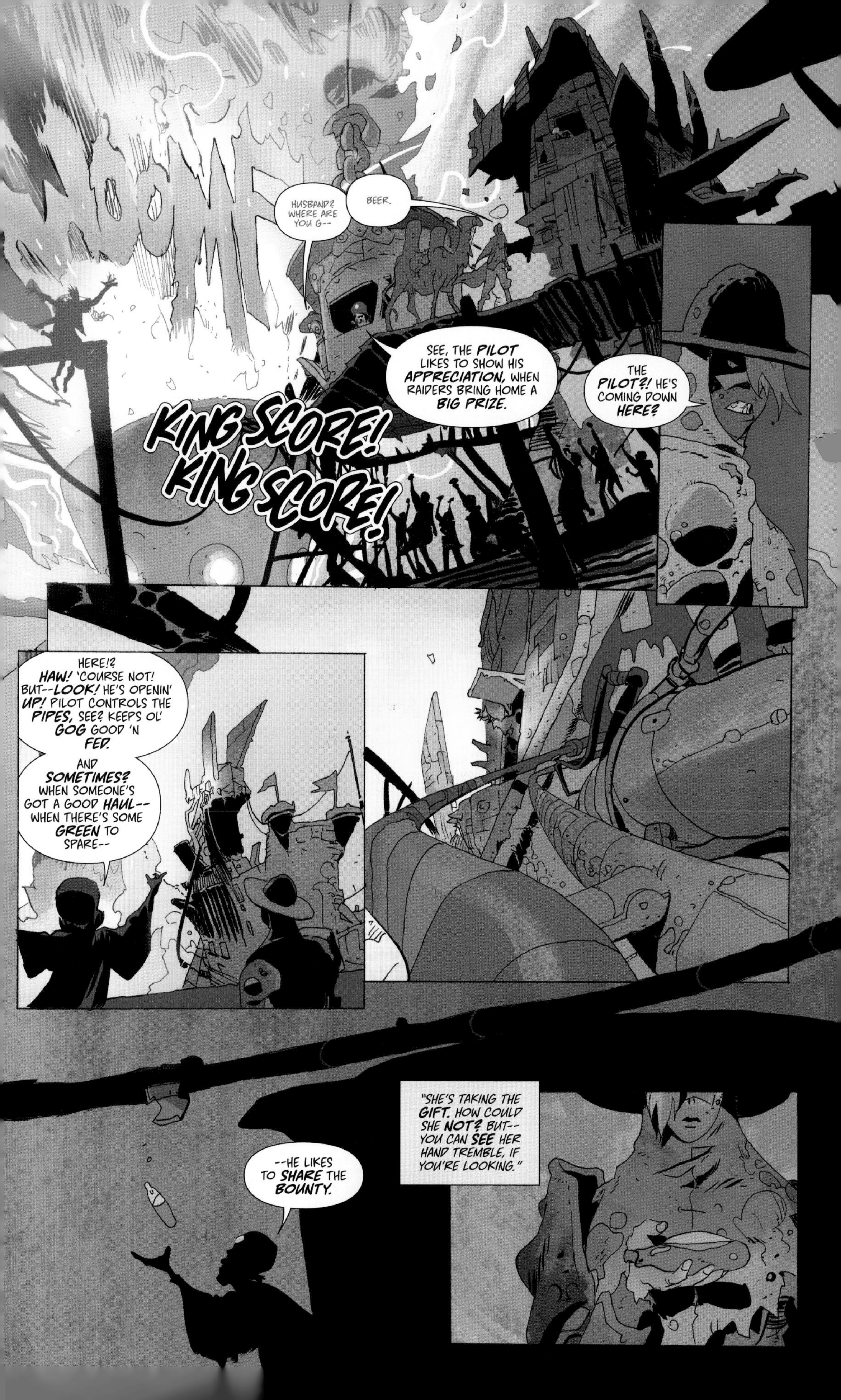

HUSBAND? WHERE ARE YOU G--
BEER.
SEE, THE PILOT LIKES TO SHOW HIS APPRECIATION, WHEN RAIDERS BRING HOME A BIG PRIZE.
KING SCORE! KING SCORE!
THE PILOT?! HE'S COMING DOWN HERE?
HERE!? HAW! 'COURSE NOT! BUT--LOOK! HE'S OPENIN' UP! PILOT CONTROLS THE PIPES, SEE? KEEPS OL' GOG GOOD 'N FED.
AND SOMETIMES? WHEN SOMEONE'S GOT A GOOD HAUL-- WHEN THERE'S SOME GREEN TO SPARE--
--HE LIKES TO SHARE THE BOUNTY.
"SHE'S TAKING THE GIFT. HOW COULD SHE NOT? BUT-- YOU CAN SEE HER HAND TREMBLE, IF YOU'RE LOOKING."

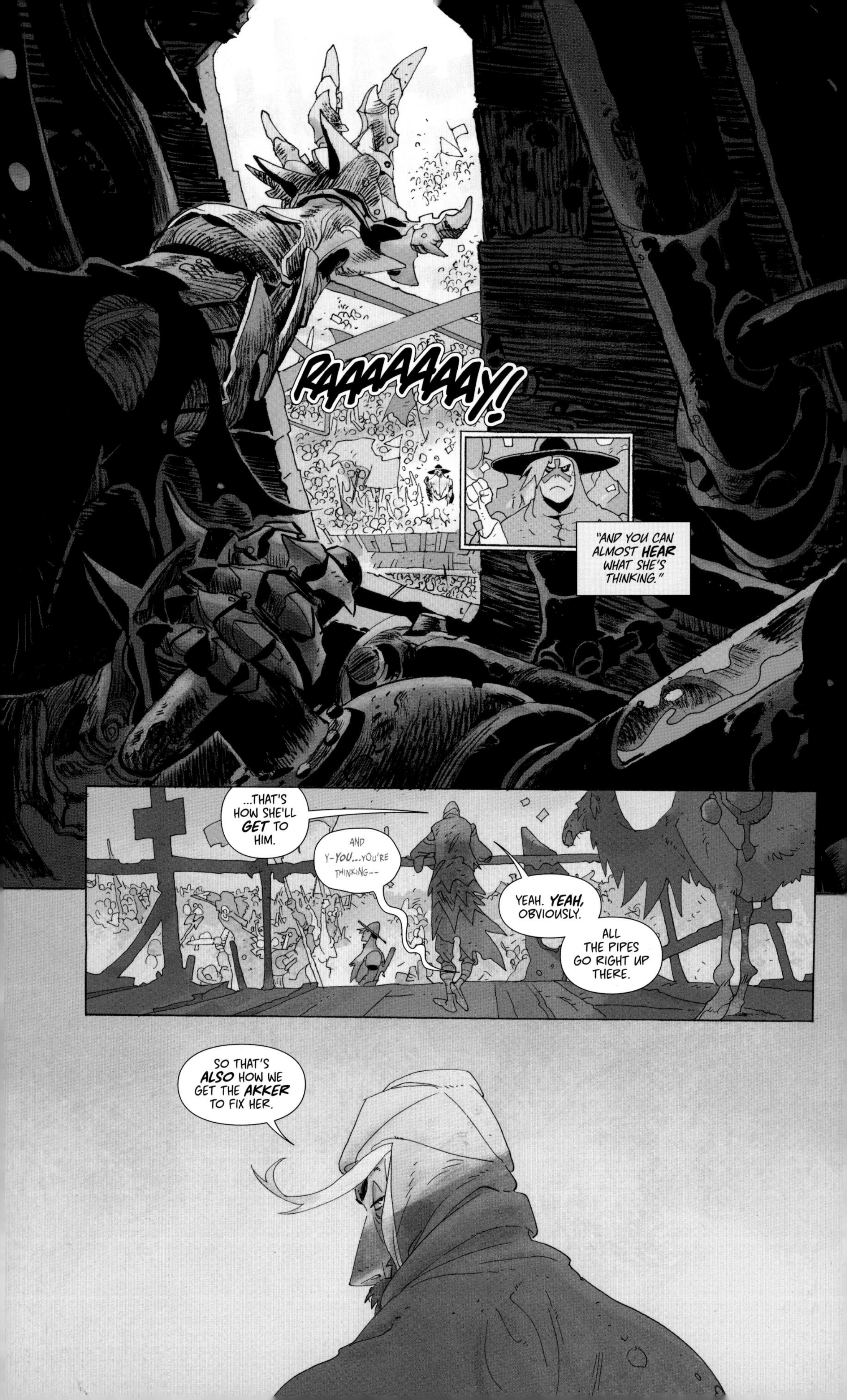
RAAAAAAAY!
"AND YOU CAN ALMOST **HEAR** WHAT SHE'S THINKING."
...THAT'S HOW SHE'LL **GET** TO HIM.
AND Y-**YOU**...YOU'RE THINKING--
YEAH. **YEAH,** OBVIOUSLY.
ALL THE PIPES GO RIGHT UP THERE.
SO THAT'S **ALSO** HOW WE GET THE **AKKER** TO FIX HER.

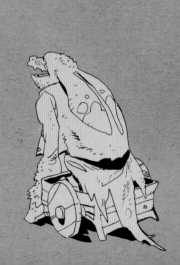

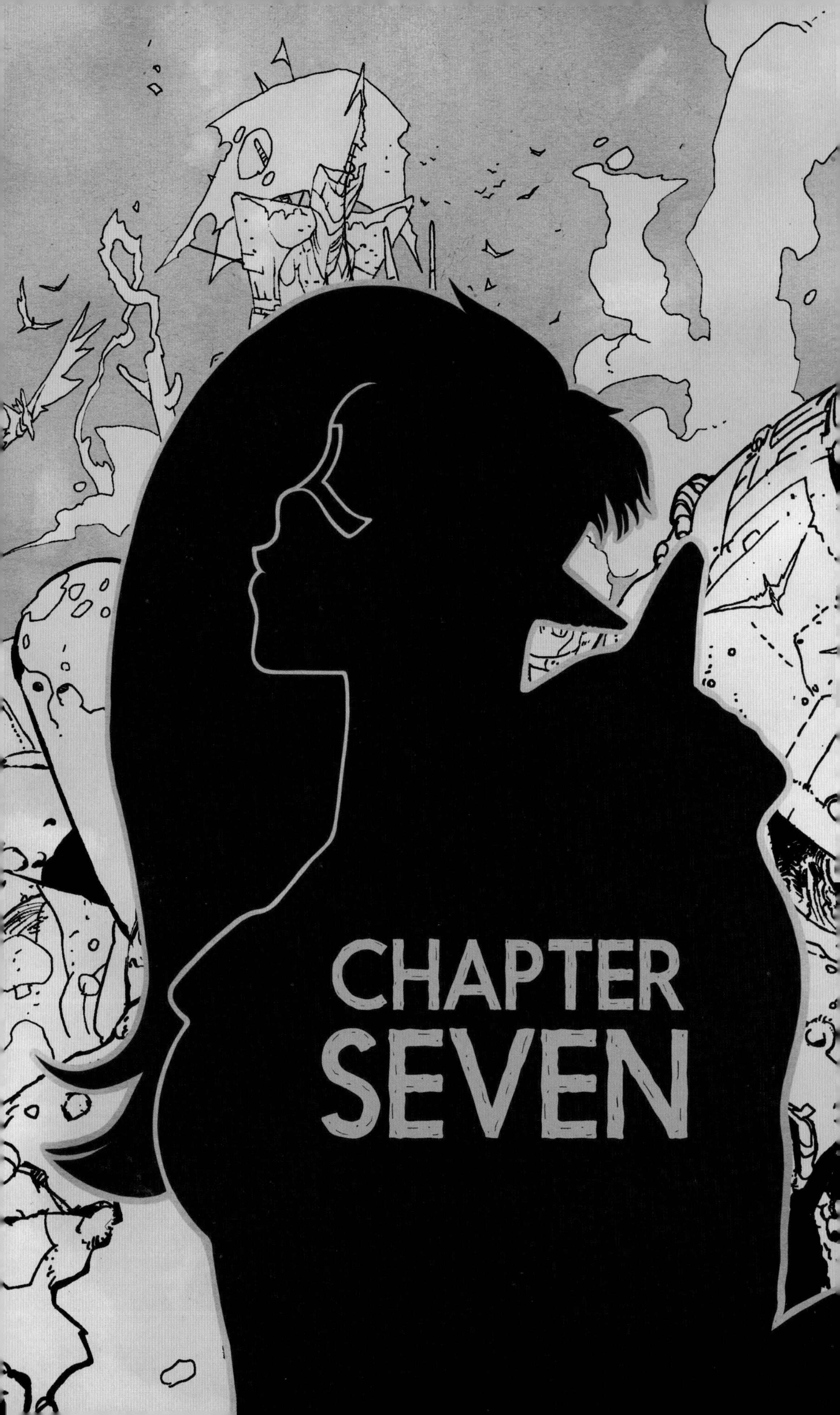
CHAPTER
SEVEN

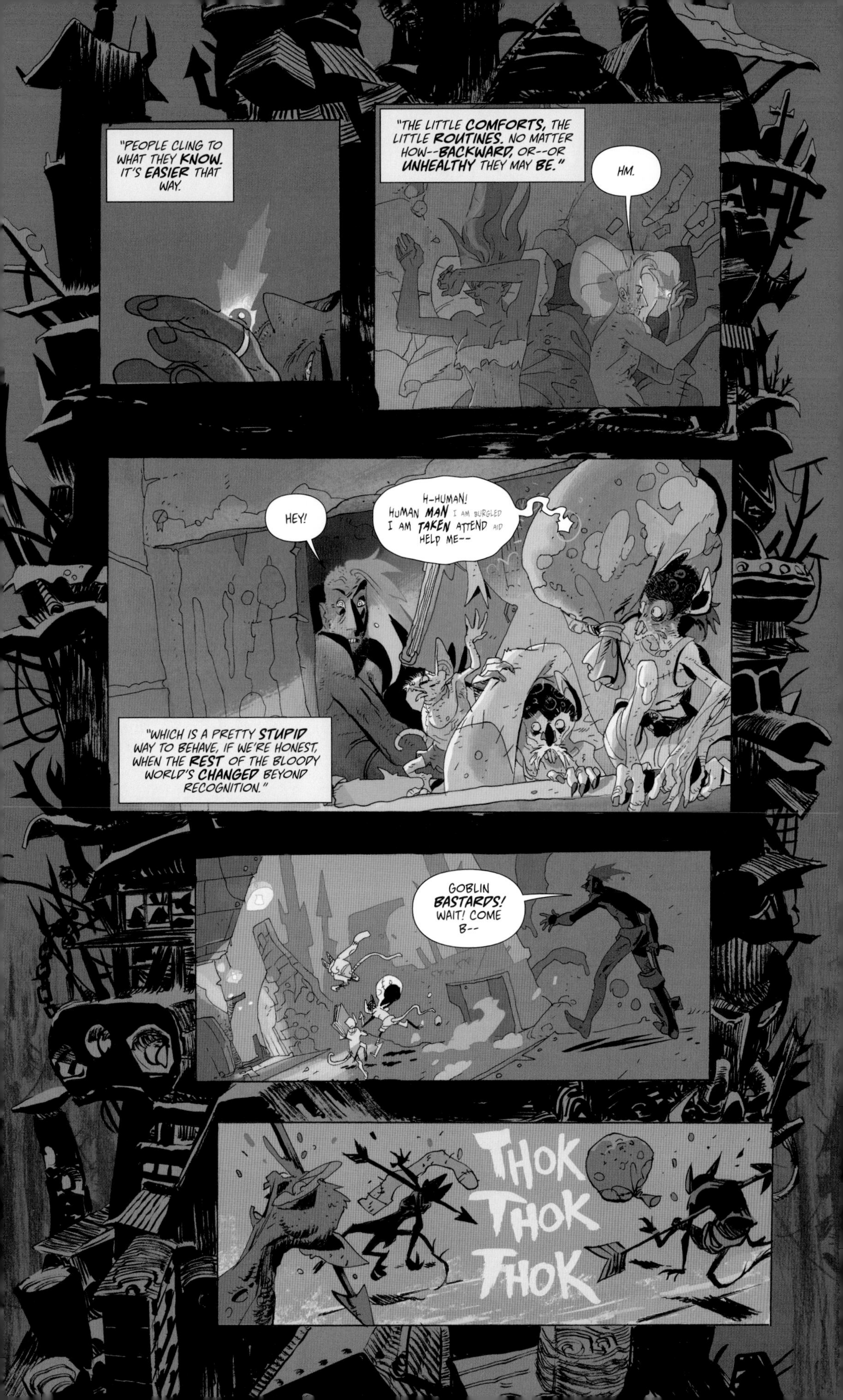
"PEOPLE CLING TO WHAT THEY KNOW. IT'S EASIER THAT WAY.
"THE LITTLE COMFORTS, THE LITTLE ROUTINES. NO MATTER HOW--BACKWARD, OR--OR UNHEALTHY THEY MAY BE."
HM.
HEY!
H-HUMAN! HUMAN MAN I AM BURGLED I AM TAKEN ATTEND AID HELP ME--
"WHICH IS A PRETTY STUPID WAY TO BEHAVE, IF WE'RE HONEST, WHEN THE REST OF THE BLOODY WORLD'S CHANGED BEYOND RECOGNITION."
GOBLIN BASTARDS! WAIT! COME B--
THOK THOK THOK

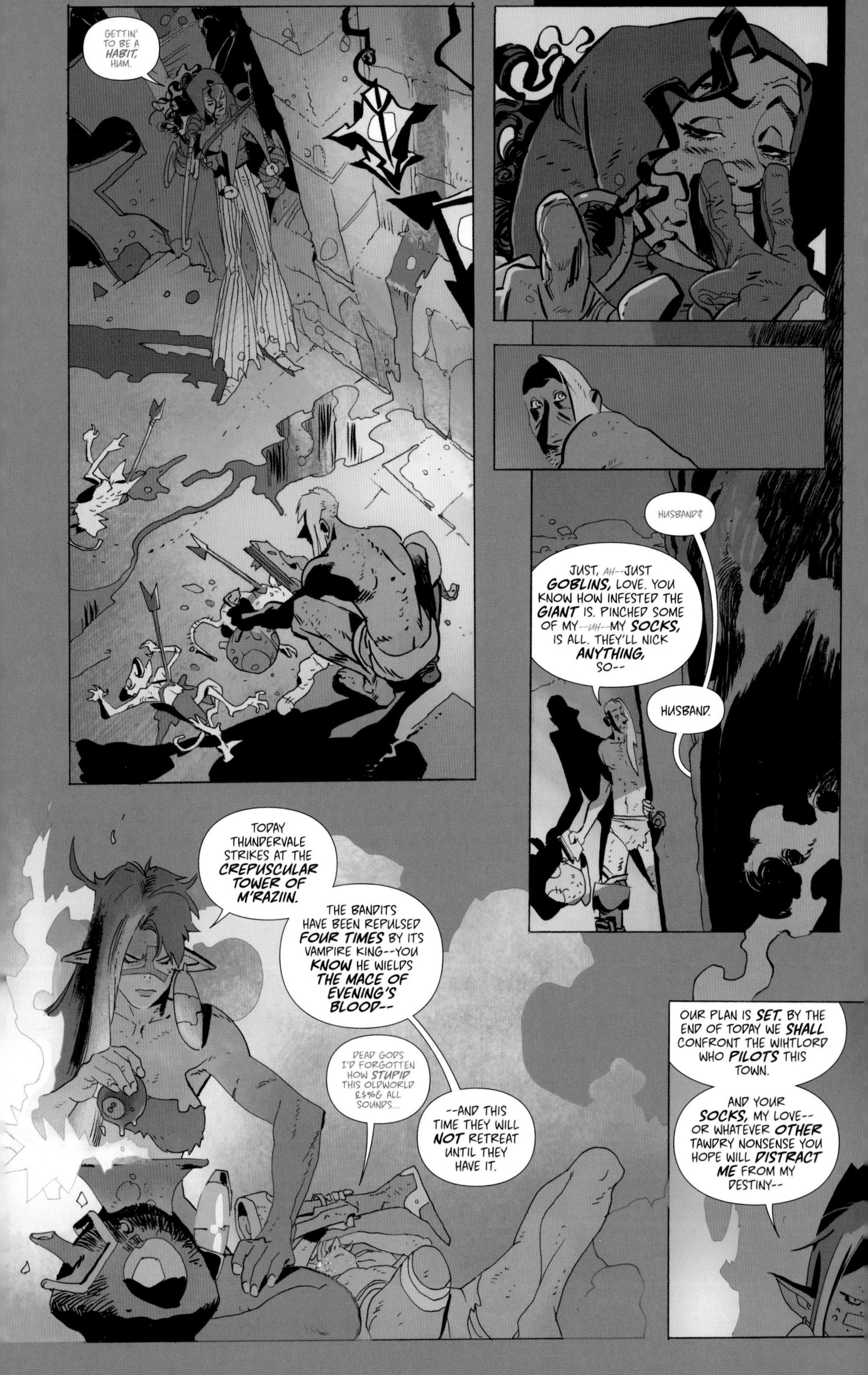
GETTIN' TO BE A HABIT, HUM.
HUSBAND?
JUST, AH--JUST GOBLINS, LOVE. YOU KNOW HOW INFESTED THE GIANT IS. PINCHED SOME OF MY--UH--MY SOCKS, IS ALL. THEY'LL NICK ANYTHING, SO--
HUSBAND.
TODAY THUNDERVALE STRIKES AT THE CREPUSCULAR TOWER OF M'RAZIIN.
THE BANDITS HAVE BEEN REPULSED FOUR TIMES BY ITS VAMPIRE KING--YOU KNOW HE WIELDS THE MACE OF EVENING'S BLOOD--
DEAD GODS I'D FORGOTTEN HOW STUPID THIS OLDWORLD £$%& ALL SOUNDS...
--AND THIS TIME THEY WILL NOT RETREAT UNTIL THEY HAVE IT.
OUR PLAN IS SET. BY THE END OF TODAY WE SHALL CONFRONT THE WIHTLORD WHO PILOTS THIS TOWN.
AND YOUR SOCKS, MY LOVE--OR WHATEVER OTHER TAWDRY NONSENSE YOU HOPE WILL DISTRACT ME FROM MY DESTINY--

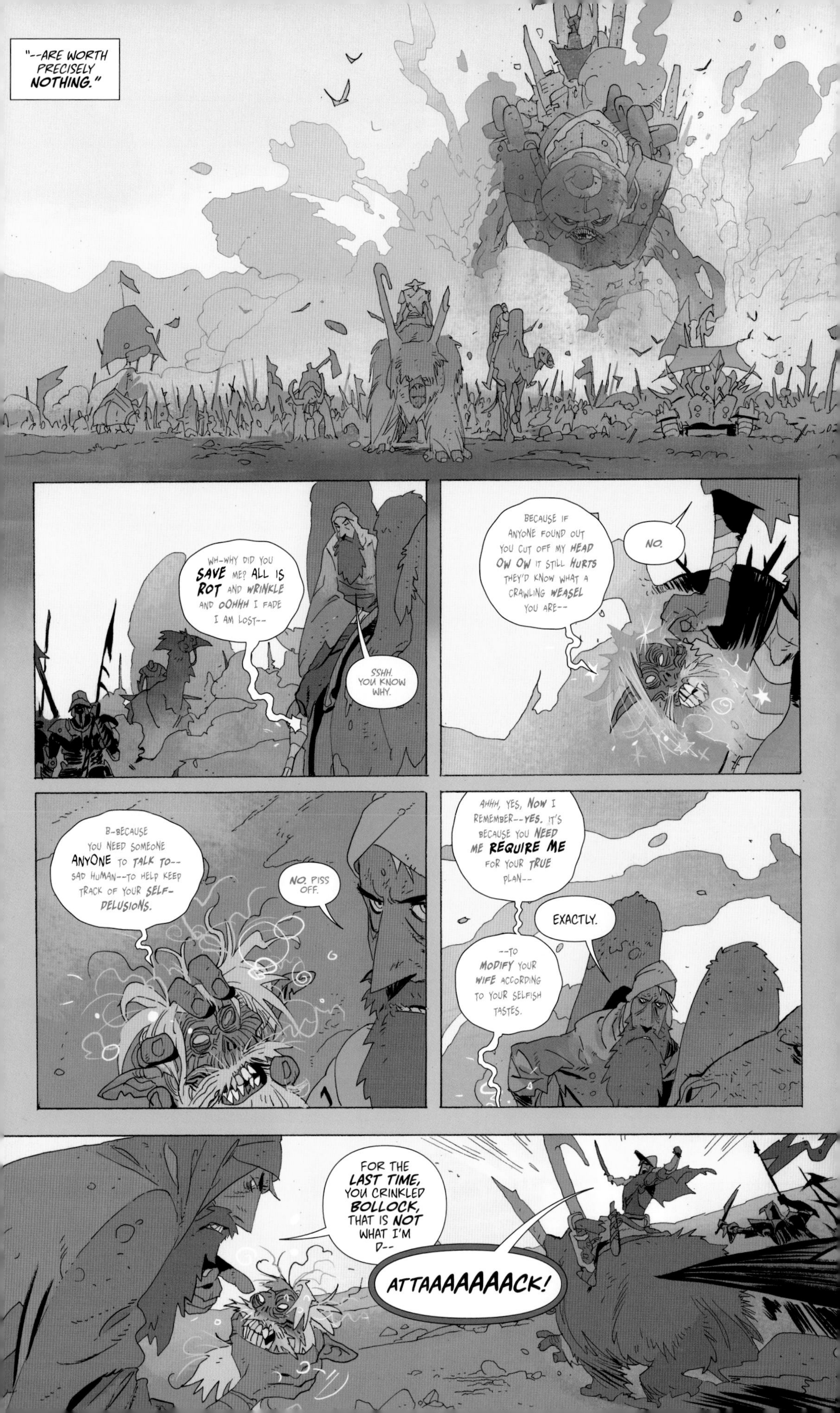
"--ARE WORTH PRECISELY NOTHING."
WH-WHY DID YOU SAVE ME? ALL IS ROT AND WRINKLE AND OOHHH I FADE I AM LOST--
SSHH. YOU KNOW WHY.
BECAUSE IF ANYONE FOUND OUT YOU CUT OFF MY HEAD OW OW IT STILL HURTS THEY'D KNOW WHAT A CRAWLING WEASEL YOU ARE--
NO.
B-BECAUSE YOU NEED SOMEONE ANYONE TO TALK TO--SAD HUMAN--TO HELP KEEP TRACK OF YOUR SELF-DELUSIONS.
NO. PISS OFF.
AHHH, YES, NOW I REMEMBER--YES. IT'S BECAUSE YOU NEED ME REQUIRE ME FOR YOUR TRUE PLAN--
EXACTLY.
--TO MODIFY YOUR WIFE ACCORDING TO YOUR SELFISH TASTES.
FOR THE LAST TIME, YOU CRINKLED BOLLOCK, THAT IS NOT WHAT I'M D--
ATTAAAAAAACK!

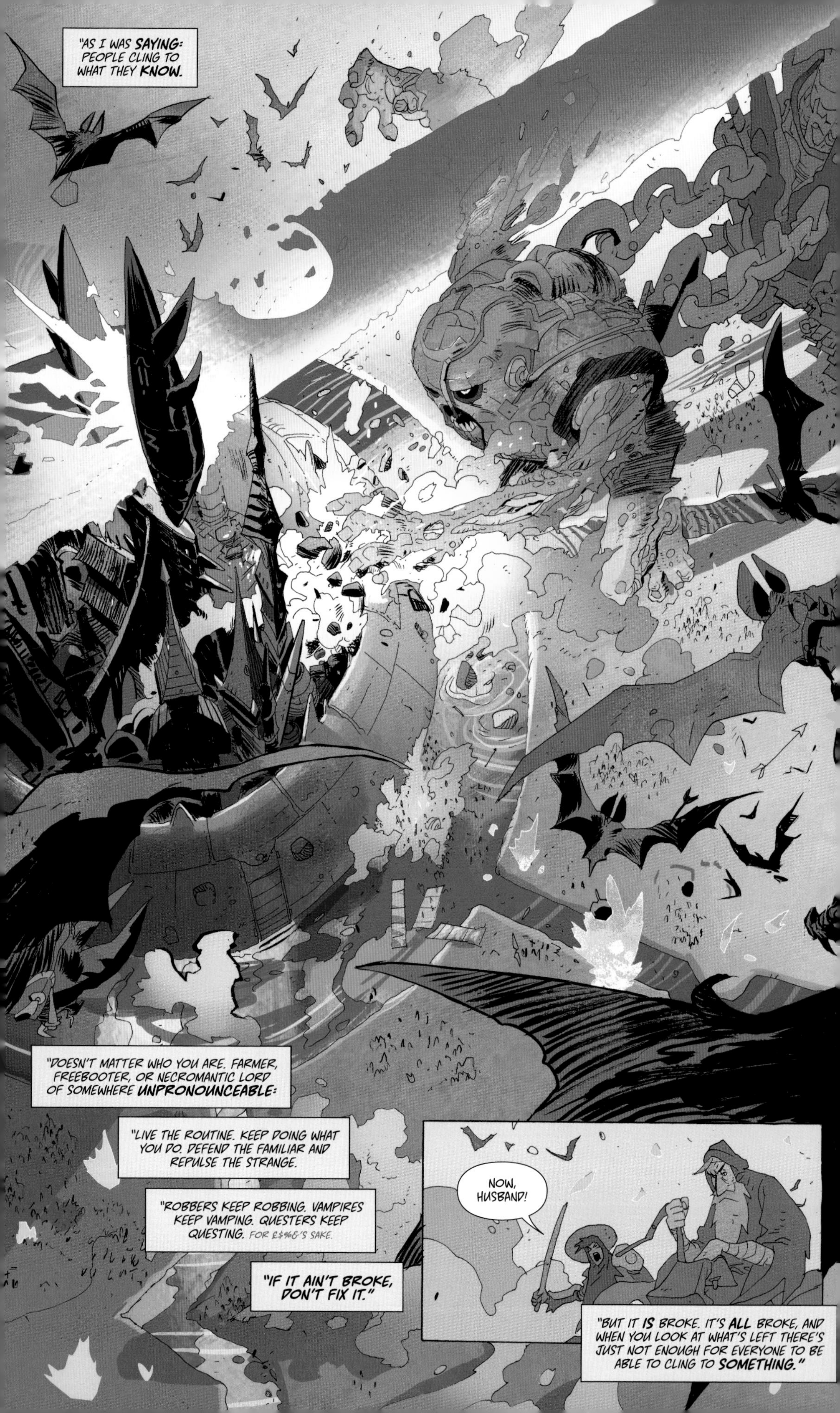
"AS I WAS SAYING: PEOPLE CLING TO WHAT THEY KNOW.
"DOESN'T MATTER WHO YOU ARE. FARMER, FREEBOOTER, OR NECROMANTIC LORD OF SOMEWHERE UNPRONOUNCEABLE:
"LIVE THE ROUTINE. KEEP DOING WHAT YOU DO. DEFEND THE FAMILIAR AND REPULSE THE STRANGE.
"ROBBERS KEEP ROBBING. VAMPIRES KEEP VAMPING. QUESTERS KEEP QUESTING. FOR £$%&'S SAKE.
"IF IT AIN'T BROKE, DON'T FIX IT."
NOW, HUSBAND!
"BUT IT IS BROKE. IT'S ALL BROKE, AND WHEN YOU LOOK AT WHAT'S LEFT THERE'S JUST NOT ENOUGH FOR EVERYONE TO BE ABLE TO CLING TO SOMETHING."

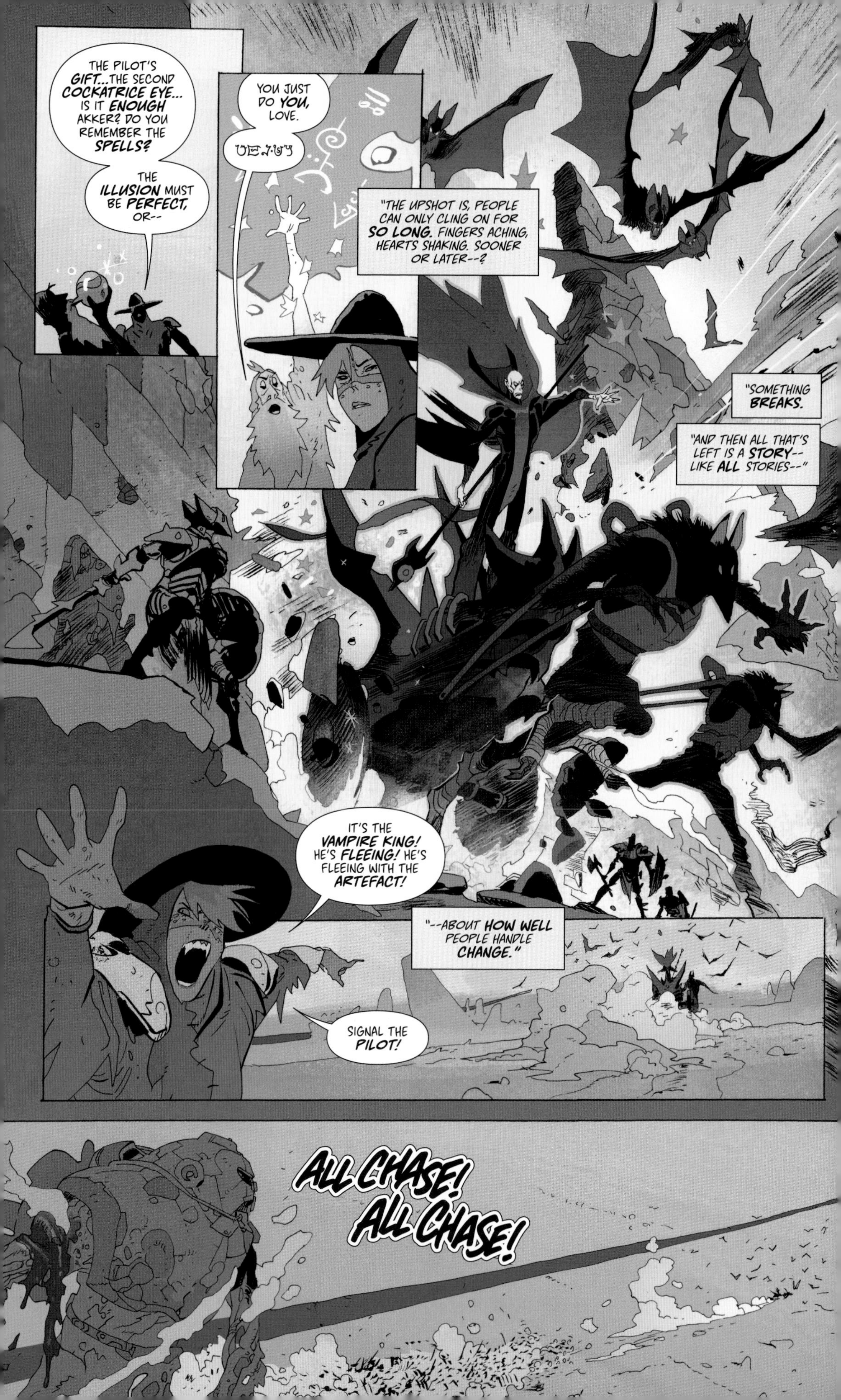

THE PILOT'S GIFT...THE SECOND COCKATRICE EYE... IS IT ENOUGH AKKER? DO YOU REMEMBER THE SPELLS?
THE ILLUSION MUST BE PERFECT, OR--
YOU JUST DO YOU, LOVE.
"THE UPSHOT IS, PEOPLE CAN ONLY CLING ON FOR SO LONG. FINGERS ACHING, HEARTS SHAKING. SOONER OR LATER--?
"SOMETHING BREAKS.
"AND THEN ALL THAT'S LEFT IS A STORY-- LIKE ALL STORIES--"
IT'S THE VAMPIRE KING! HE'S FLEEING! HE'S FLEEING WITH THE ARTEFACT!
"--ABOUT HOW WELL PEOPLE HANDLE CHANGE."
SIGNAL THE PILOT!
ALL CHASE! ALL CHASE!

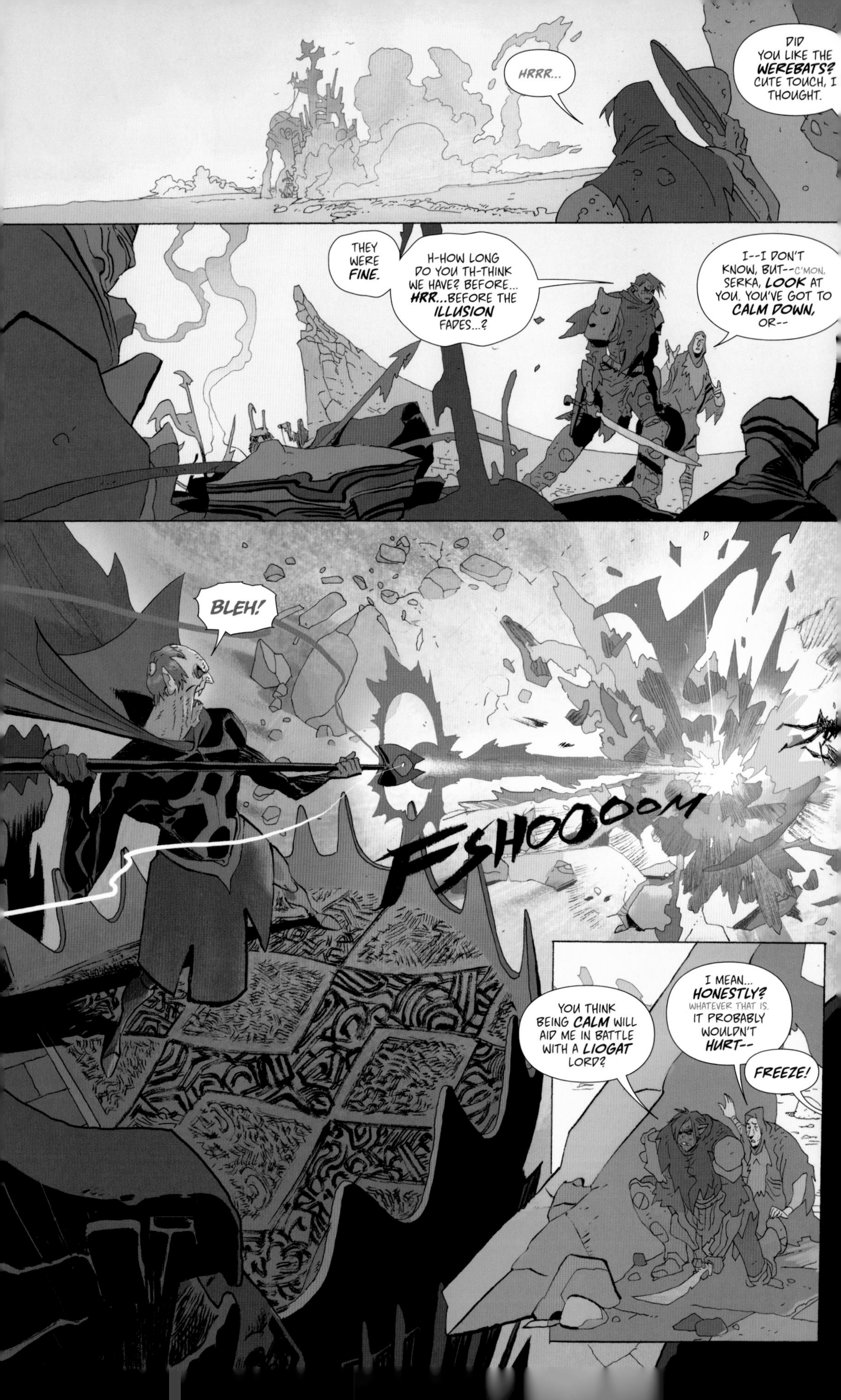
HRRR...
DID YOU LIKE THE WEREBATS? CUTE TOUCH, I THOUGHT.
THEY WERE FINE.
H-HOW LONG DO YOU TH-THINK WE HAVE? BEFORE... HRR...BEFORE THE ILLUSION FADES...?
I--I DON'T KNOW, BUT--C'MON, SERKA, LOOK AT YOU. YOU'VE GOT TO CALM DOWN, OR--
BLEH!
FSHOOOOOM
YOU THINK BEING CALM WILL AID ME IN BATTLE WITH A LIOGAT LORD?
I MEAN... HONESTLY? WHATEVER THAT IS. IT PROBABLY WOULDN'T HURT--
FREEZE!

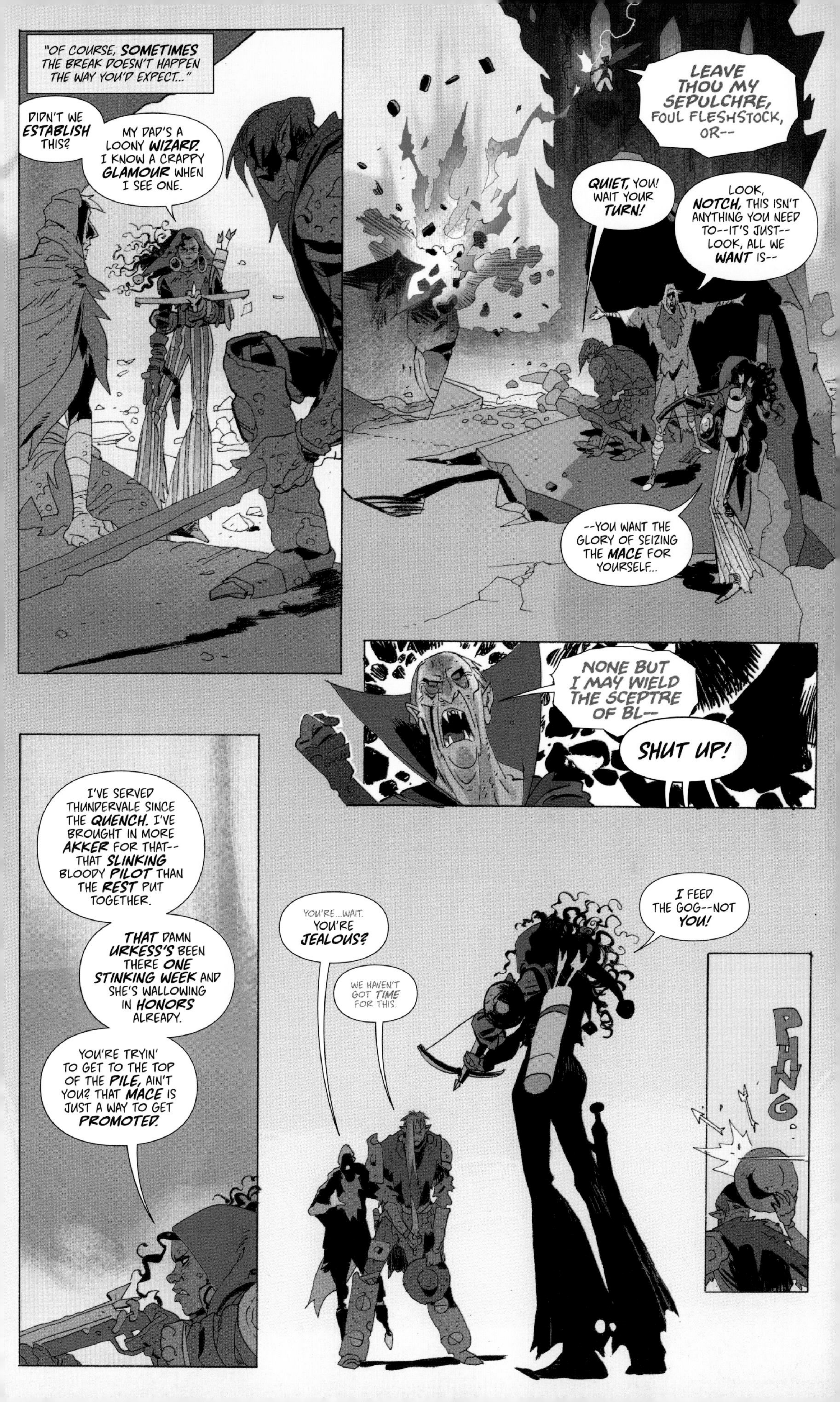
"OF COURSE, SOMETIMES THE BREAK DOESN'T HAPPEN THE WAY YOU'D EXPECT..."
DIDN'T WE ESTABLISH THIS?
MY DAD'S A LOONY WIZARD. I KNOW A CRAPPY GLAMOUR WHEN I SEE ONE.
LEAVE THOU MY SEPULCHRE, FOUL FLESHSTOCK, OR--
QUIET, YOU! WAIT YOUR TURN!
LOOK, NOTCH, THIS ISN'T ANYTHING YOU NEED TO--IT'S JUST--LOOK, ALL WE WANT IS--
--YOU WANT THE GLORY OF SEIZING THE MACE FOR YOURSELF...
NONE BUT I MAY WIELD THE SCEPTRE OF BL--
SHUT UP!
I'VE SERVED THUNDERVALE SINCE THE QUENCH. I'VE BROUGHT IN MORE AKKER FOR THAT--THAT SLINKING BLOODY PILOT THAN THE REST PUT TOGETHER.
THAT DAMN URKESS'S BEEN THERE ONE STINKING WEEK AND SHE'S WALLOWING IN HONORS ALREADY.
YOU'RE TRYIN' TO GET TO THE TOP OF THE PILE, AIN'T YOU? THAT MACE IS JUST A WAY TO GET PROMOTED.
YOU'RE...WAIT. YOU'RE JEALOUS?
WE HAVEN'T GOT TIME FOR THIS.
I FEED THE GOG--NOT YOU!
PHNG

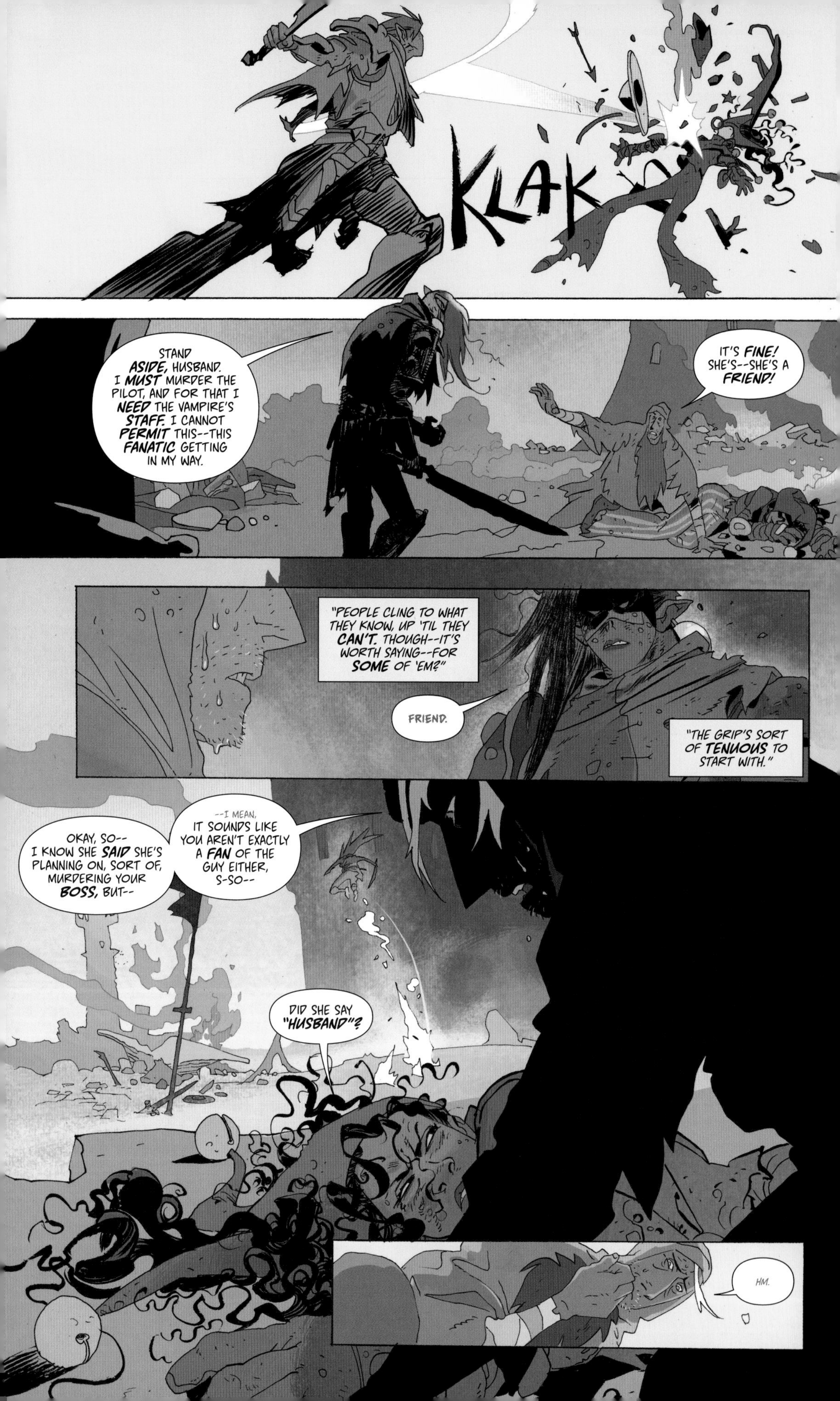
KLAK
STAND ASIDE, HUSBAND. I MUST MURDER THE PILOT, AND FOR THAT I NEED THE VAMPIRE'S STAFF. I CANNOT PERMIT THIS--THIS FANATIC GETTING IN MY WAY.
IT'S FINE! SHE'S--SHE'S A FRIEND!
"PEOPLE CLING TO WHAT THEY KNOW, UP 'TIL THEY CAN'T. THOUGH--IT'S WORTH SAYING--FOR SOME OF 'EM?"
FRIEND.
"THE GRIP'S SORT OF TENUOUS TO START WITH."
OKAY, SO-- I KNOW SHE SAID SHE'S PLANNING ON, SORT OF, MURDERING YOUR BOSS, BUT--
--I MEAN, IT SOUNDS LIKE YOU AREN'T EXACTLY A FAN OF THE GUY EITHER, S-SO--
DID SHE SAY "HUSBAND"?
HM.

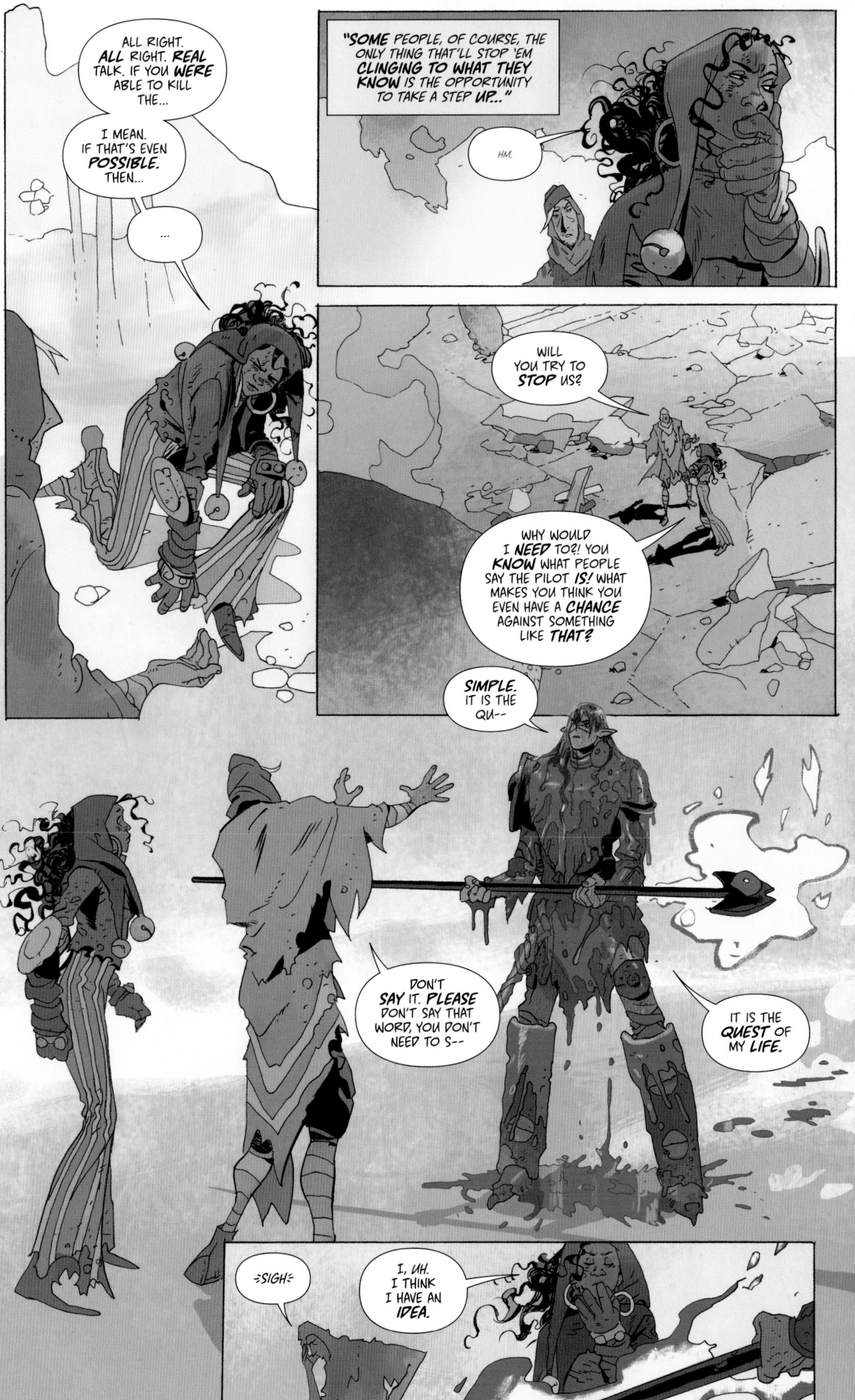
ALL RIGHT. ALL RIGHT. REAL TALK. IF YOU WERE ABLE TO KILL THE...
I MEAN. IF THAT'S EVEN POSSIBLE. THEN...
...
"SOME PEOPLE, OF COURSE, THE ONLY THING THAT'LL STOP 'EM CLINGING TO WHAT THEY KNOW IS THE OPPORTUNITY TO TAKE A STEP UP..."
HM.
WILL YOU TRY TO STOP US?
WHY WOULD I NEED TO?! YOU KNOW WHAT PEOPLE SAY THE PILOT IS! WHAT MAKES YOU THINK YOU EVEN HAVE A CHANCE AGAINST SOMETHING LIKE THAT?
SIMPLE. IT IS THE QU--
DON'T SAY IT. PLEASE DON'T SAY THAT WORD, YOU DON'T NEED TO S--
IT IS THE QUEST OF MY LIFE.
=SIGH=
I, UH. I THINK I HAVE AN IDEA.

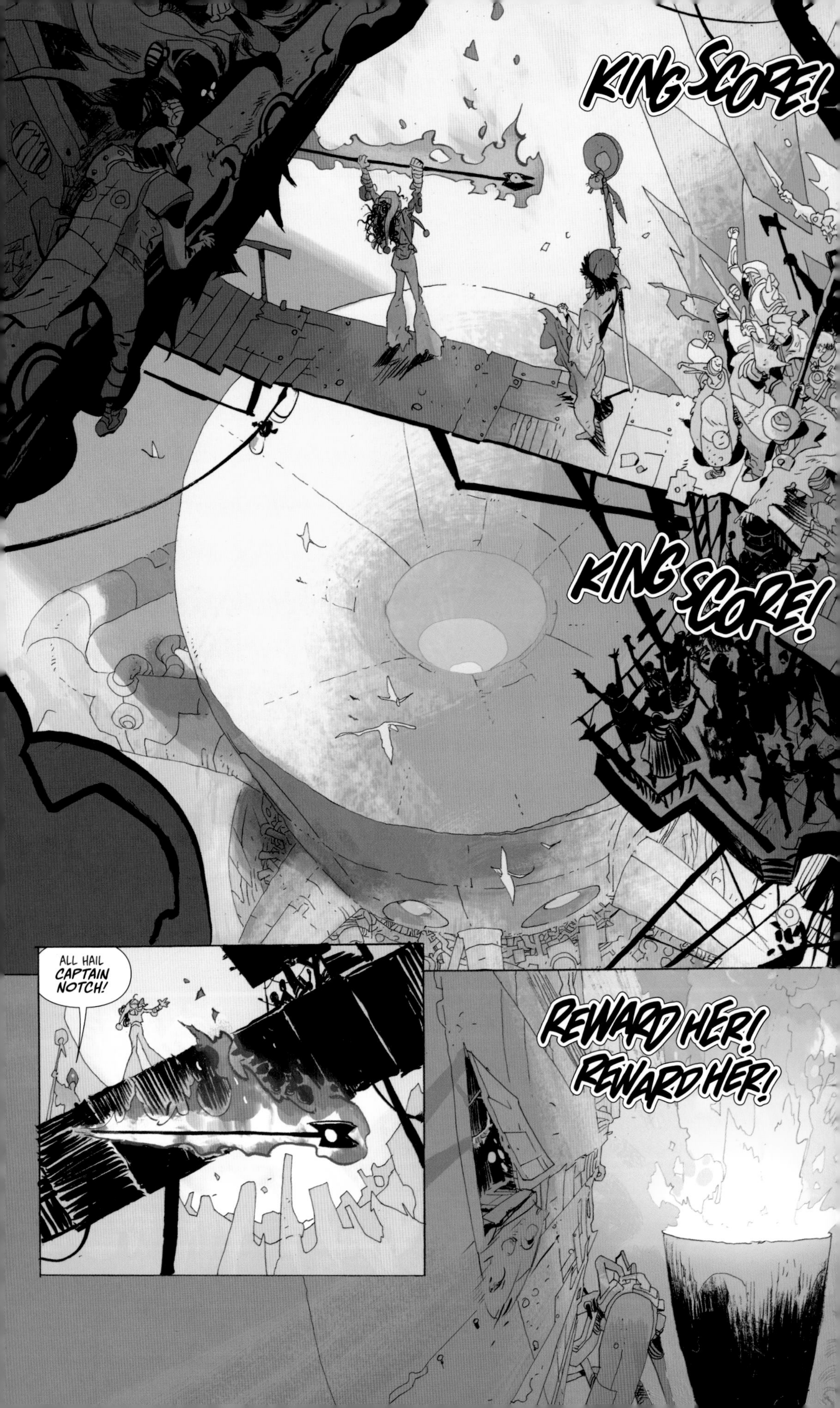

KING SCORE!
KING SCORE!
ALL HAIL CAPTAIN NOTCH!
REWARD HER! REWARD HER!

"SO, YEAH, PEOPLE CLING TO WHAT THEY **KNOW**. EVEN THE STUFF THEY DON'T **REALLY** KNOW AT ALL.

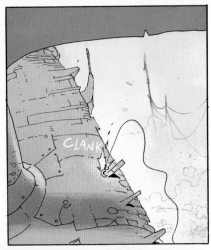

CLANK

"LIKE...THEY CLING TO THEIR **MYSTERIES**...

"...THEY CLING TO THEIR **GOALS**, WITHOUT STOPPING TO WONDER WHAT'LL HAPPEN IF THEY EVER **GET** THERE...

"...THEY CLING TO **WEALTH**, WITHOUT A THOUGHT FOR THE **SOURCE**..."

RAAAAAAY!

NOW.

"...AND **OH**, BY ALL THE MOLDERING GODS, THEY CLING TO **IDEAS**.

"THEY CLING TO IDEAS THAT HAVE NO **POINT**. NO **FUTURE**. NO **HAPPY ENDING**."

...AND WITH THE GREATEST OF **RESPECT**, IT'S TAKING **TOO LONG**.

"YOU WANT THE TRUTH? PEOPLE CLING TO THE **UGLIEST** IDEAS HARDEST OF ALL."

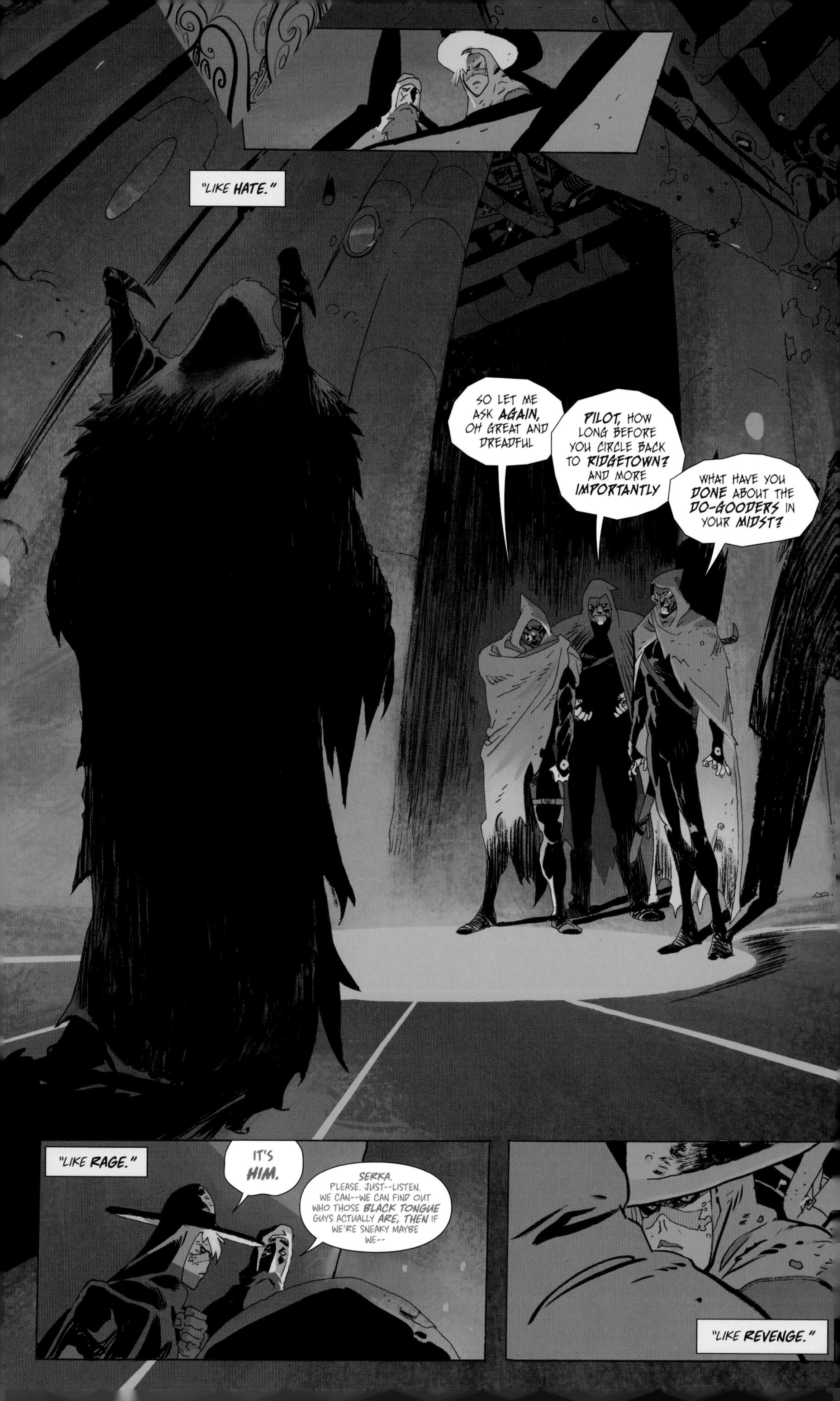
"LIKE HATE."
SO LET ME ASK AGAIN, OH GREAT AND DREADFUL
PILOT, HOW LONG BEFORE YOU CIRCLE BACK TO RIDGETOWN? AND MORE IMPORTANTLY
WHAT HAVE YOU DONE ABOUT THE DO-GOODERS IN YOUR MIDST?
"LIKE RAGE."
IT'S HIM.
SERKA. PLEASE. JUST--LISTEN. WE CAN--WE CAN FIND OUT WHO THOSE BLACK TONGUE GUYS ACTUALLY ARE, THEN IF WE'RE SNEAKY MAYBE WE--
"LIKE REVENGE."

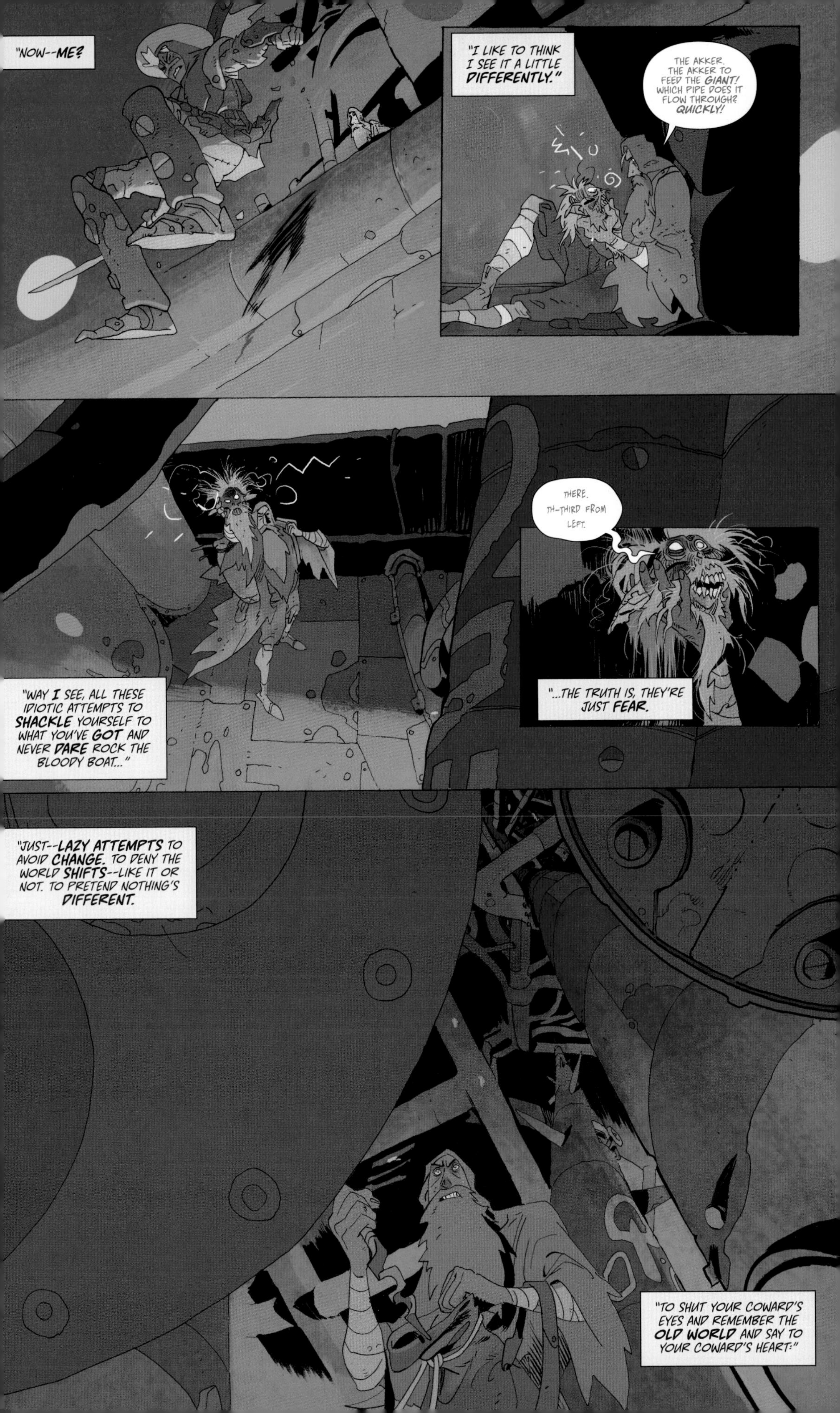
"NOW--ME?
"I LIKE TO THINK I SEE IT A LITTLE DIFFERENTLY."
THE AKKER. THE AKKER TO FEED THE GIANT! WHICH PIPE DOES IT FLOW THROUGH? QUICKLY!
"WAY I SEE, ALL THESE IDIOTIC ATTEMPTS TO SHACKLE YOURSELF TO WHAT YOU'VE GOT AND NEVER DARE ROCK THE BLOODY BOAT..."
THERE. TH-THIRD FROM LEFT.
"...THE TRUTH IS, THEY'RE JUST FEAR.
"JUST--LAZY ATTEMPTS TO AVOID CHANGE. TO DENY THE WORLD SHIFTS--LIKE IT OR NOT. TO PRETEND NOTHING'S DIFFERENT.
"TO SHUT YOUR COWARD'S EYES AND REMEMBER THE OLD WORLD AND SAY TO YOUR COWARD'S HEART:"

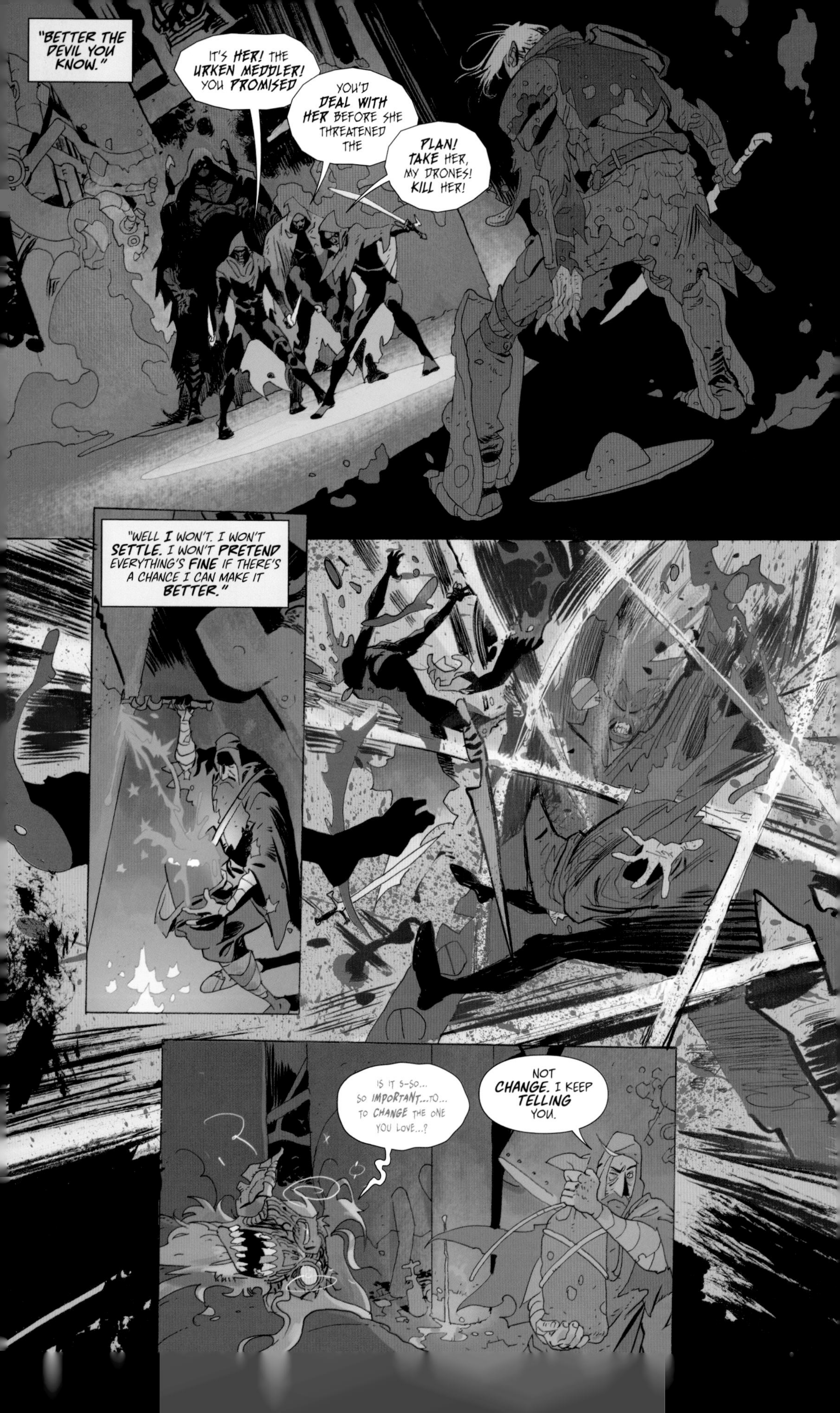
"BETTER THE DEVIL YOU KNOW."
IT'S HER! THE URKEN MEDDLER! YOU PROMISED
YOU'D DEAL WITH HER BEFORE SHE THREATENED THE
PLAN! TAKE HER, MY DRONES! KILL HER!
"WELL I WON'T. I WON'T SETTLE. I WON'T PRETEND EVERYTHING'S FINE IF THERE'S A CHANCE I CAN MAKE IT BETTER."
IS IT S-SO... SO IMPORTANT...TO... TO CHANGE THE ONE YOU LOVE...?
NOT CHANGE. I KEEP TELLING YOU.

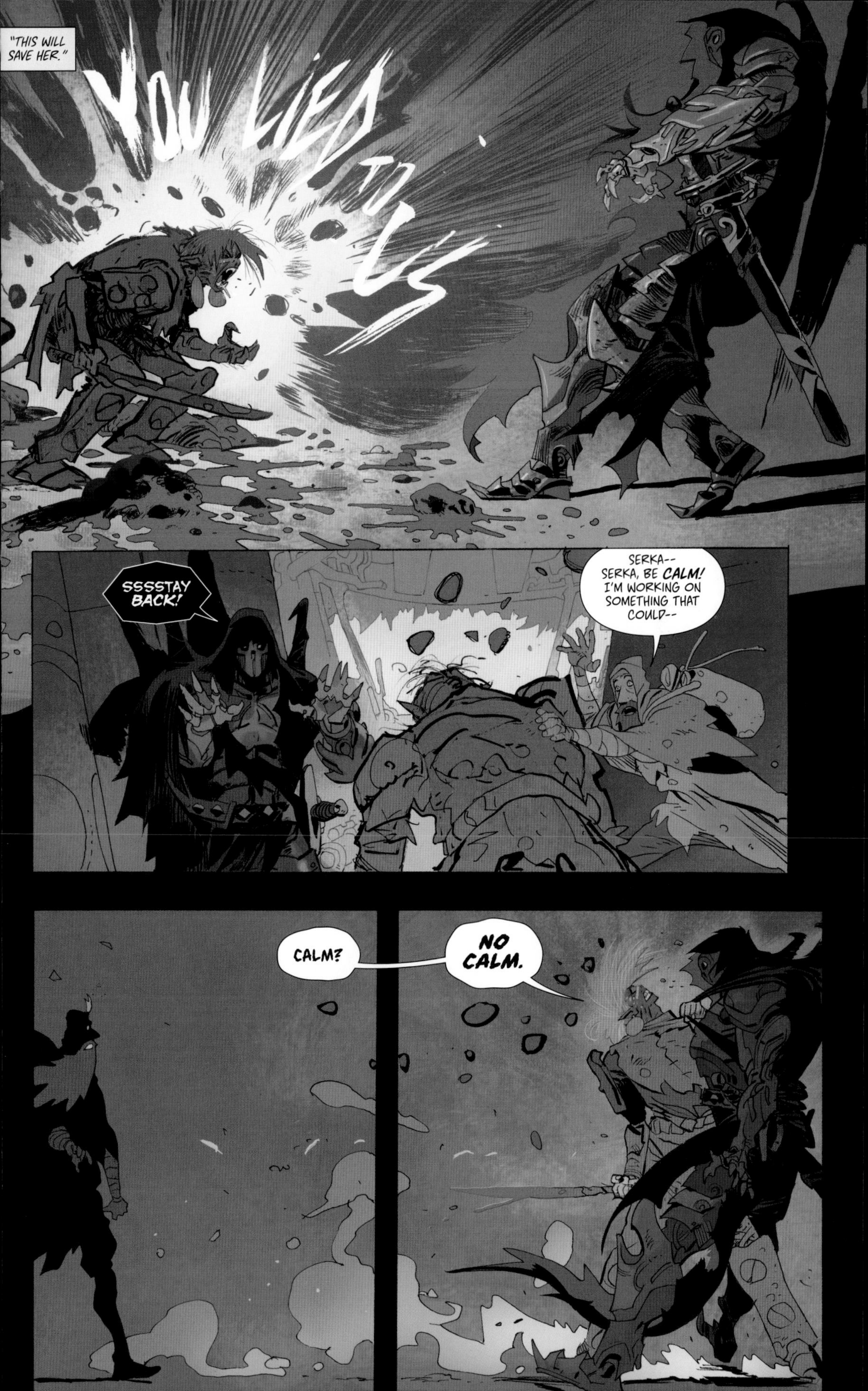
"THIS WILL SAVE HER."
YOU LIED TO US
SSSSTAY BACK!
SERKA-- SERKA, BE CALM! I'M WORKING ON SOMETHING THAT COULD--
CALM?
NO CALM.

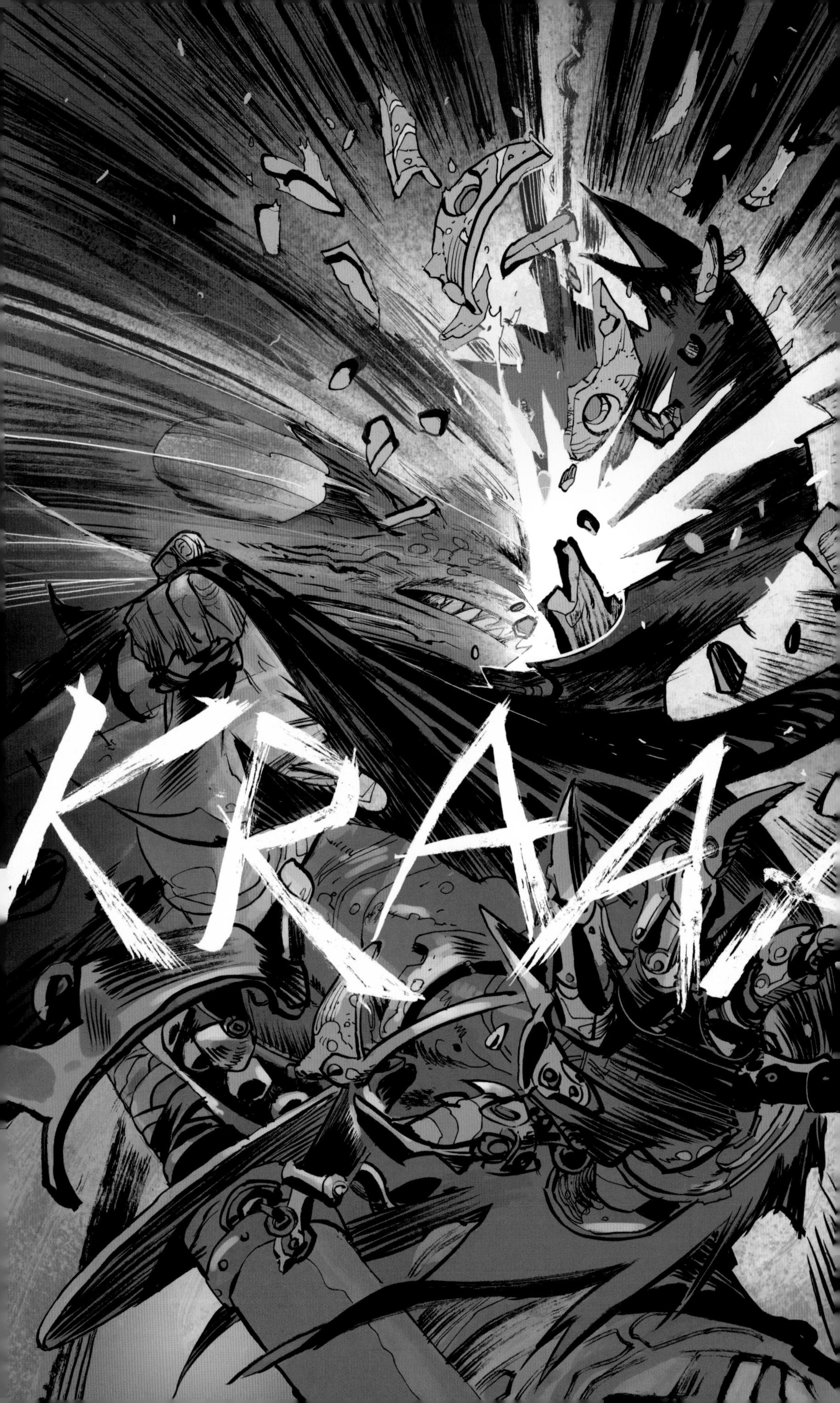
KRAA

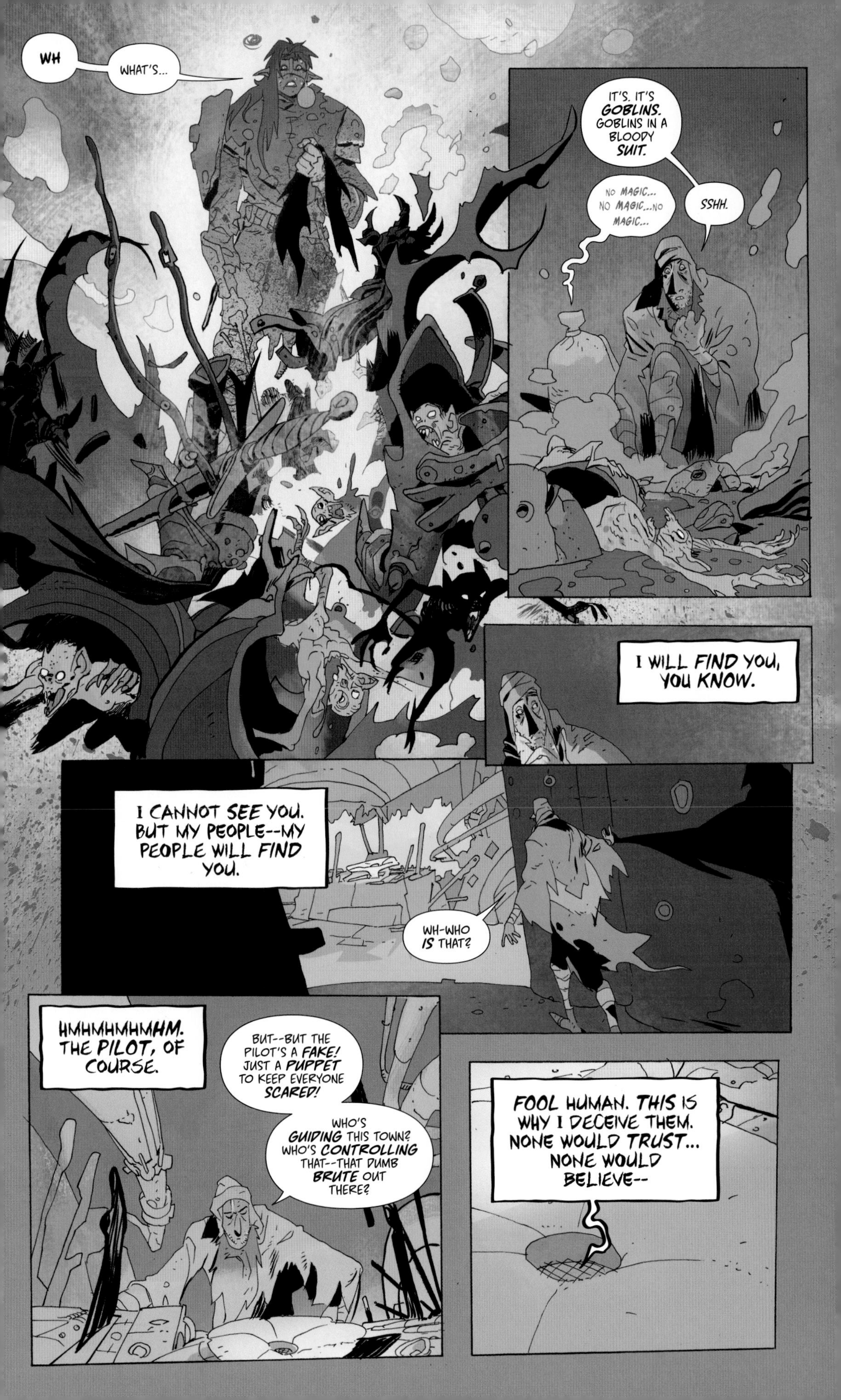
WH
WHAT'S...
IT'S. IT'S GOBLINS. GOBLINS IN A BLOODY SUIT.
SSHH.
NO MAGIC... NO MAGIC...NO MAGIC...
I WILL FIND YOU, YOU KNOW.
I CANNOT SEE YOU. BUT MY PEOPLE--MY PEOPLE WILL FIND YOU.
WH-WHO IS THAT?
HMHMHMHMHM. THE PILOT, OF COURSE.
BUT--BUT THE PILOT'S A FAKE! JUST A PUPPET TO KEEP EVERYONE SCARED!
WHO'S GUIDING THIS TOWN? WHO'S CONTROLLING THAT--THAT DUMB BRUTE OUT THERE?
FOOL HUMAN. THIS IS WHY I DECEIVE THEM. NONE WOULD TRUST... NONE WOULD BELIEVE--

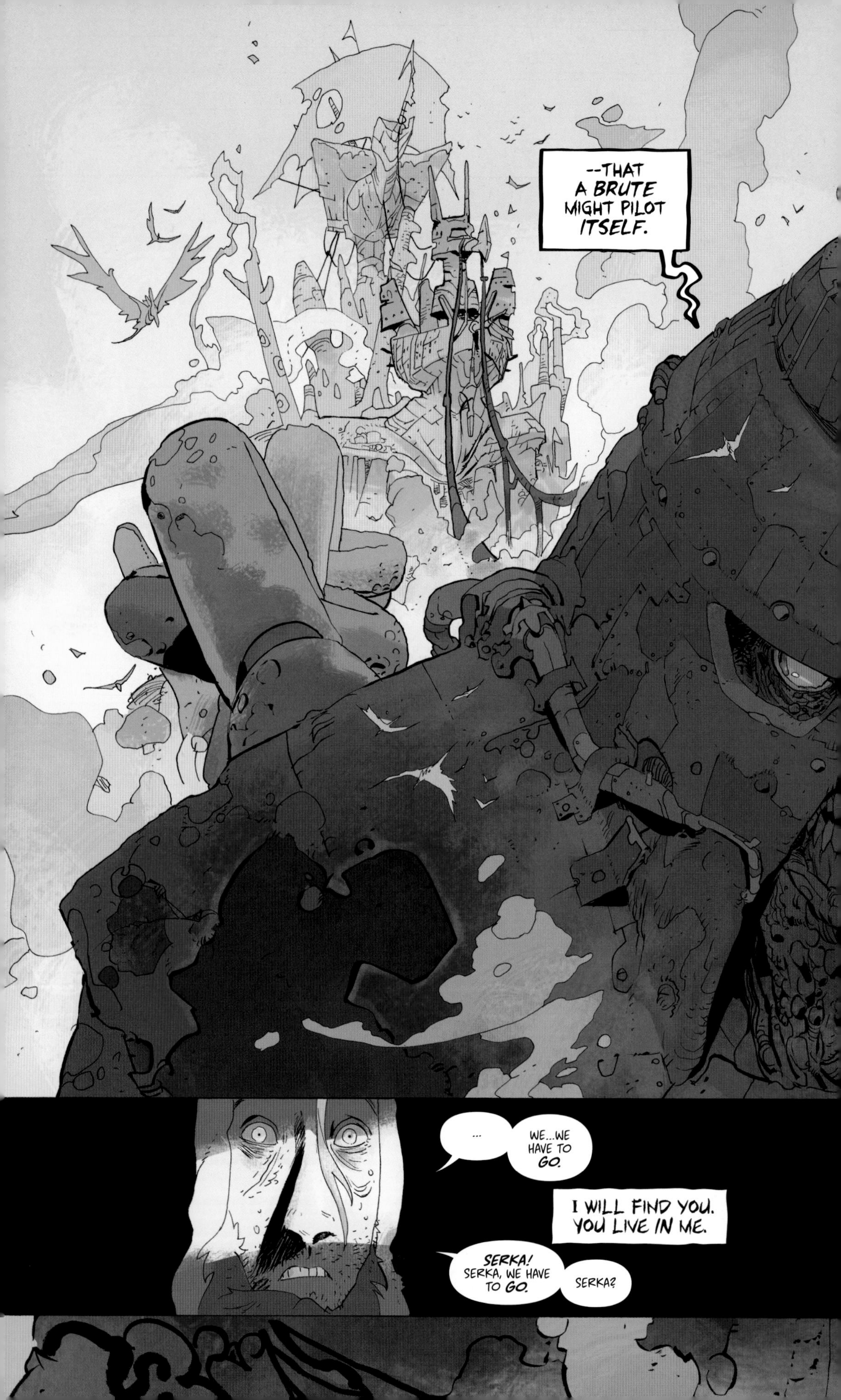
--THAT A BRUTE MIGHT PILOT ITSELF.
...
WE...WE HAVE TO GO.
I WILL FIND YOU. YOU LIVE IN ME.
SERKA! SERKA, WE HAVE TO GO.
SERKA?

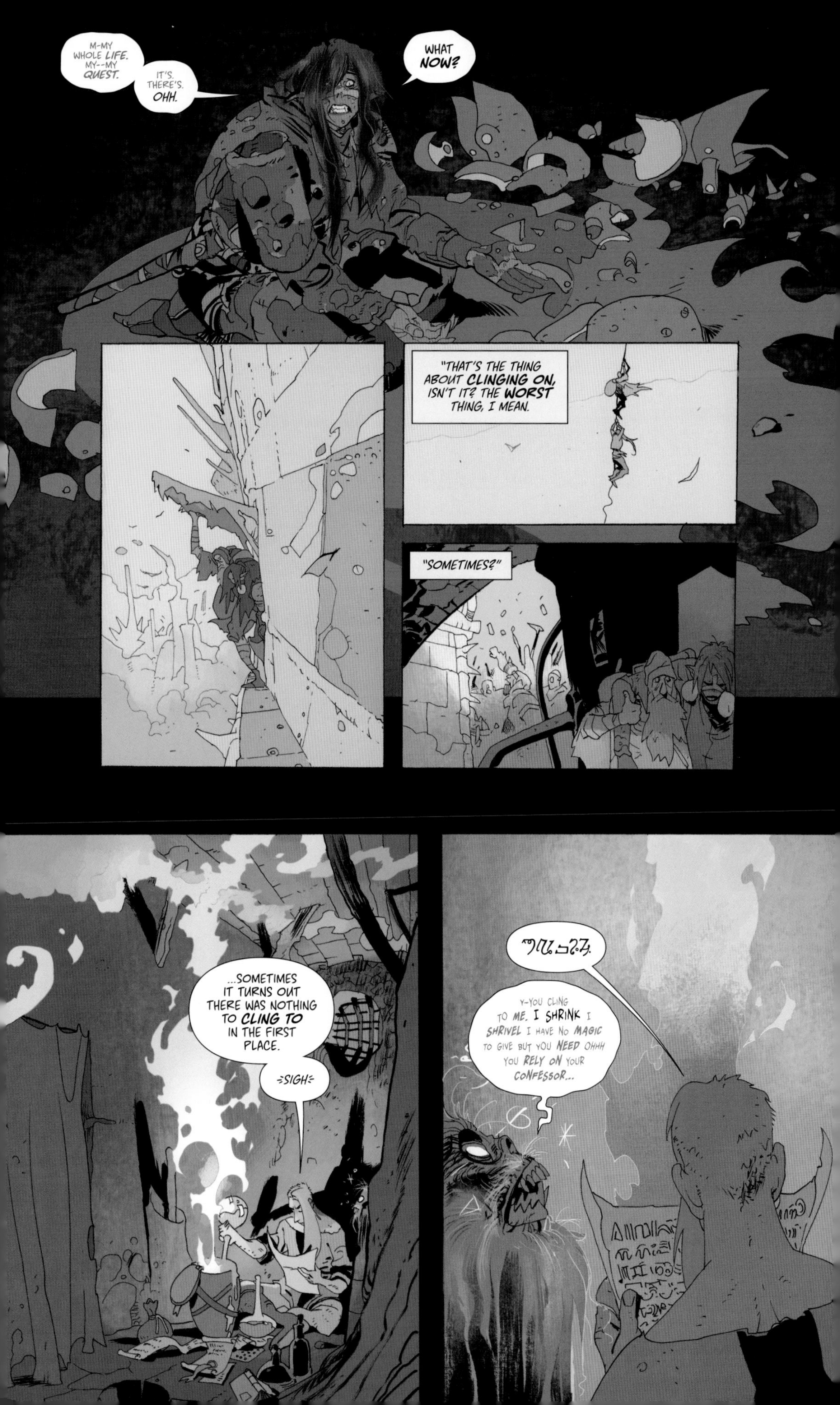
M-MY WHOLE LIFE. MY--MY QUEST.
IT'S. THERE'S. OHH.
WHAT NOW?
"THAT'S THE THING ABOUT CLINGING ON, ISN'T IT? THE WORST THING, I MEAN.
"SOMETIMES?"
...SOMETIMES IT TURNS OUT THERE WAS NOTHING TO CLING TO IN THE FIRST PLACE.
=SIGH=
Y-YOU CLING TO ME. I SHRINK I SHRIVEL I HAVE NO MAGIC TO GIVE BUT YOU NEED OHHH YOU RELY ON YOUR CONFESSOR...

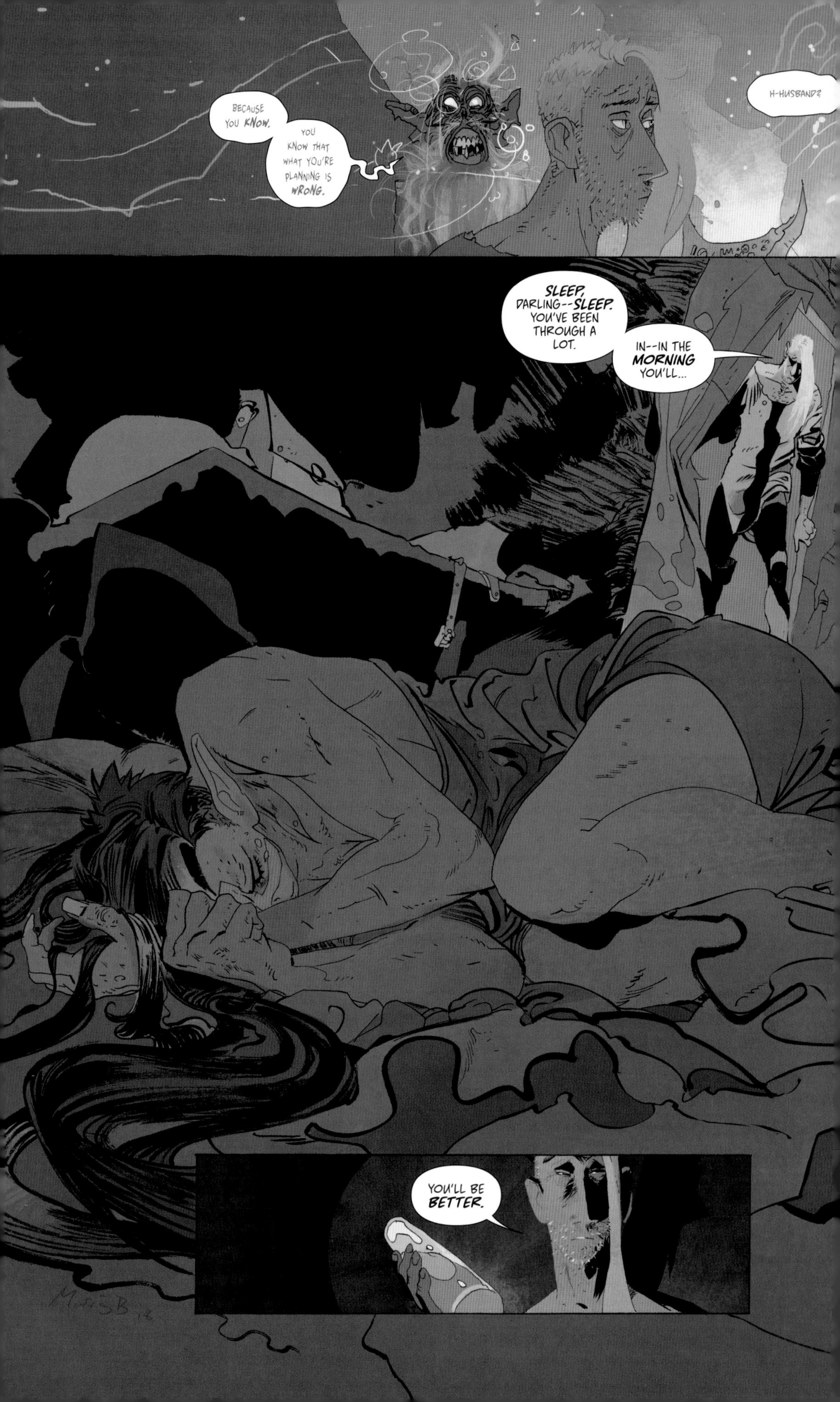

BECAUSE YOU KNOW.
YOU KNOW THAT WHAT YOU'RE PLANNING IS WRONG.
H-HUSBAND?
SLEEP, DARLING--SLEEP. YOU'VE BEEN THROUGH A LOT.
IN--IN THE MORNING YOU'LL...
YOU'LL BE BETTER.

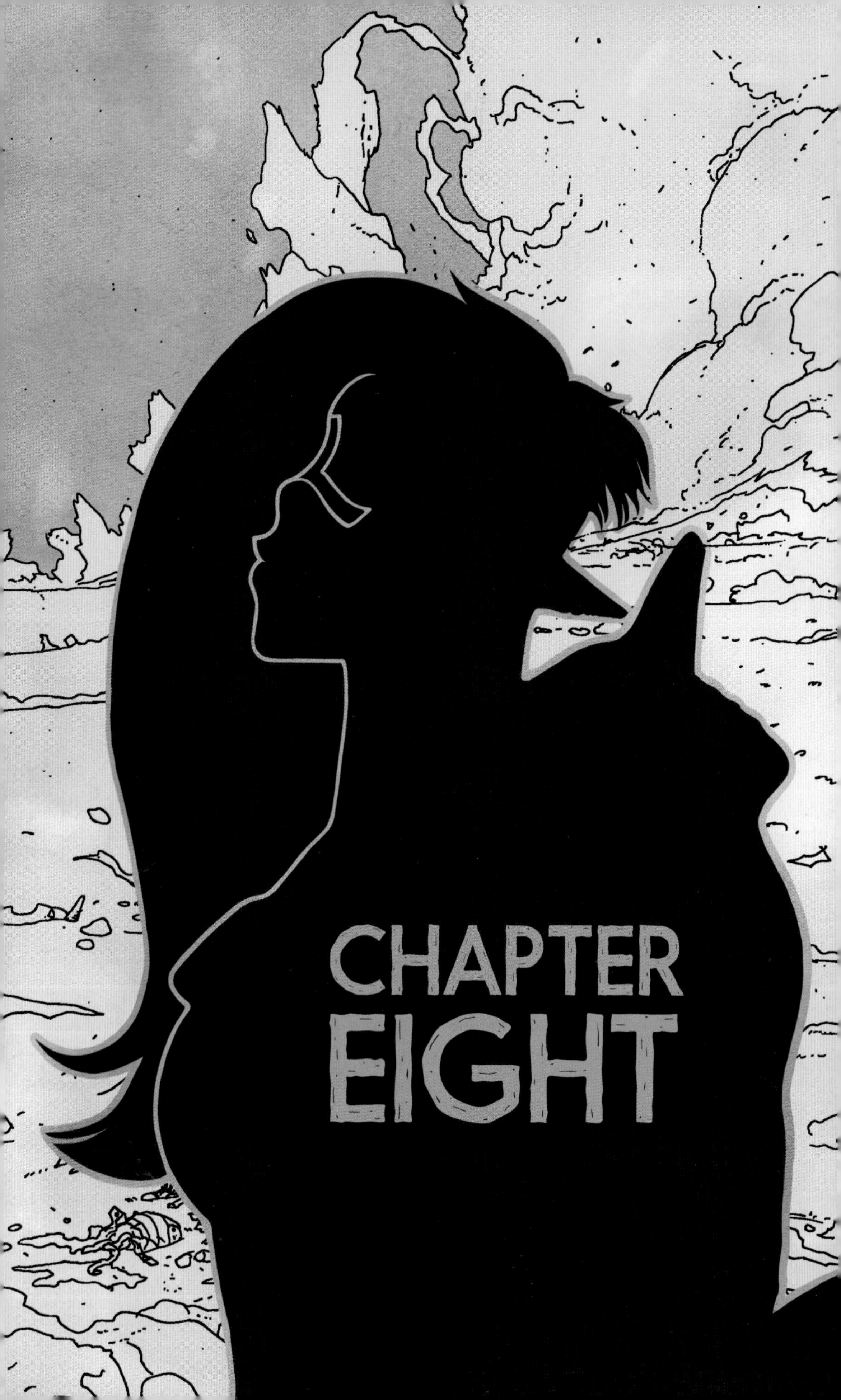
CHAPTER
EIGHT

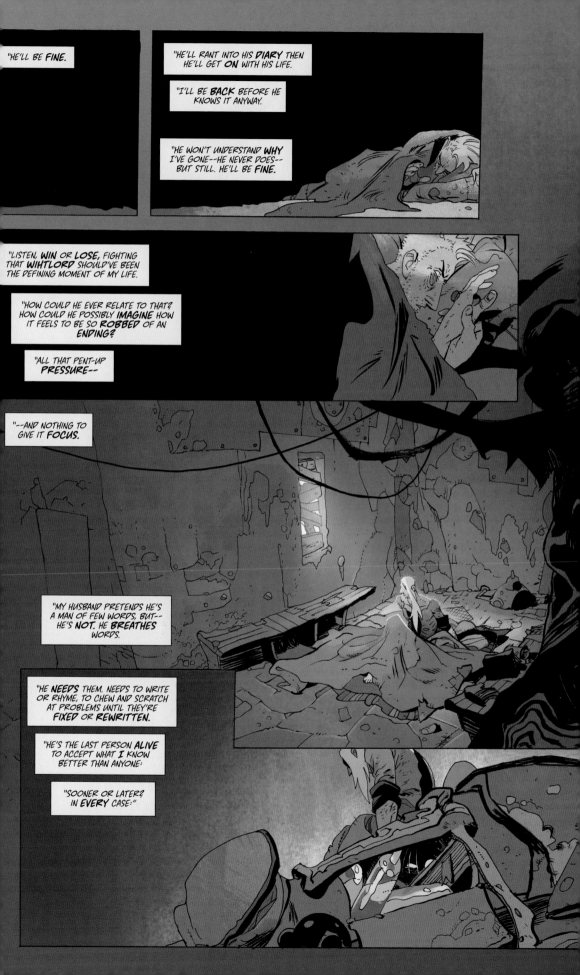

"HE'LL BE **FINE**.

"HE'LL RANT INTO HIS **DIARY** THEN HE'LL GET **ON** WITH HIS LIFE.

"I'LL BE **BACK** BEFORE HE KNOWS IT ANYWAY.

"HE WON'T UNDERSTAND **WHY** I'VE GONE--HE NEVER DOES--BUT STILL. HE'LL BE **FINE**.

"LISTEN, **WIN** OR **LOSE**, FIGHTING THAT **WIHTLORD** SHOULD'VE BEEN THE DEFINING MOMENT OF MY LIFE.

"HOW COULD HE EVER RELATE TO THAT? HOW COULD HE POSSIBLY **IMAGINE** HOW IT FEELS TO BE SO **ROBBED** OF AN **ENDING**?

"ALL THAT PENT-UP **PRESSURE**--

"--AND NOTHING TO GIVE IT **FOCUS**.

"MY HUSBAND PRETENDS HE'S A MAN OF FEW WORDS, BUT-- HE'S **NOT**. HE **BREATHES** WORDS.

"HE **NEEDS** THEM. NEEDS TO WRITE OR RHYME, TO CHEW AND SCRATCH AT PROBLEMS UNTIL THEY'RE **FIXED** OR **REWRITTEN**.

"HE'S THE LAST PERSON **ALIVE** TO ACCEPT WHAT **I** KNOW BETTER THAN ANYONE:

"SOONER OR LATER? IN **EVERY** CASE:"

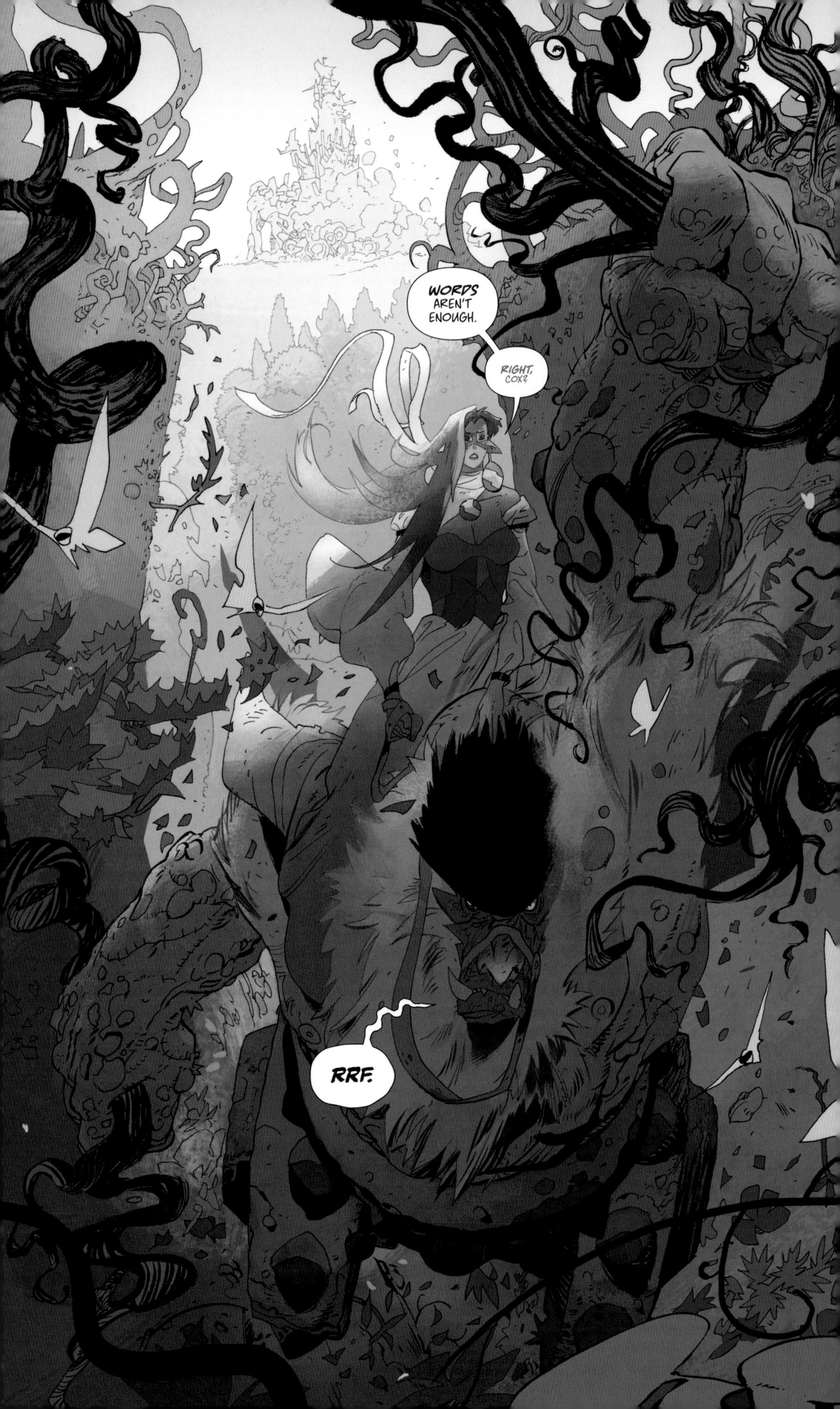
WORDS AREN'T ENOUGH.
RIGHT, COX?
RRF.

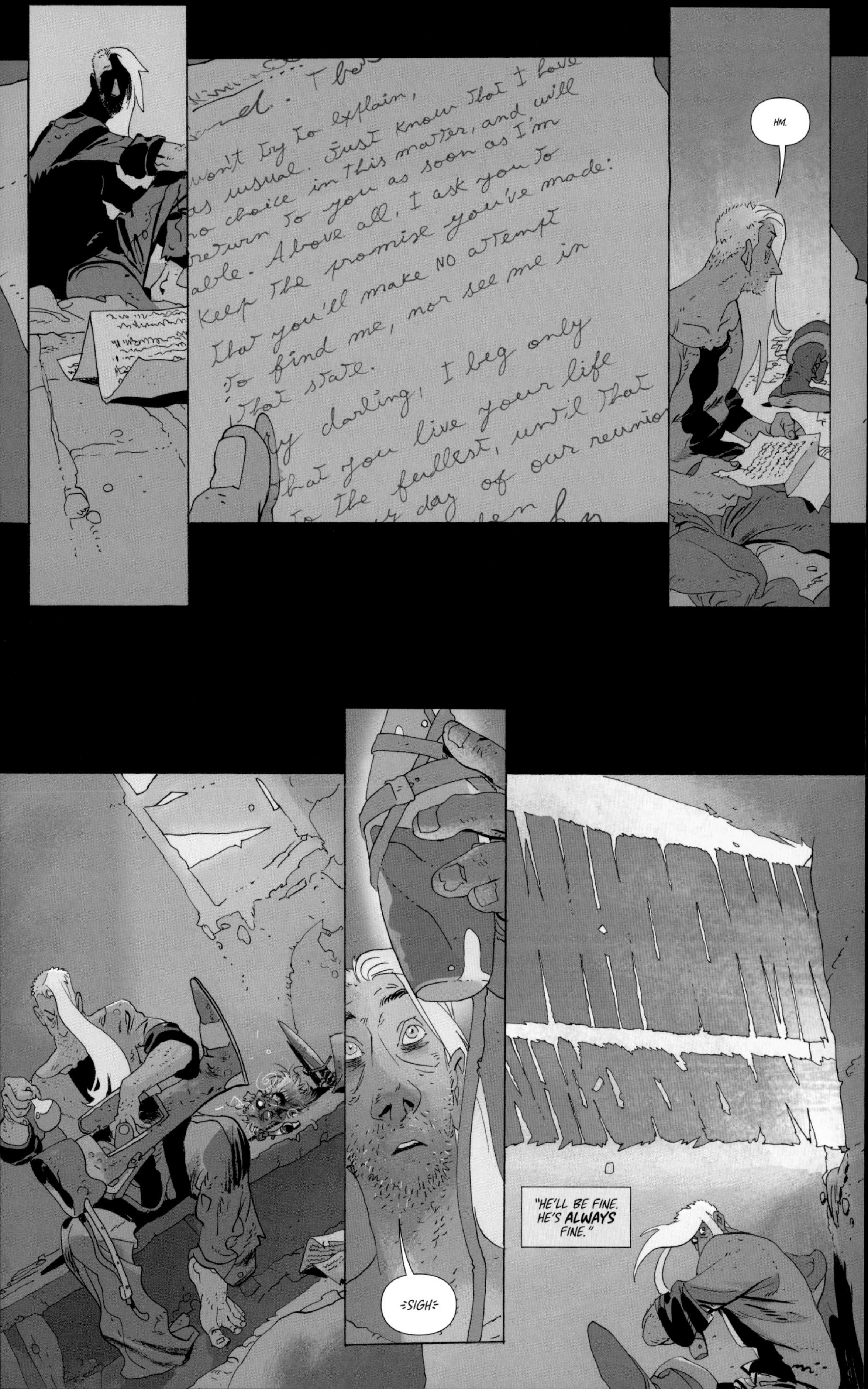
won't try to explain,
as usual. Just know that I love
no choice in this matter, and will
return to you as soon as I'm
able. Above all, I ask you to
keep the promise you've made:
that you'll make NO attempt
to find me, nor see me in
that state.
y darling, I beg only
that you live your life
to the fullest, until that
day of our reunio
HM.
SIGH
"HE'LL BE FINE. HE'S ALWAYS FINE."

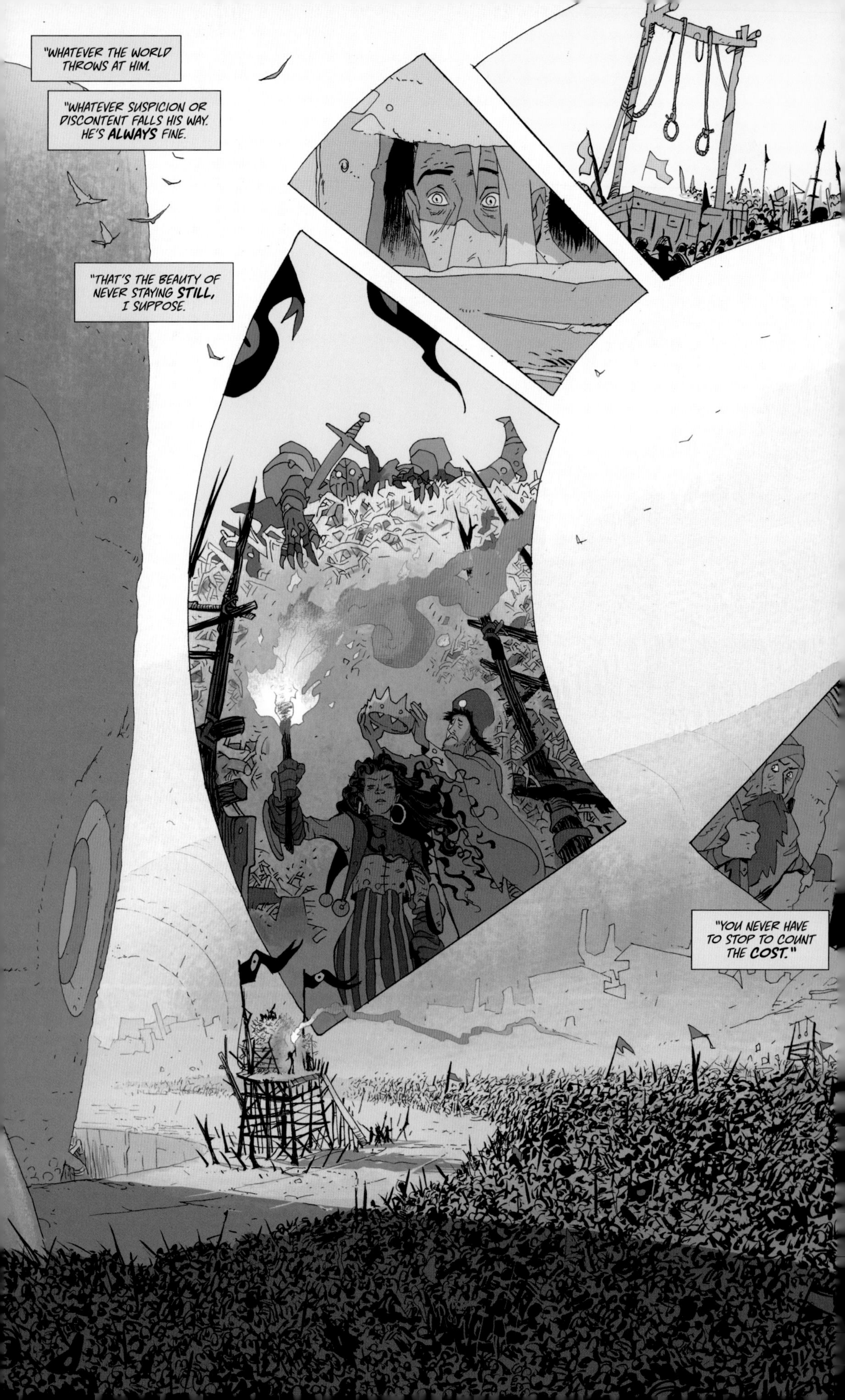
"WHATEVER THE WORLD THROWS AT HIM.
"WHATEVER SUSPICION OR DISCONTENT FALLS HIS WAY. HE'S **ALWAYS** FINE.
"THAT'S THE BEAUTY OF NEVER STAYING **STILL**, I SUPPOSE.
"YOU NEVER HAVE TO STOP TO COUNT THE **COST**."

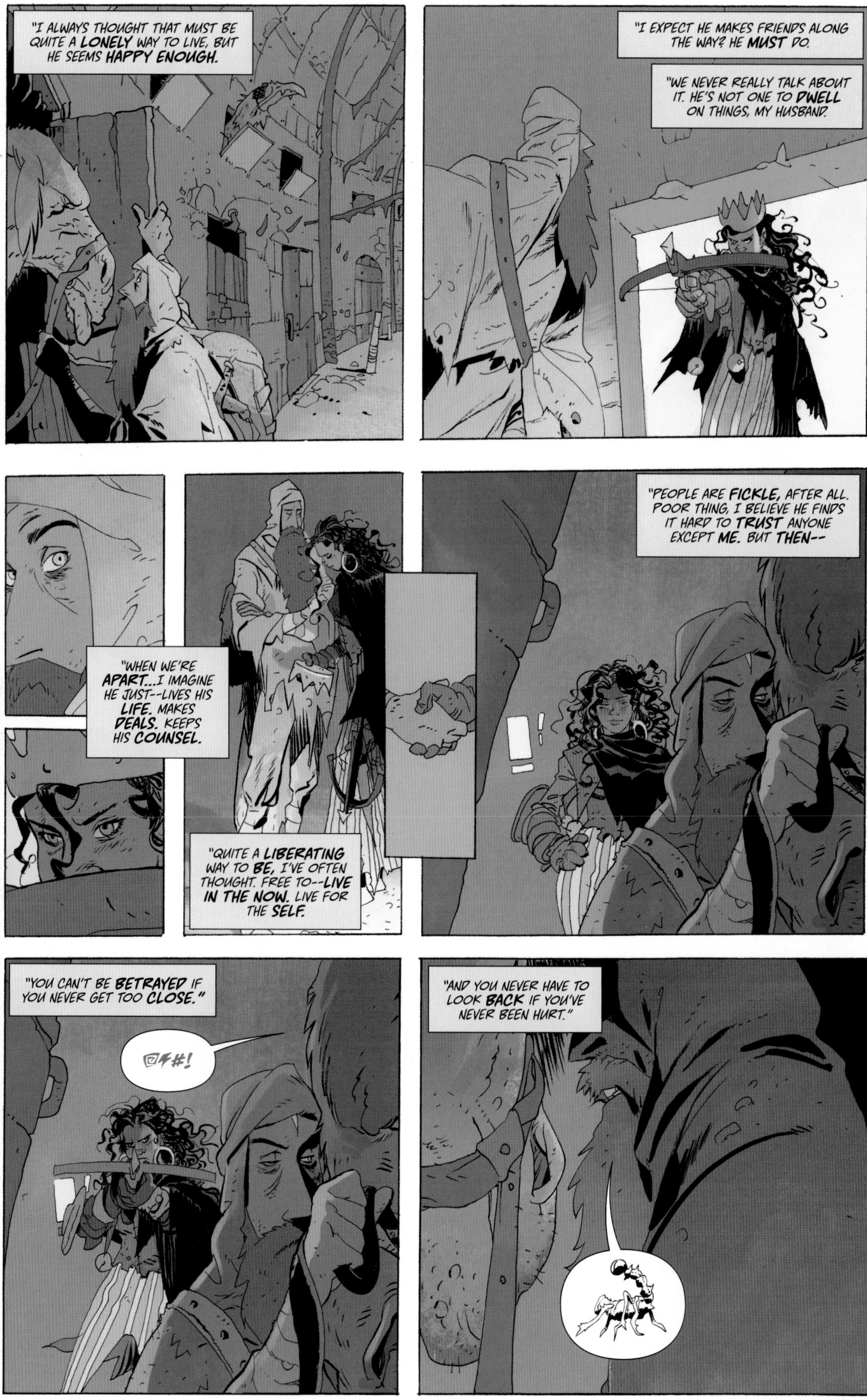
"I ALWAYS THOUGHT THAT MUST BE QUITE A LONELY WAY TO LIVE, BUT HE SEEMS HAPPY ENOUGH.
"I EXPECT HE MAKES FRIENDS ALONG THE WAY? HE MUST DO.
"WE NEVER REALLY TALK ABOUT IT. HE'S NOT ONE TO DWELL ON THINGS, MY HUSBAND.
"WHEN WE'RE APART...I IMAGINE HE JUST--LIVES HIS LIFE. MAKES DEALS. KEEPS HIS COUNSEL.
"QUITE A LIBERATING WAY TO BE, I'VE OFTEN THOUGHT. FREE TO--LIVE IN THE NOW. LIVE FOR THE SELF.
"PEOPLE ARE FICKLE, AFTER ALL. POOR THING, I BELIEVE HE FINDS IT HARD TO TRUST ANYONE EXCEPT ME. BUT THEN--
!
"YOU CAN'T BE BETRAYED IF YOU NEVER GET TOO CLOSE."
@#!
"AND YOU NEVER HAVE TO LOOK BACK IF YOU'VE NEVER BEEN HURT."

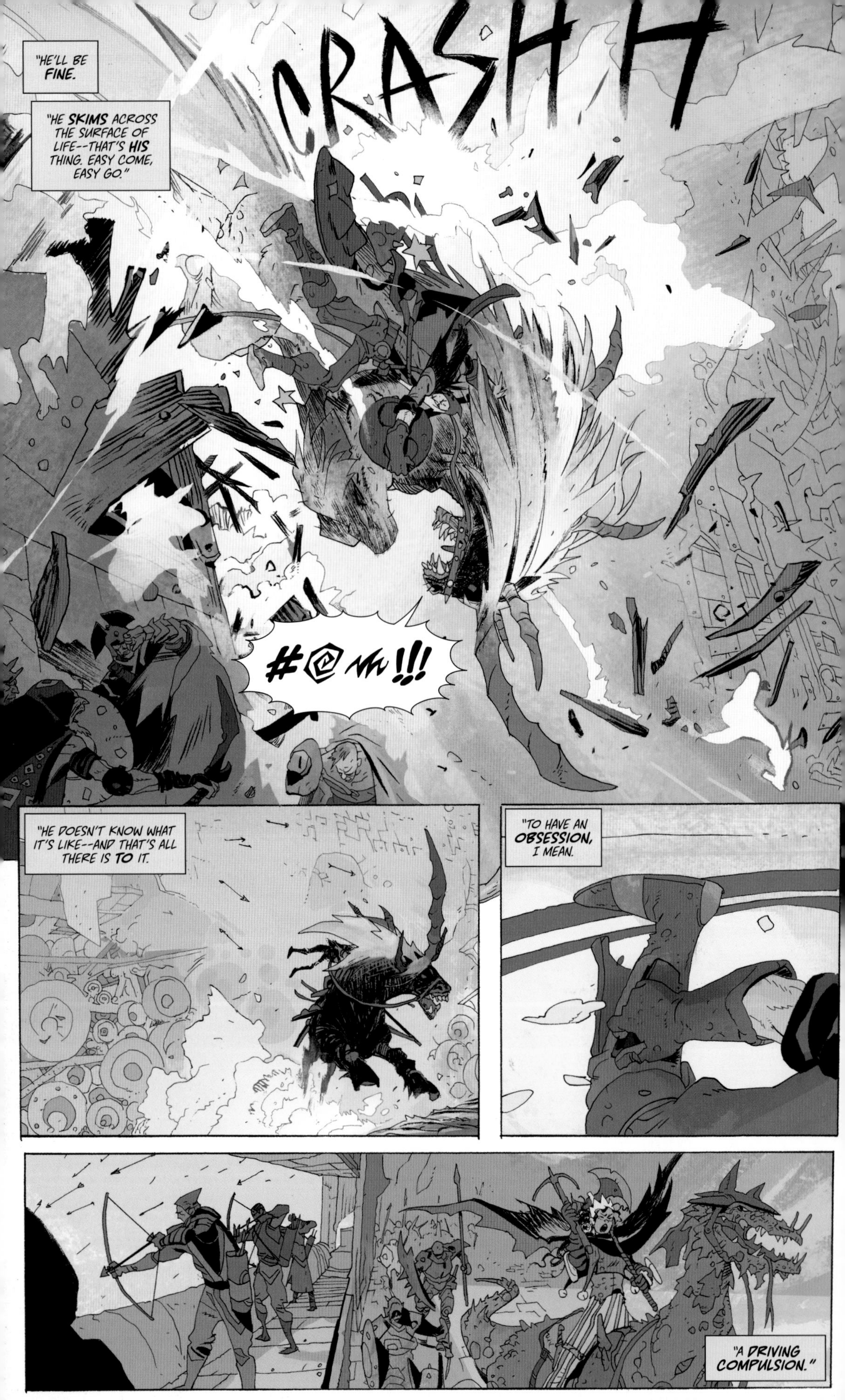
"HE'LL BE FINE.
"HE SKIMS ACROSS THE SURFACE OF LIFE--THAT'S HIS THING. EASY COME, EASY GO."
CRASHH
#@%!!!
"HE DOESN'T KNOW WHAT IT'S LIKE--AND THAT'S ALL THERE IS TO IT.
"TO HAVE AN OBSESSION, I MEAN.
"A DRIVING COMPULSION."

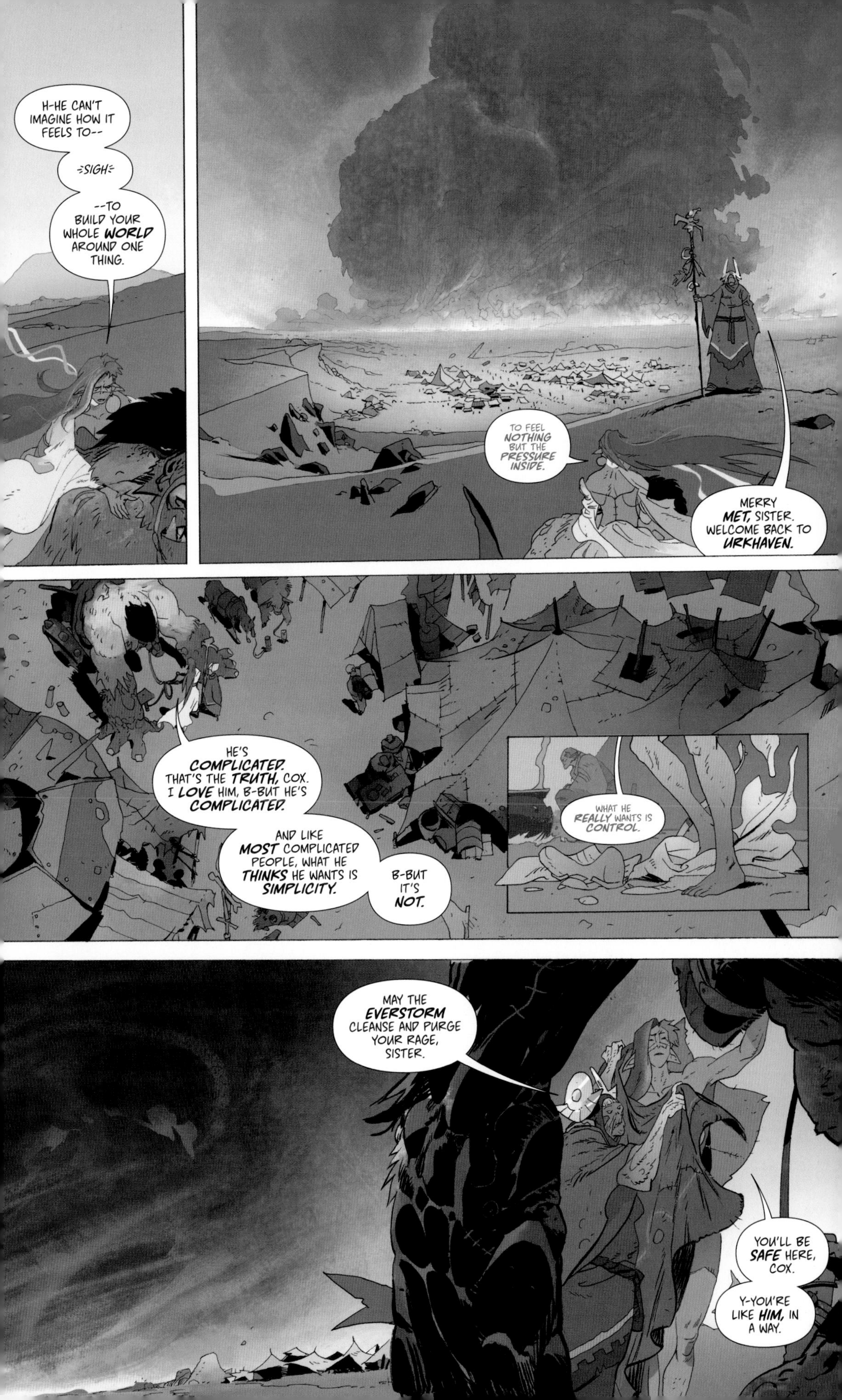

H-HE CAN'T IMAGINE HOW IT FEELS TO--
=SIGH=
--TO BUILD YOUR WHOLE WORLD AROUND ONE THING.
TO FEEL NOTHING BUT THE PRESSURE INSIDE.
MERRY MET, SISTER. WELCOME BACK TO URKHAVEN.
HE'S COMPLICATED. THAT'S THE TRUTH, COX. I LOVE HIM, B-BUT HE'S COMPLICATED.
AND LIKE MOST COMPLICATED PEOPLE, WHAT HE THINKS HE WANTS IS SIMPLICITY.
B-BUT IT'S NOT.
WHAT HE REALLY WANTS IS CONTROL.
MAY THE EVERSTORM CLEANSE AND PURGE YOUR RAGE, SISTER.
YOU'LL BE SAFE HERE, COX.
Y-YOU'RE LIKE HIM, IN A WAY.

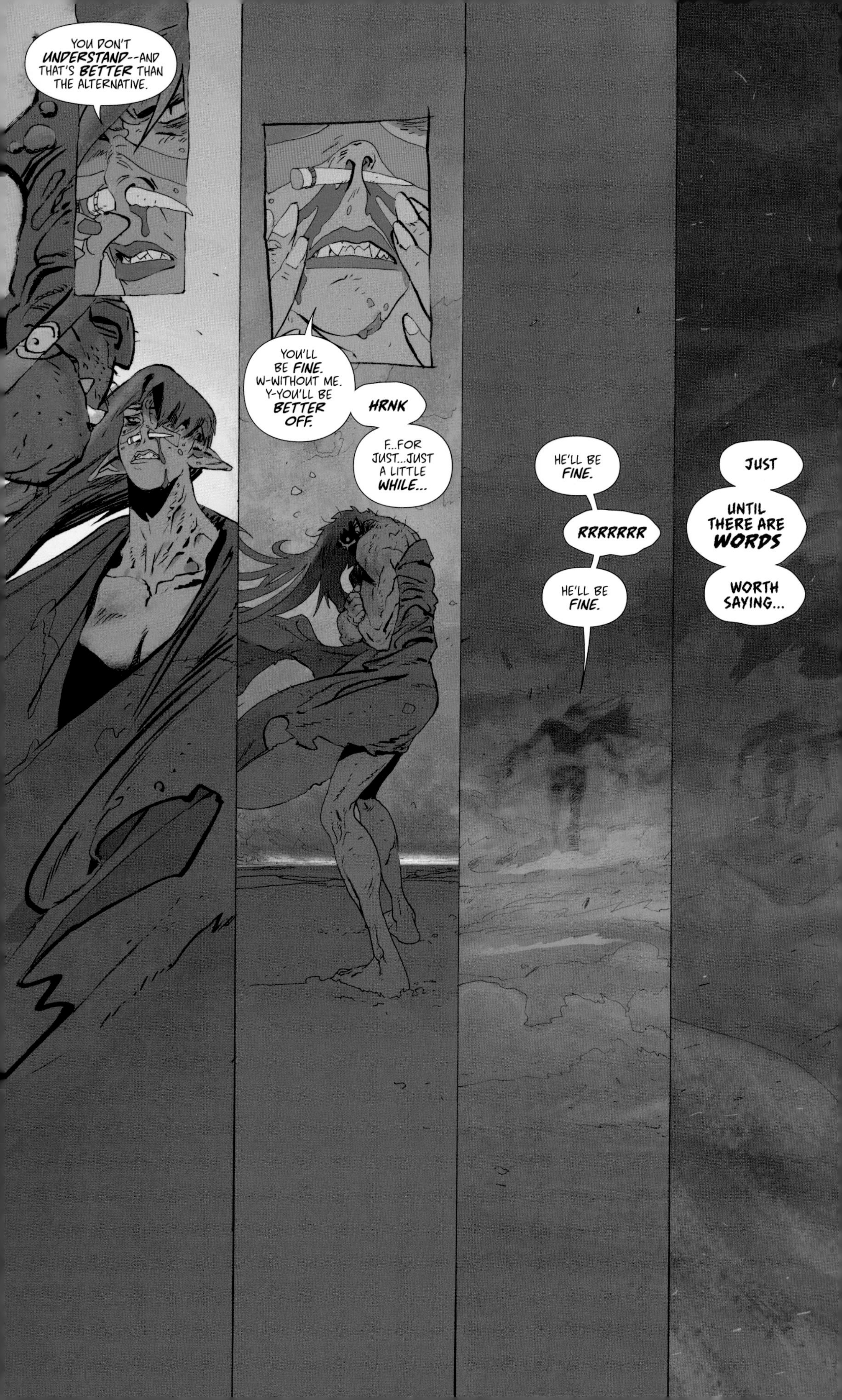

YOU DON'T UNDERSTAND--AND THAT'S BETTER THAN THE ALTERNATIVE.
YOU'LL BE FINE. W-WITHOUT ME. Y-YOU'LL BE BETTER OFF.
HRNK
F...FOR JUST...JUST A LITTLE WHILE...
HE'LL BE FINE.
RRRRRRR
HE'LL BE FINE.
JUST
UNTIL THERE ARE WORDS
WORTH SAYING...

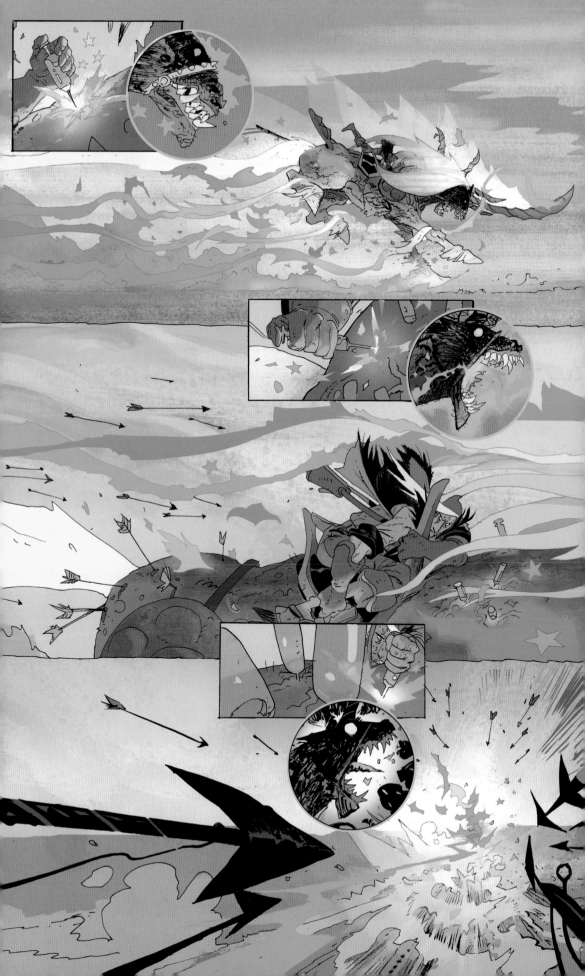

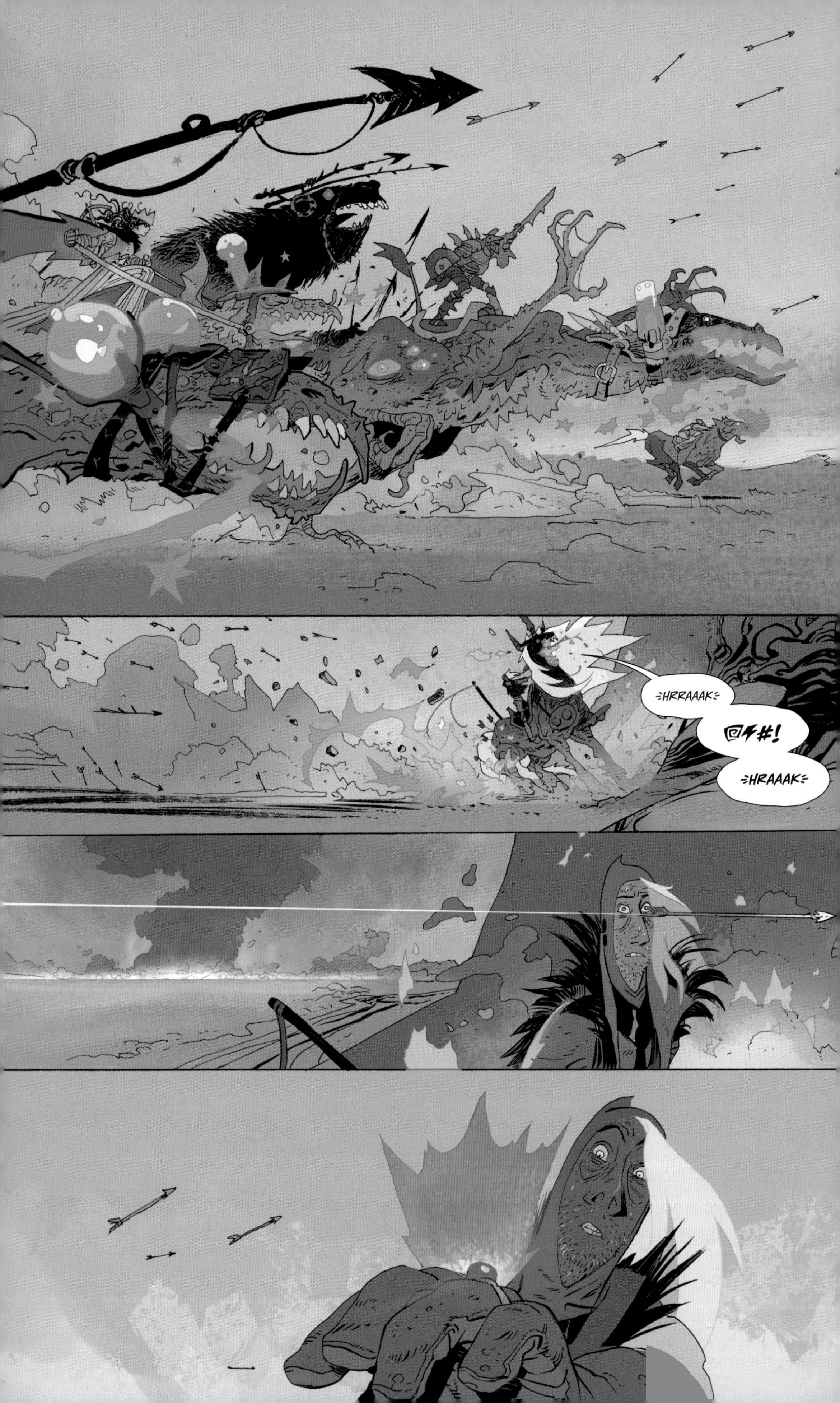
HRRAAAK
#!
HRAAAK

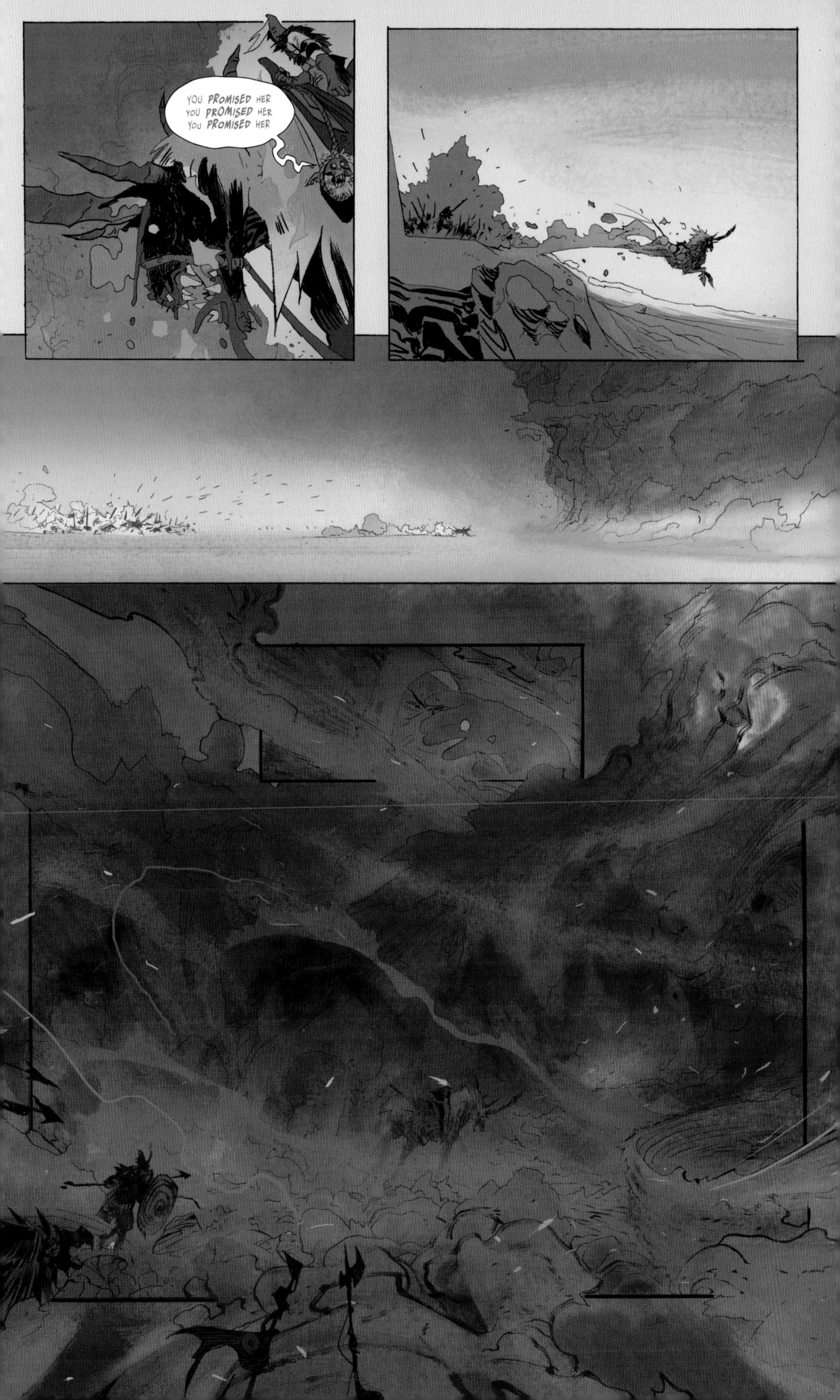
YOU PROMISED HER YOU PROMISED HER YOU PROMISED HER

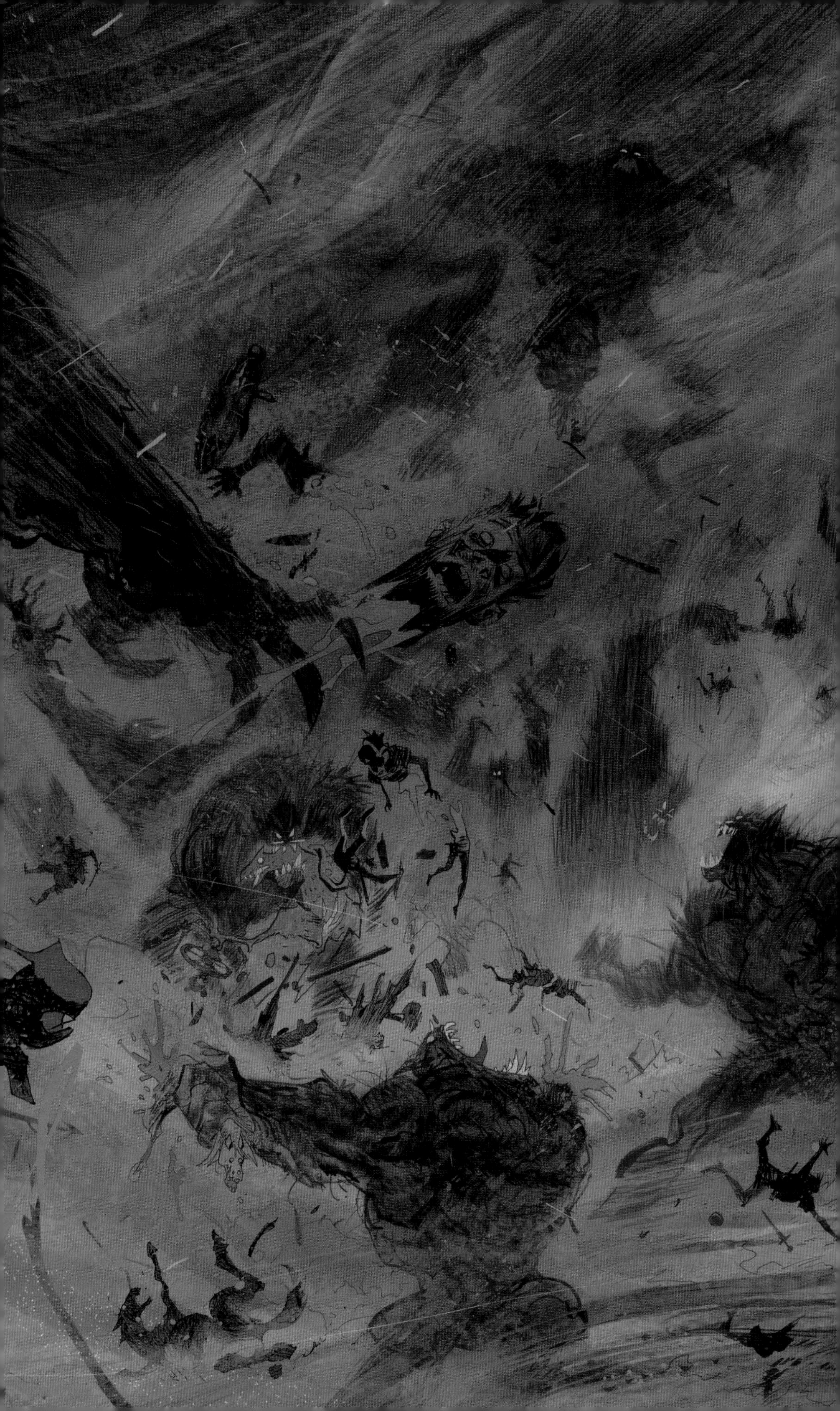

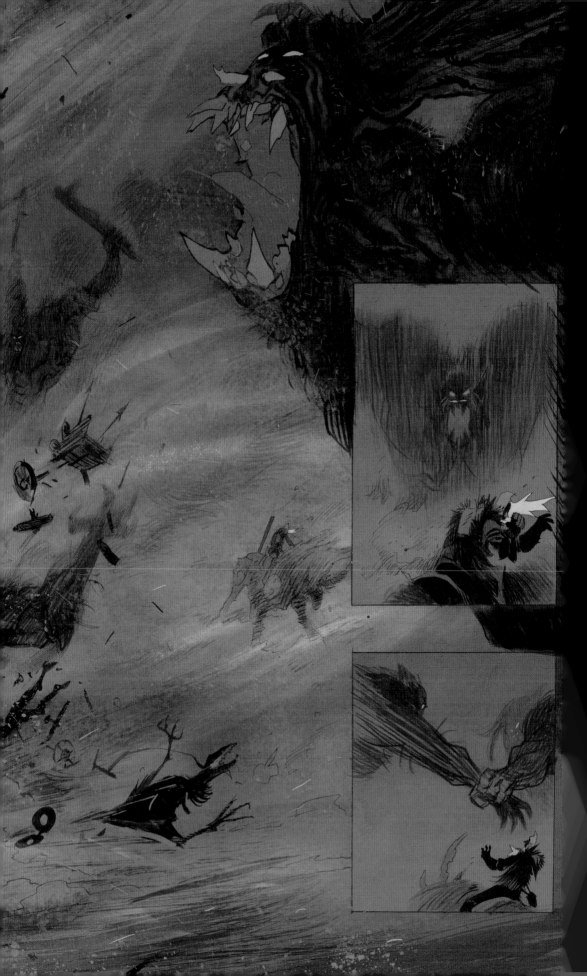

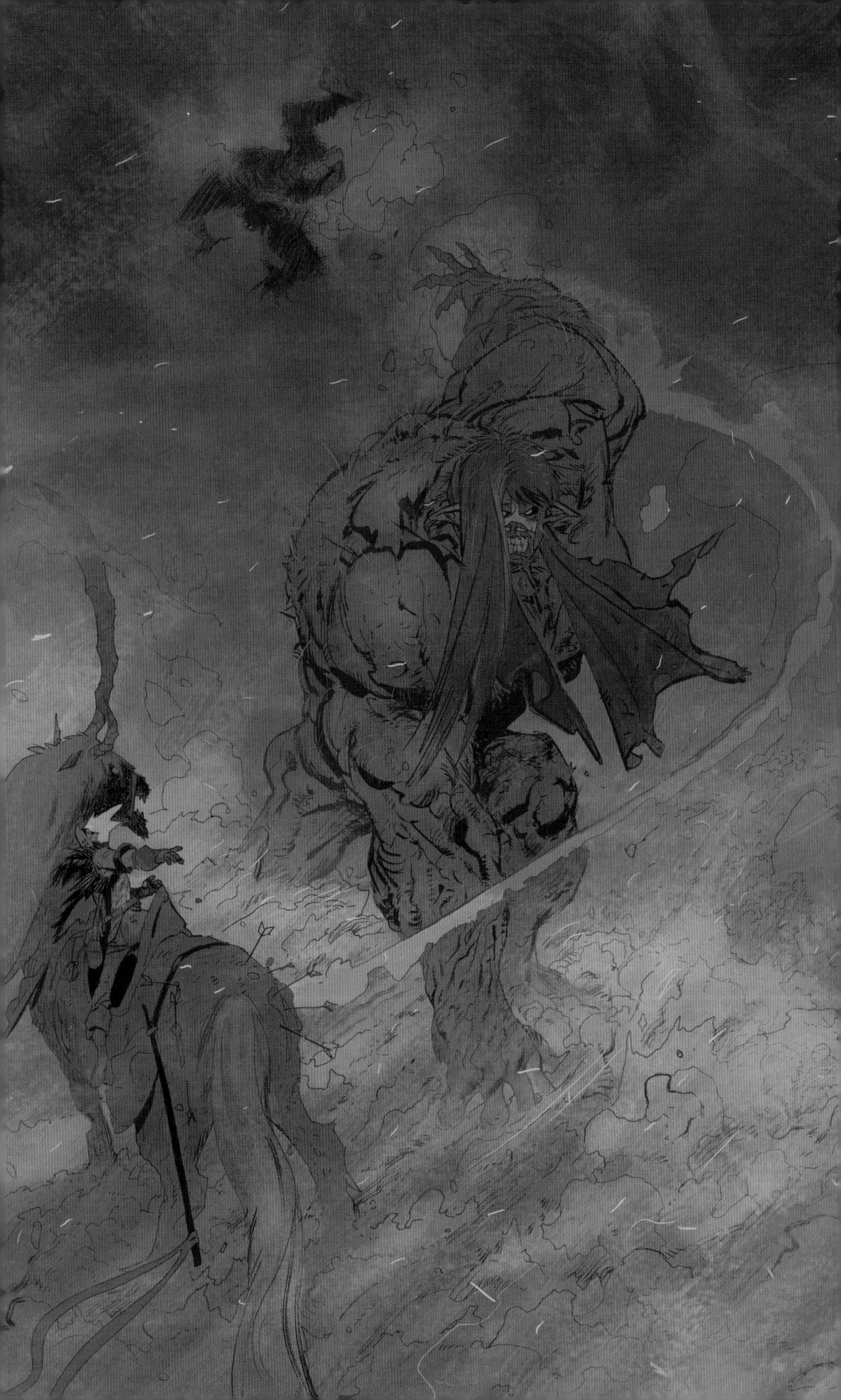

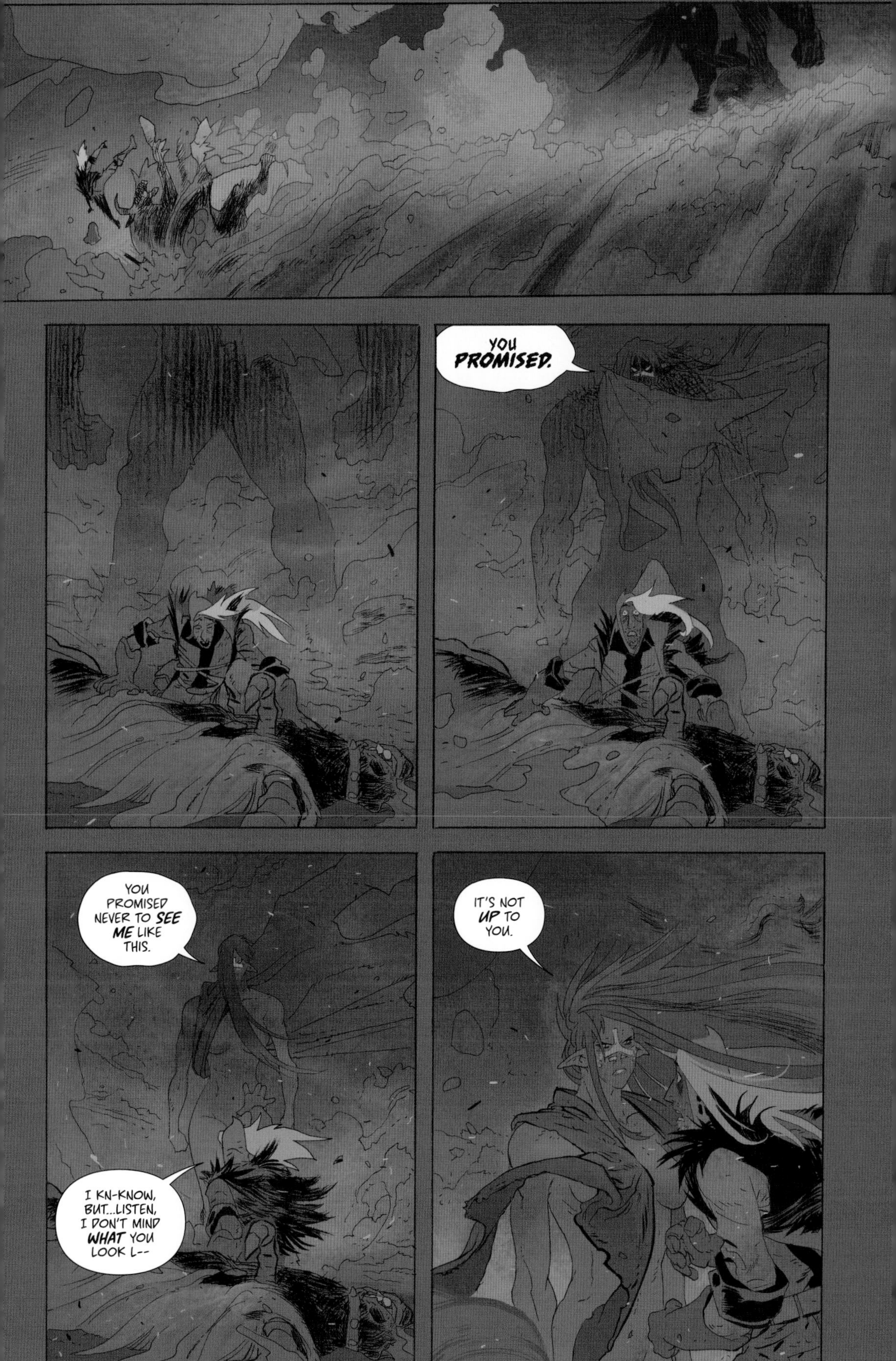
YOU PROMISED.
YOU PROMISED NEVER TO SEE ME LIKE THIS.
I KN-KNOW, BUT...LISTEN, I DON'T MIND WHAT YOU LOOK L--
IT'S NOT UP TO YOU.

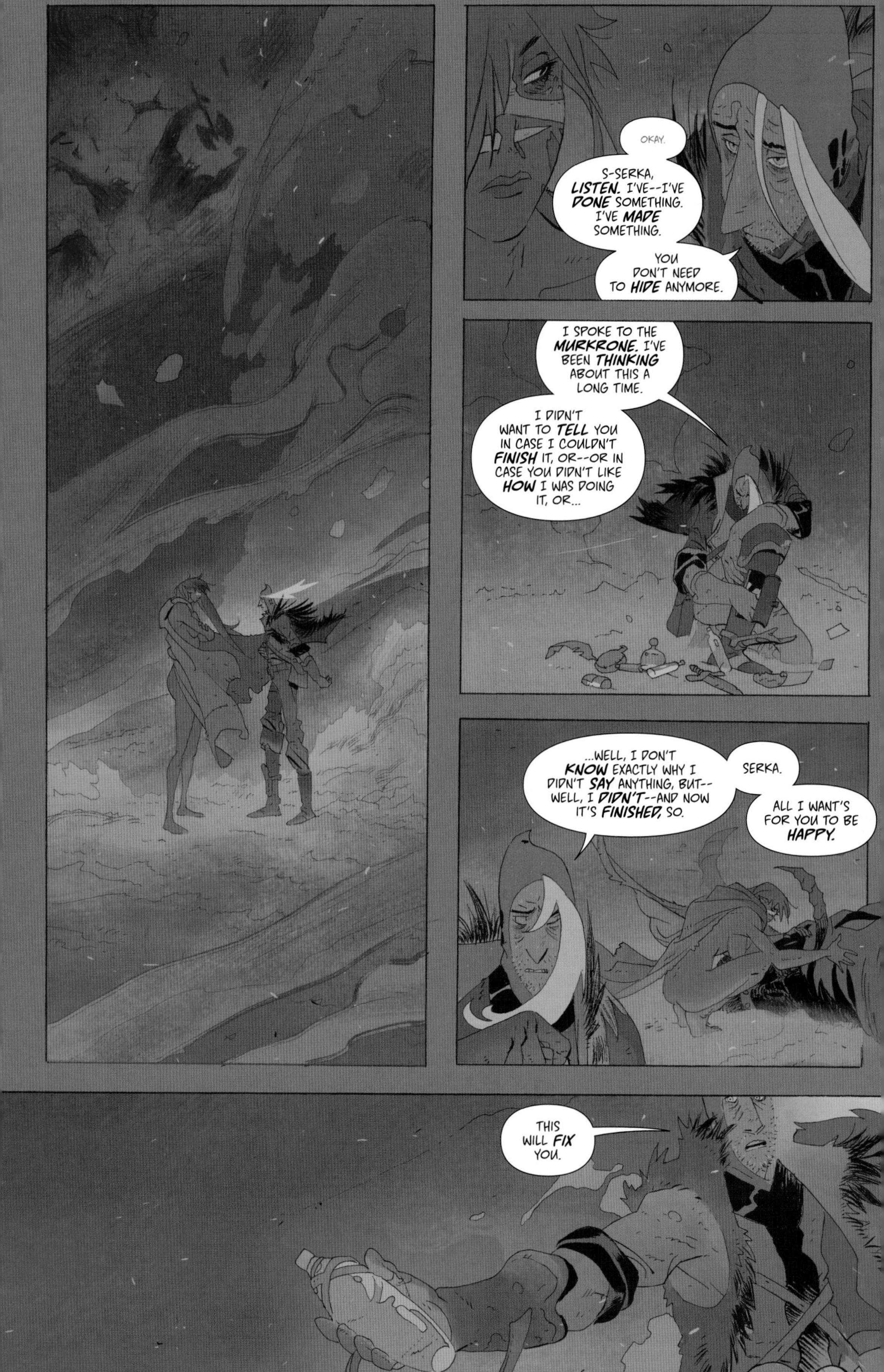

OKAY.
S-SERKA, LISTEN. I'VE--I'VE DONE SOMETHING. I'VE MADE SOMETHING.
YOU DON'T NEED TO HIDE ANYMORE.
I SPOKE TO THE MURKRONE. I'VE BEEN THINKING ABOUT THIS A LONG TIME.
I DIDN'T WANT TO TELL YOU IN CASE I COULDN'T FINISH IT, OR--OR IN CASE YOU DIDN'T LIKE HOW I WAS DOING IT, OR...
...WELL, I DON'T KNOW EXACTLY WHY I DIDN'T SAY ANYTHING, BUT--WELL, I DIDN'T--AND NOW IT'S FINISHED, SO.
SERKA.
ALL I WANT'S FOR YOU TO BE HAPPY.
THIS WILL FIX YOU.

"FIX."

I WONDER.

IF **THIS** HADN'T HAPPENED. IF YOU HADN'T **RUN** HERE TO **SAVE** YOURSELF.

IF YOU HADN'T **SEEN** ME.

WOULD YOU HAVE **SNUCK** **THIS** INTO MY DRINK?

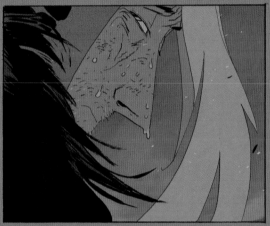

OF **COURSE** N--

WHY DO YOU THINK I **COME** HERE, HUSBAND?

...B-BECAUSE-- BECAUSE IF YOU **DIDN'T**, THE **DEMON** WOULD **TAKE OVER**, AND--

NO.

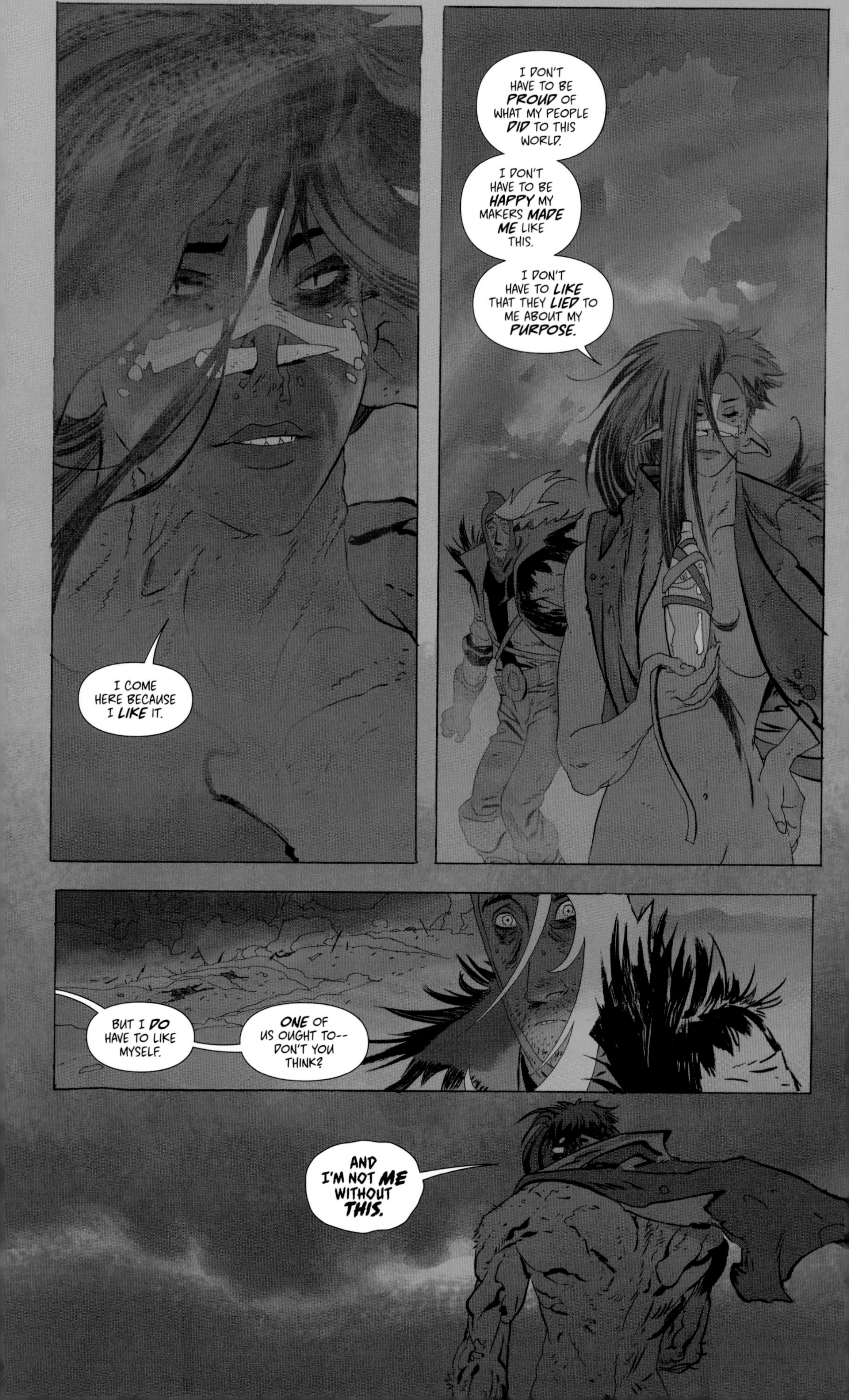
I DON'T HAVE TO BE PROUD OF WHAT MY PEOPLE DID TO THIS WORLD.
I DON'T HAVE TO BE HAPPY MY MAKERS MADE ME LIKE THIS.
I DON'T HAVE TO LIKE THAT THEY LIED TO ME ABOUT MY PURPOSE.
I COME HERE BECAUSE I LIKE IT.
BUT I DO HAVE TO LIKE MYSELF.
ONE OF US OUGHT TO-- DON'T YOU THINK?
AND I'M NOT ME WITHOUT THIS.

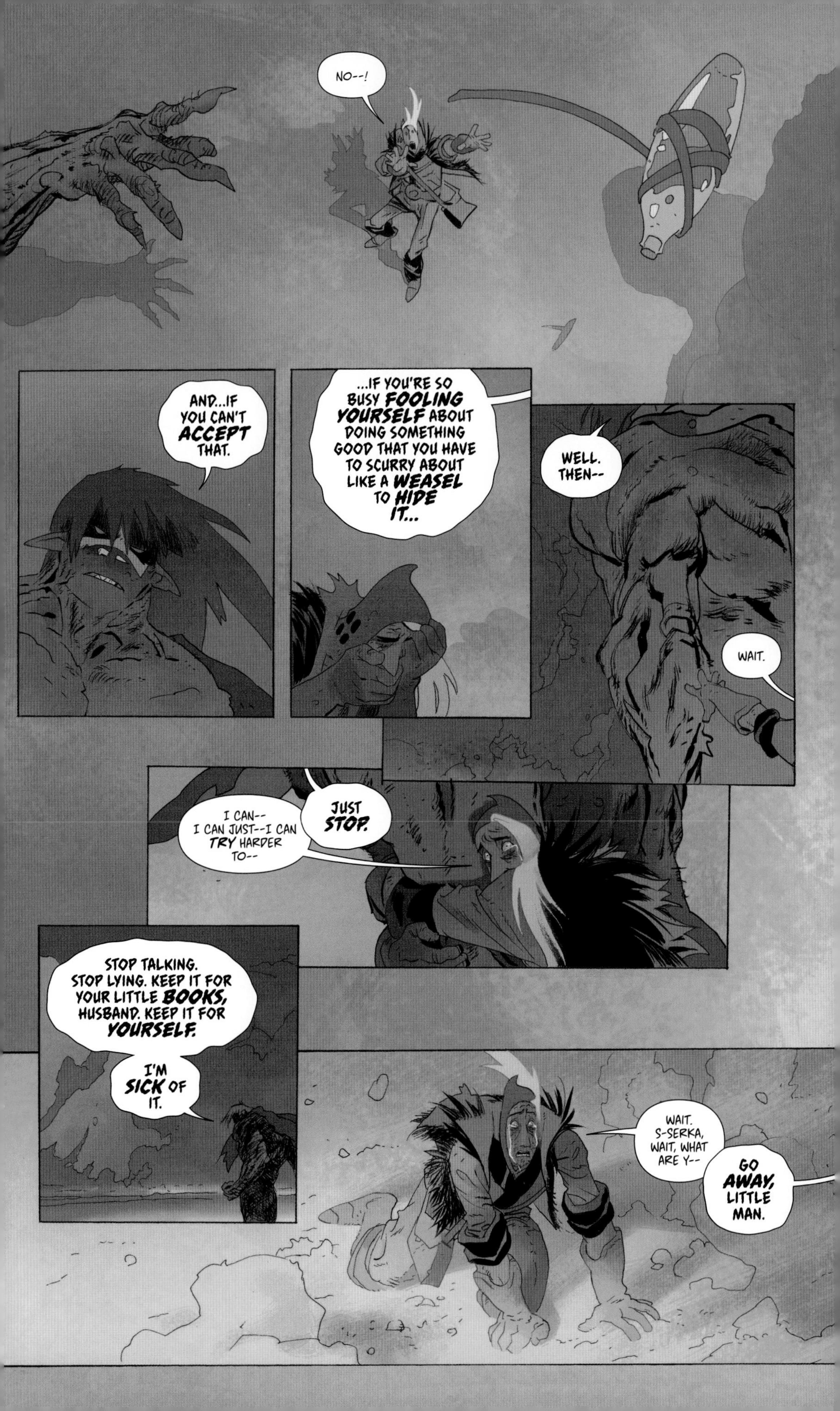
NO--!
AND...IF YOU CAN'T ACCEPT THAT.
...IF YOU'RE SO BUSY FOOLING YOURSELF ABOUT DOING SOMETHING GOOD THAT YOU HAVE TO SCURRY ABOUT LIKE A WEASEL TO HIDE IT...
WELL. THEN--
WAIT.
JUST STOP.
I CAN-- I CAN JUST--I CAN TRY HARDER TO--
STOP TALKING. STOP LYING. KEEP IT FOR YOUR LITTLE BOOKS, HUSBAND. KEEP IT FOR YOURSELF.
I'M SICK OF IT.
WAIT. S-SERKA, WAIT, WHAT ARE Y--
GO AWAY, LITTLE MAN.

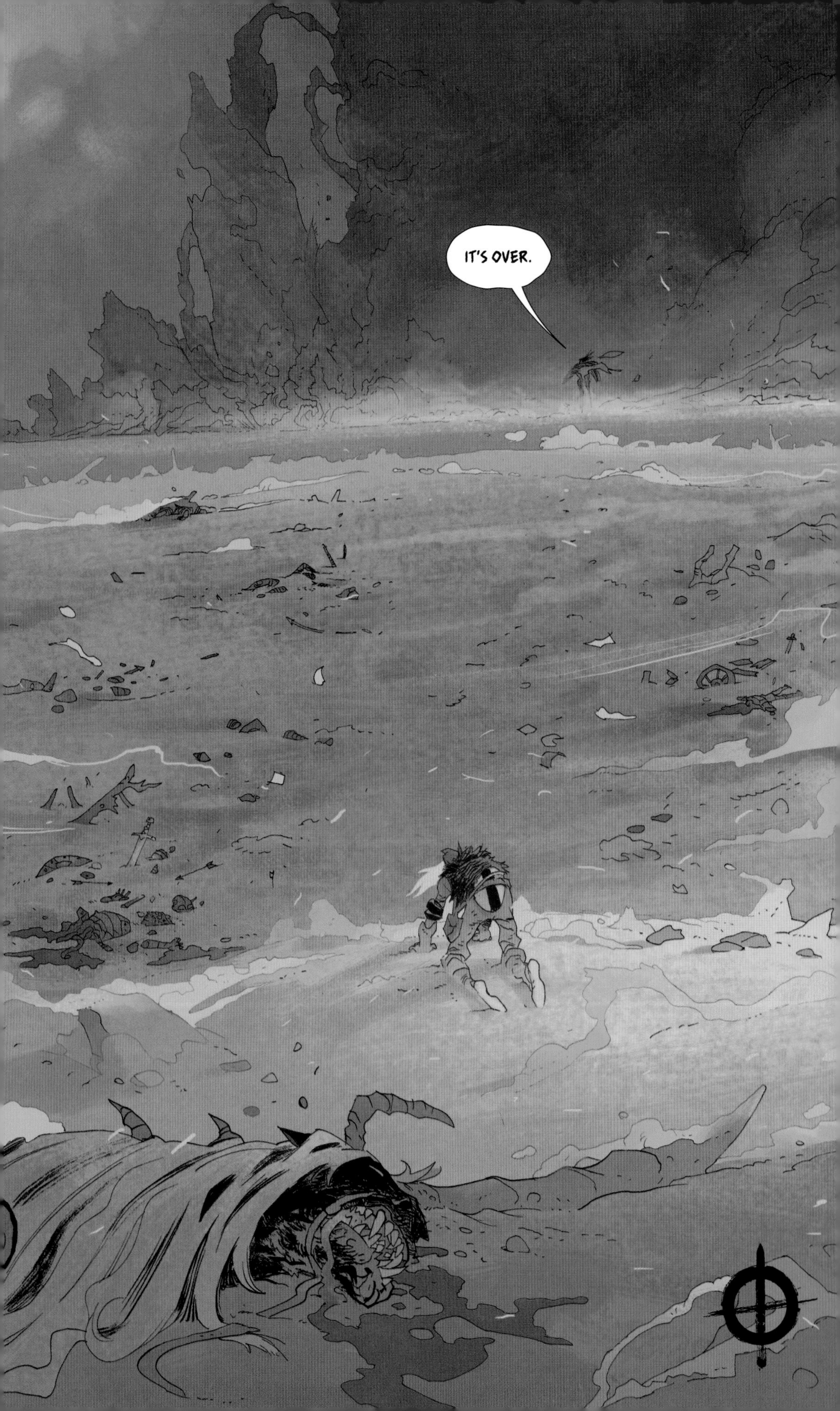
IT'S OVER.

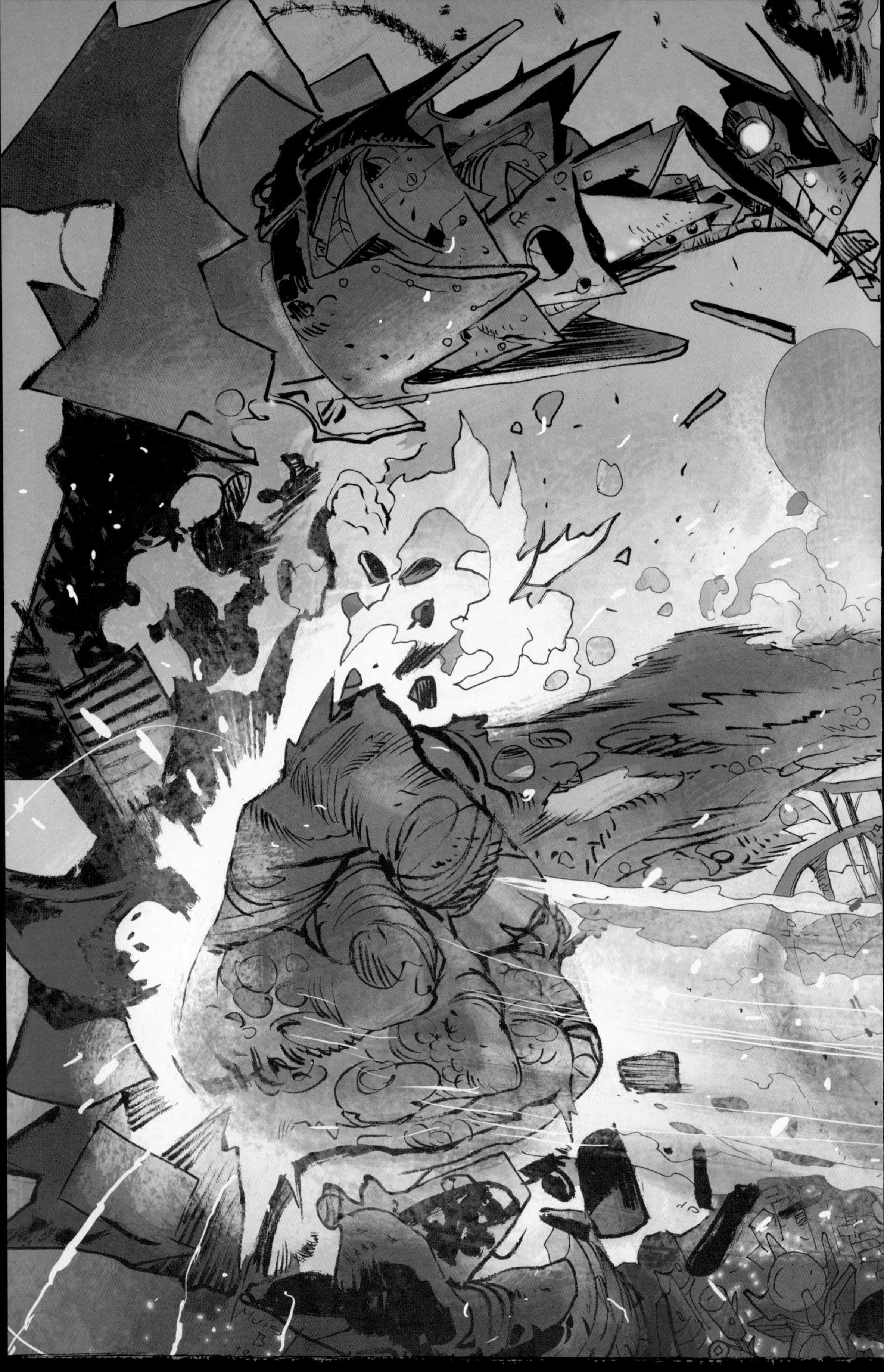

ISSUE FIVE COVER BY **MATÍAS BERGARA**

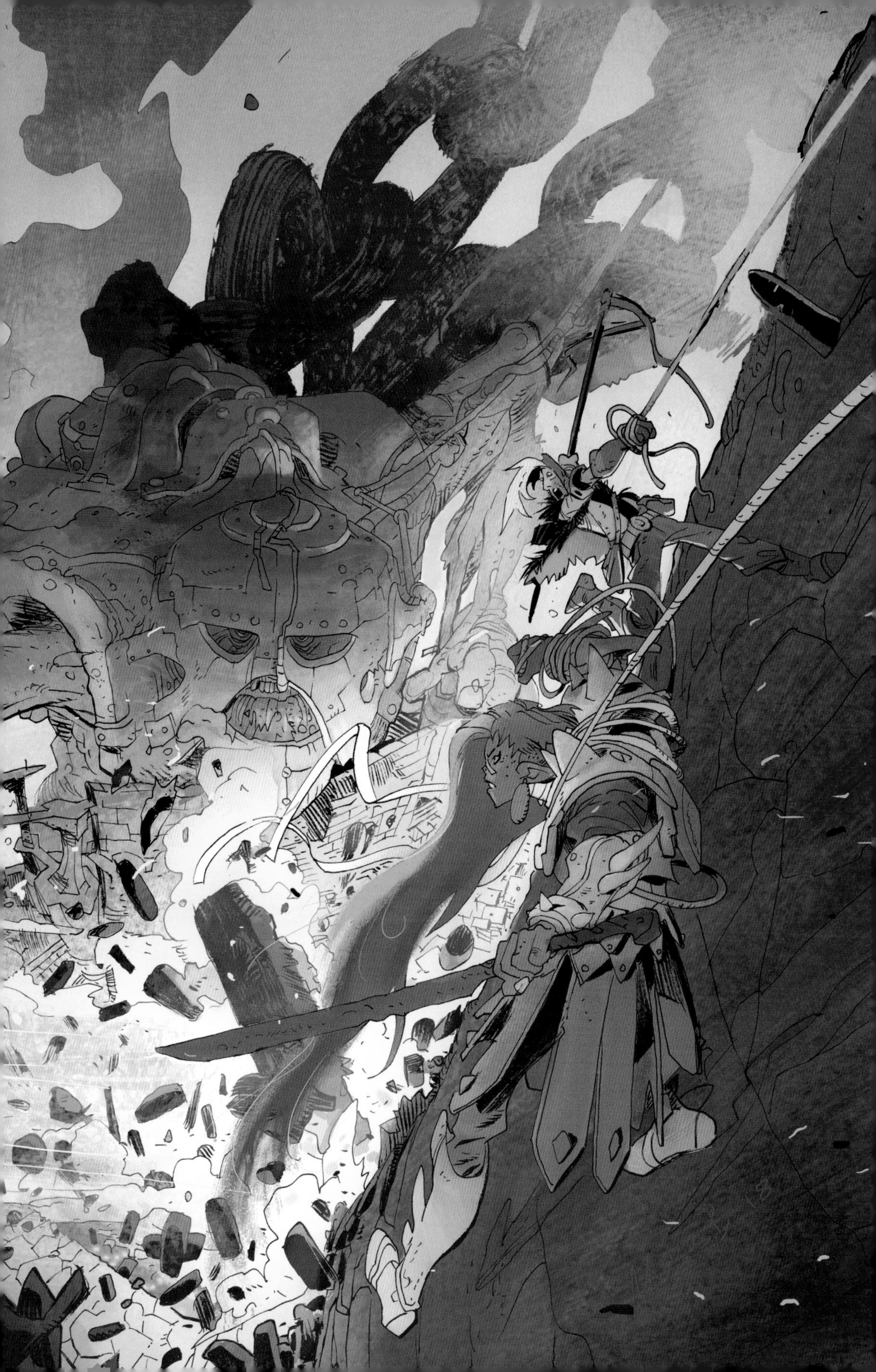

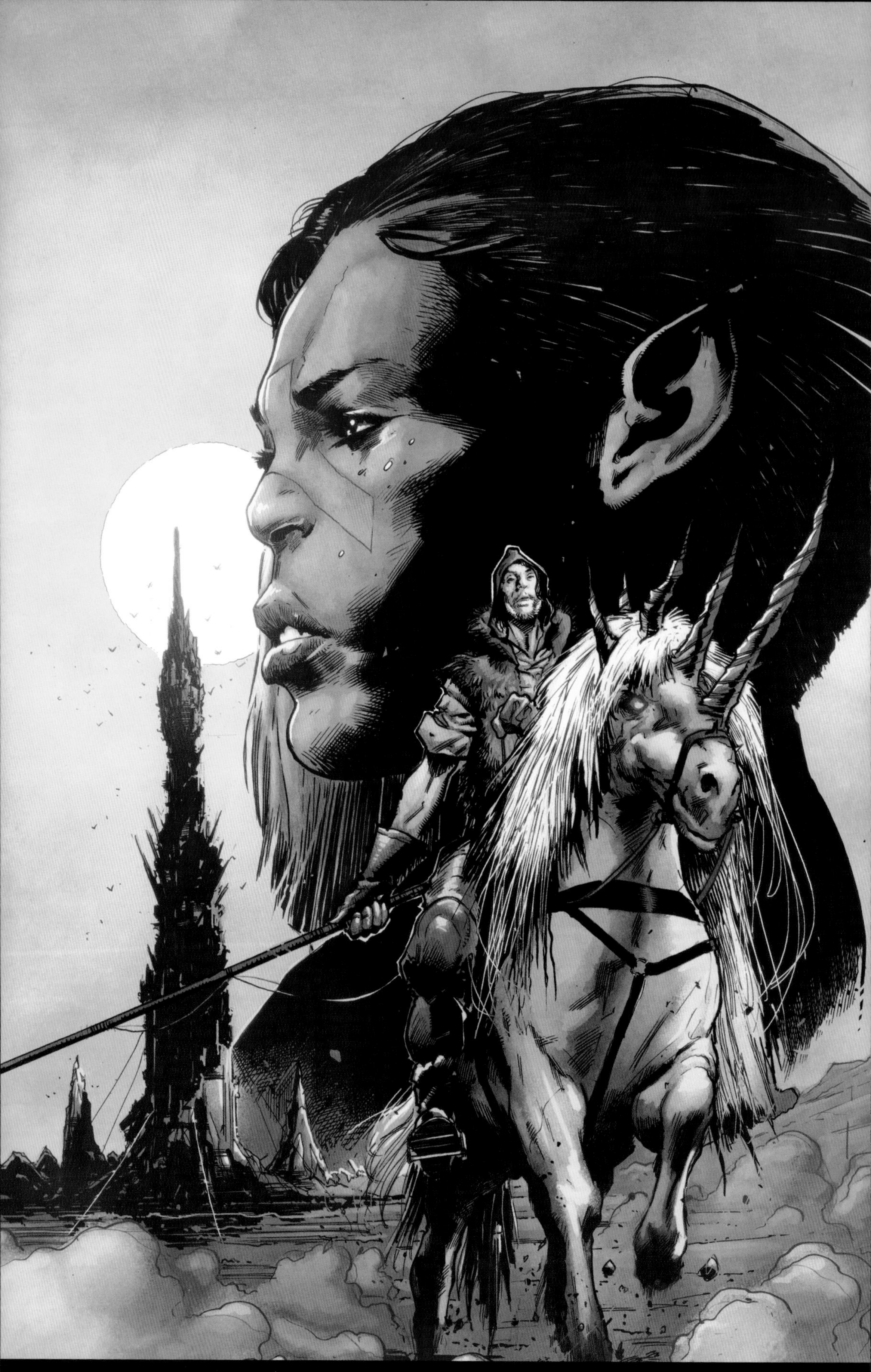

ISSUE FIVE COVER BY **TREVOR HAIRSINE** WITH COLORS BY **JORDAN BOYD**

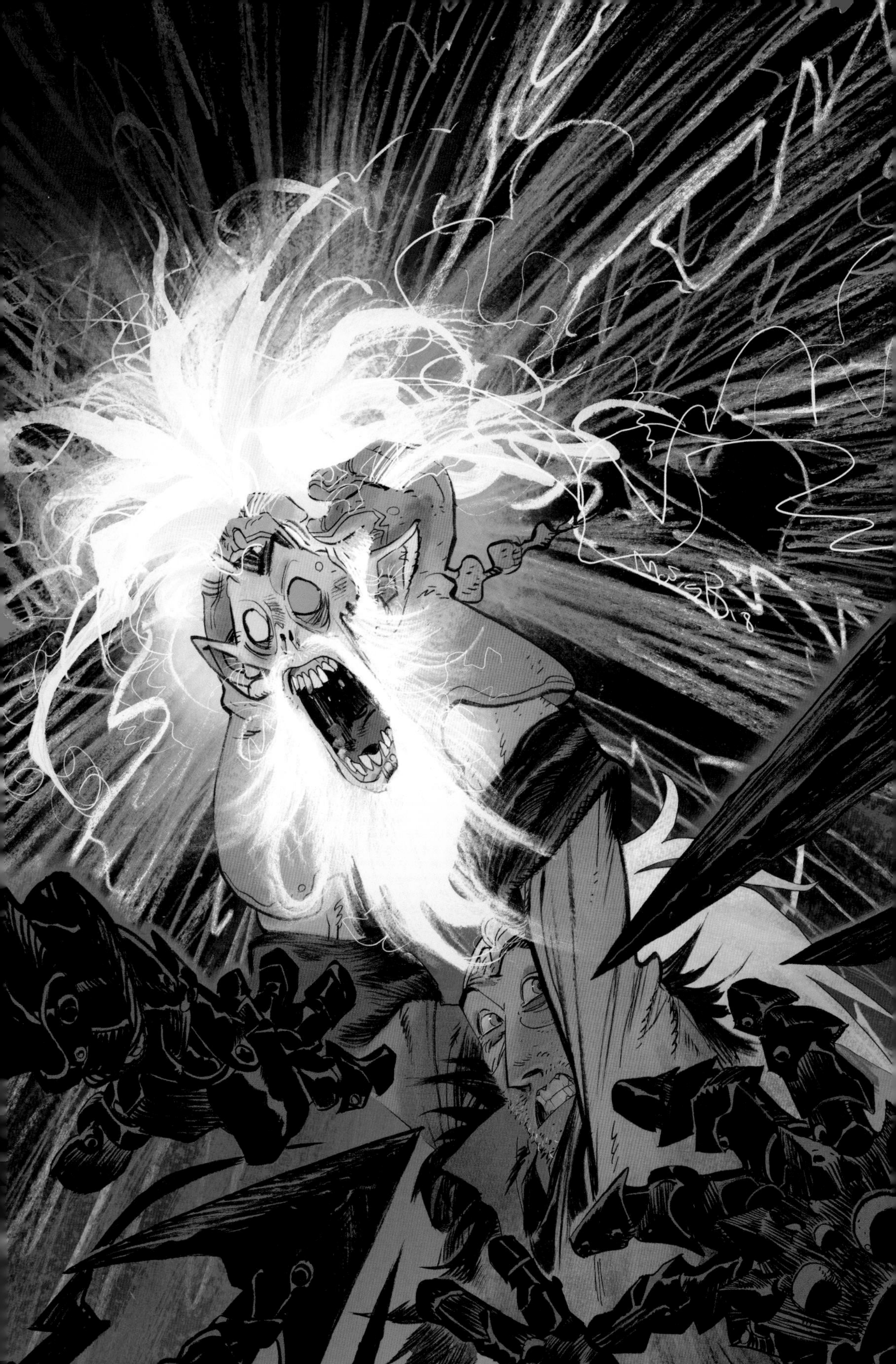

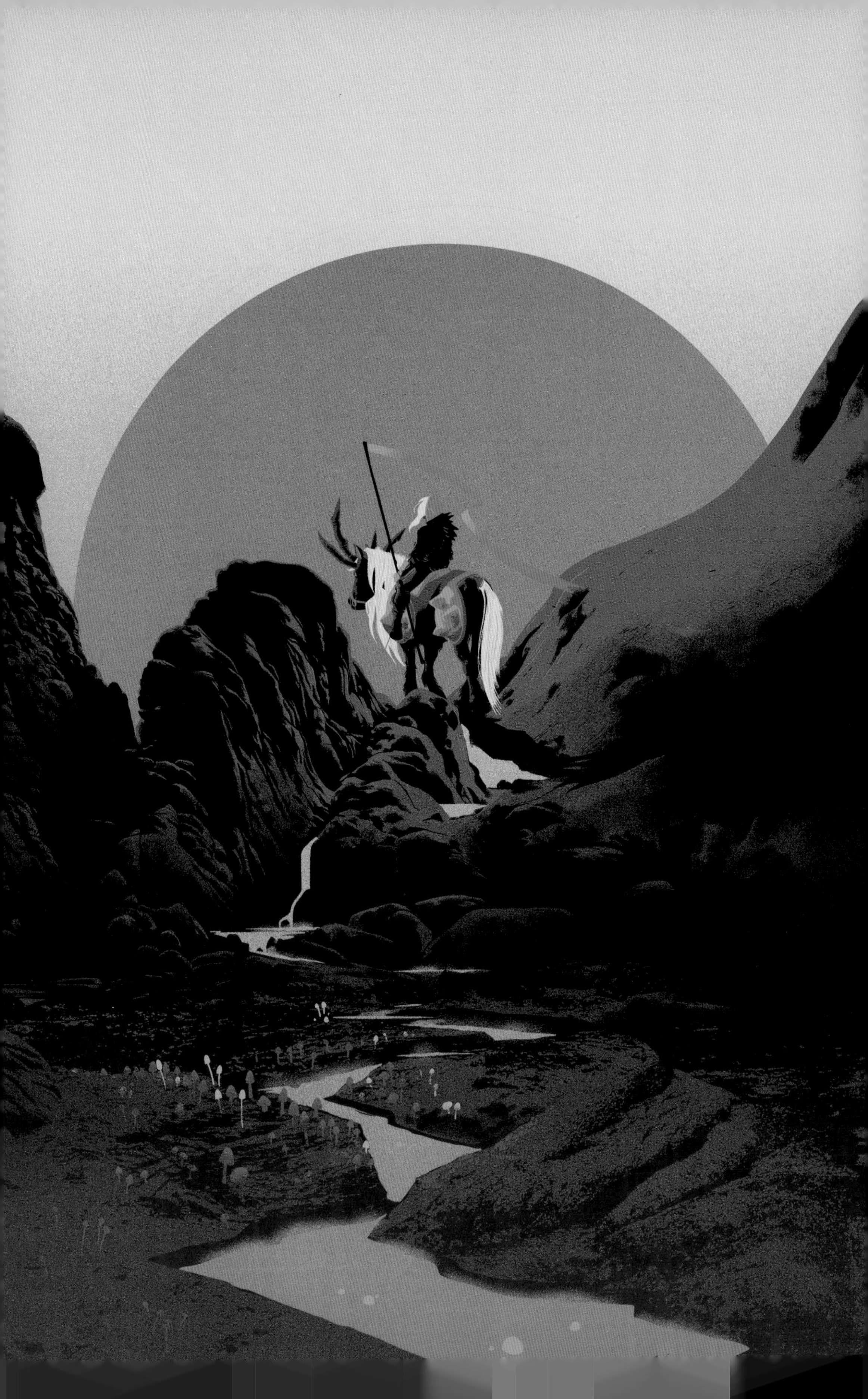

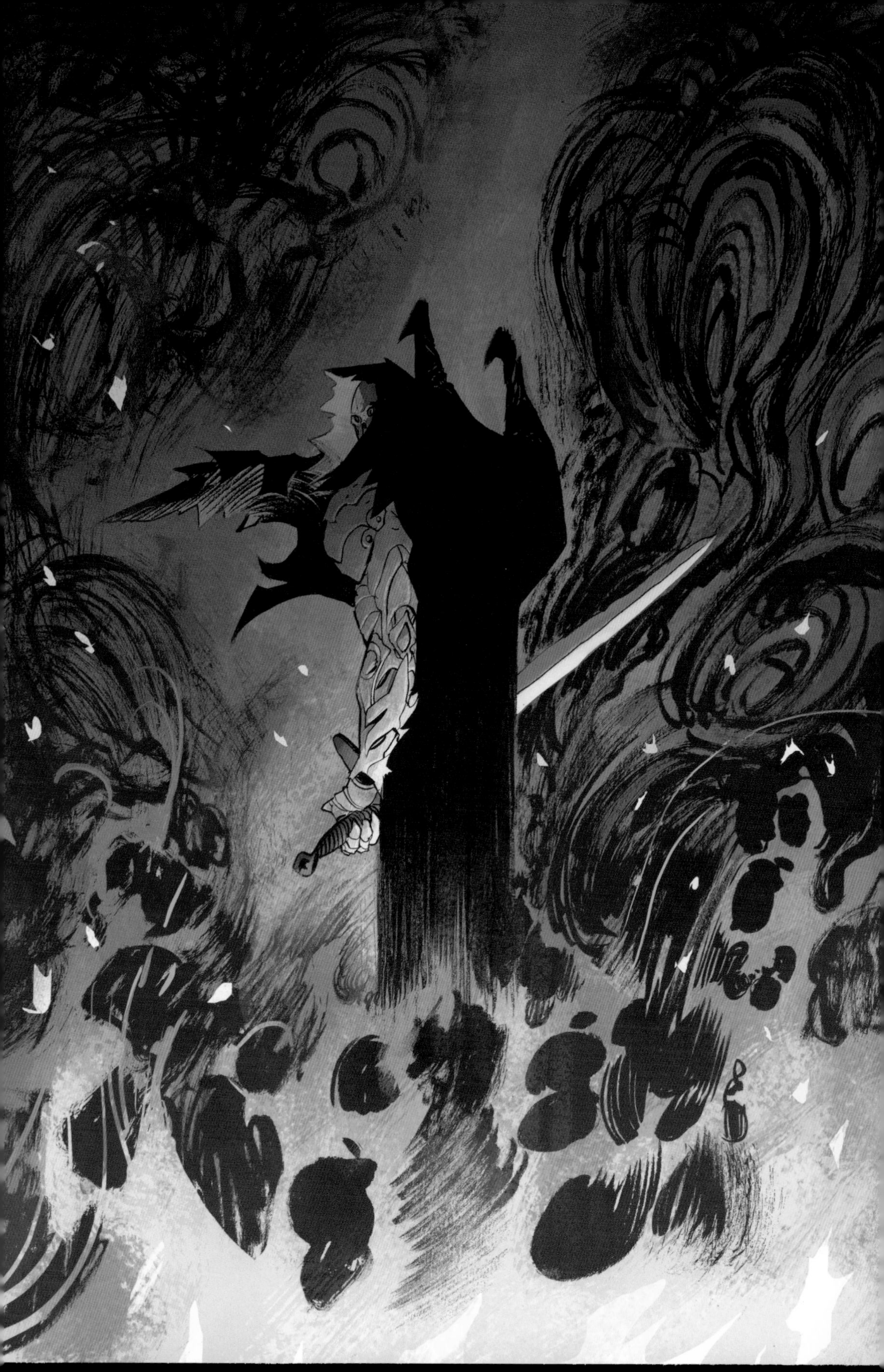

ISSUE SEVEN COVER BY **MATÍAS BERGARA**

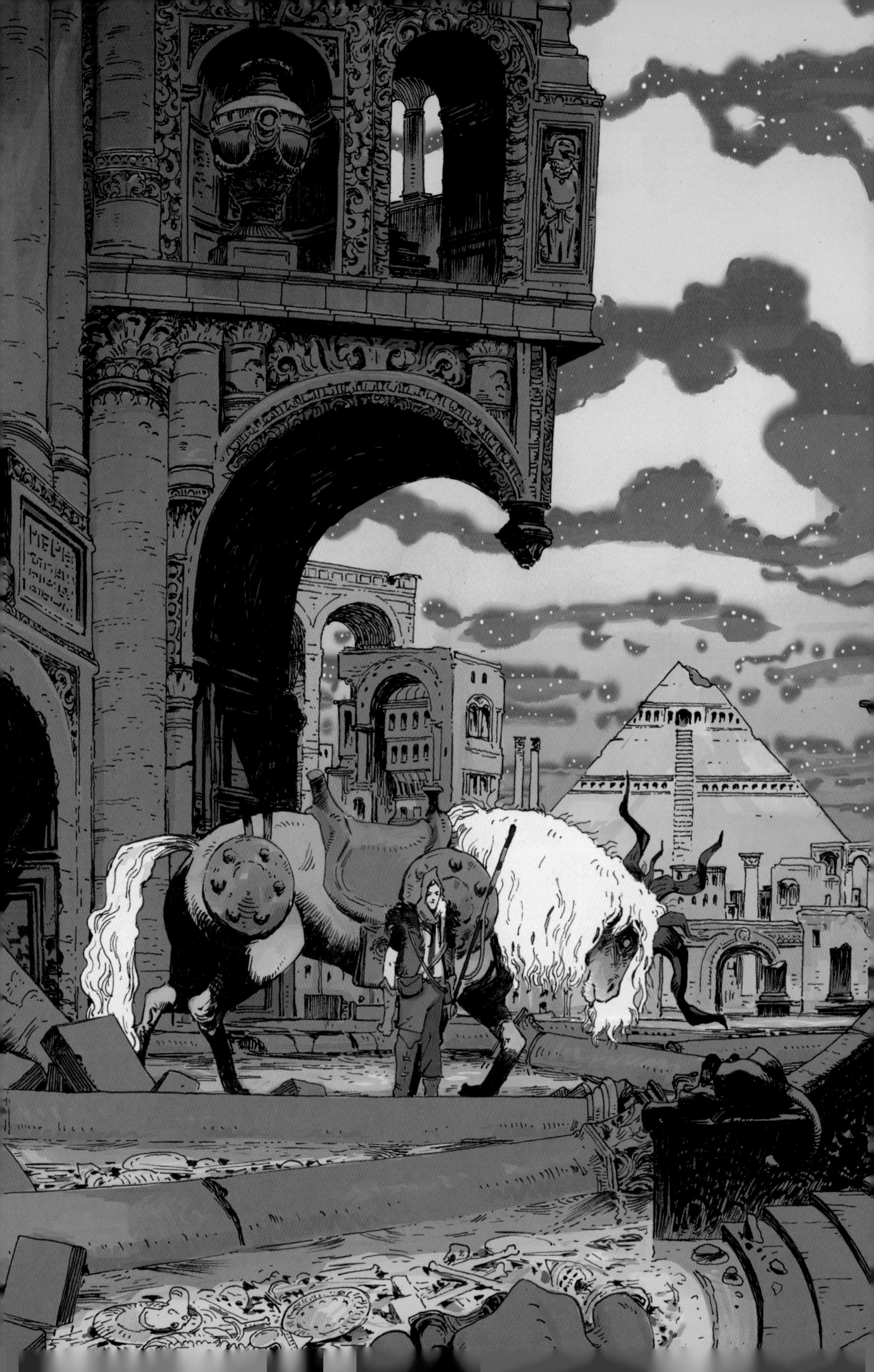

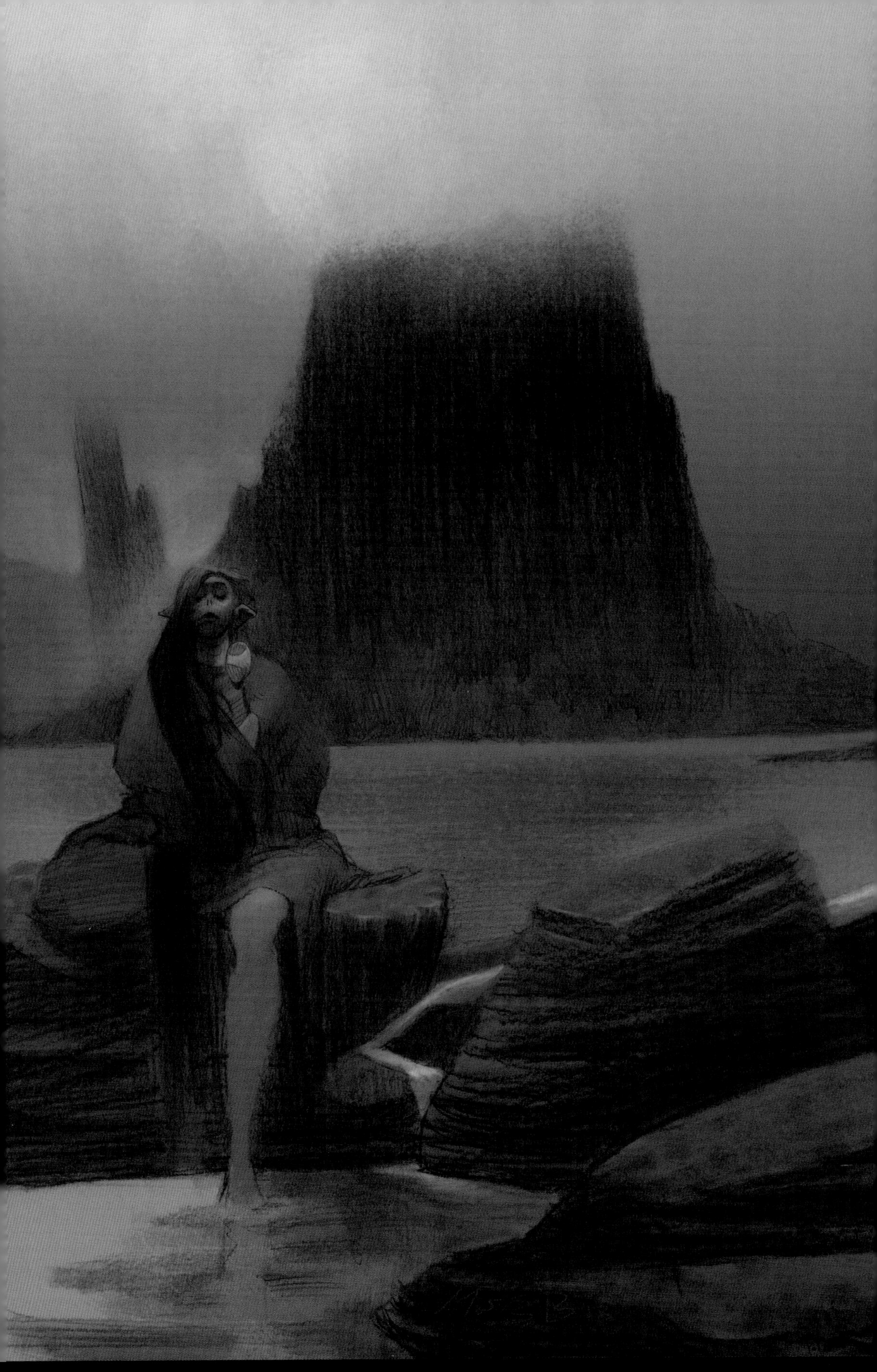

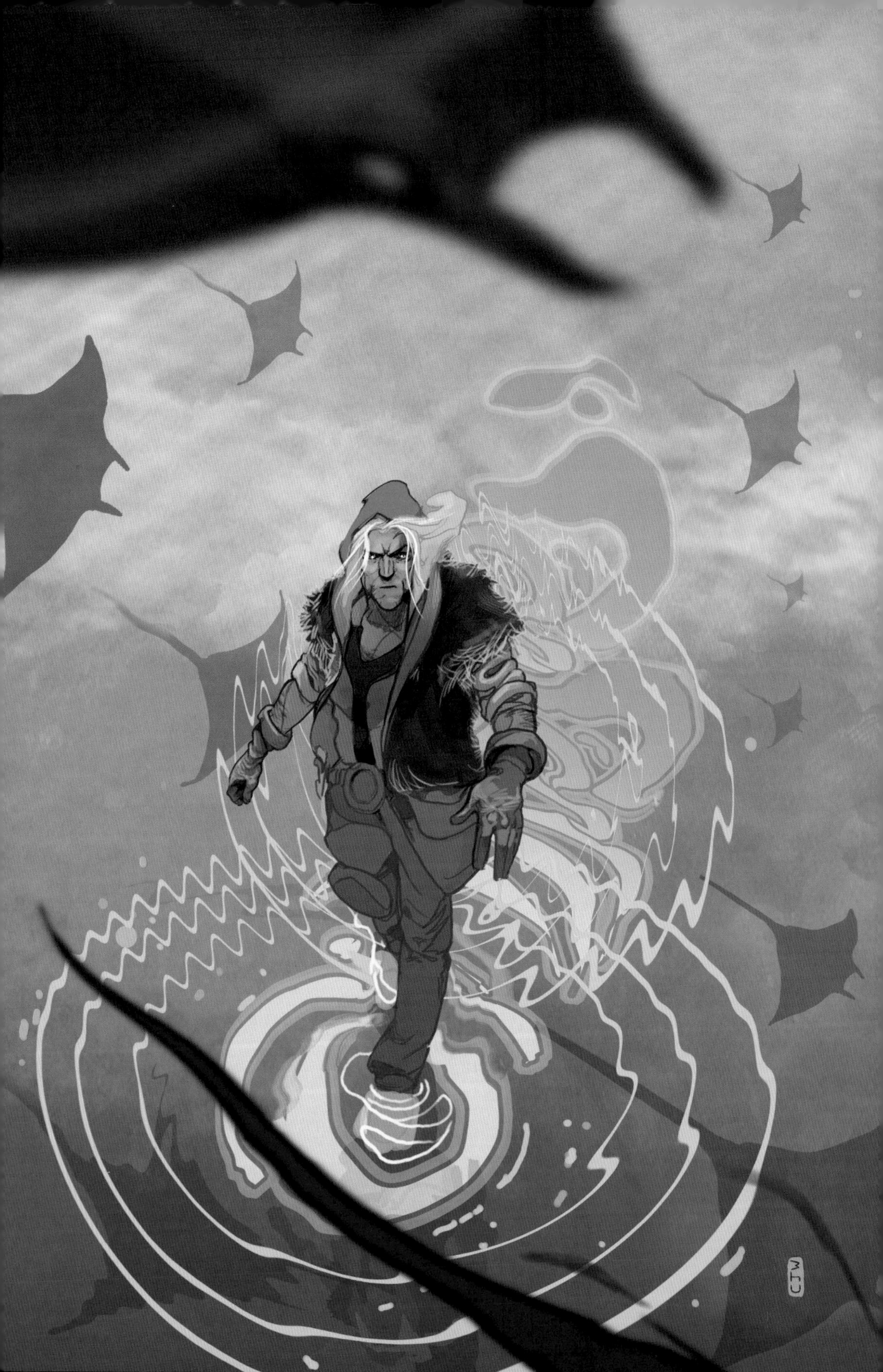
CJW

MATÍAS BERGARA SKETCHBOOK

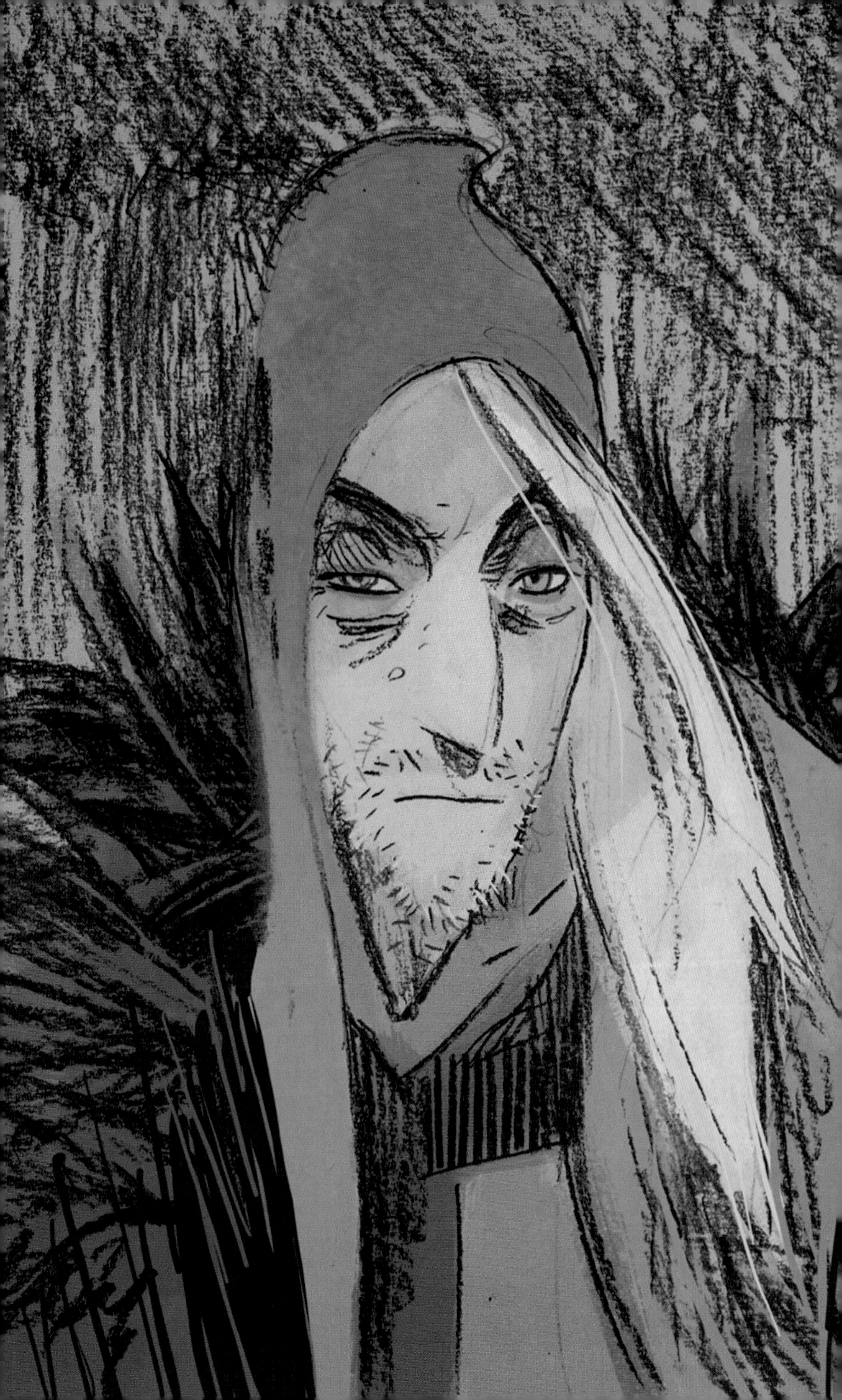

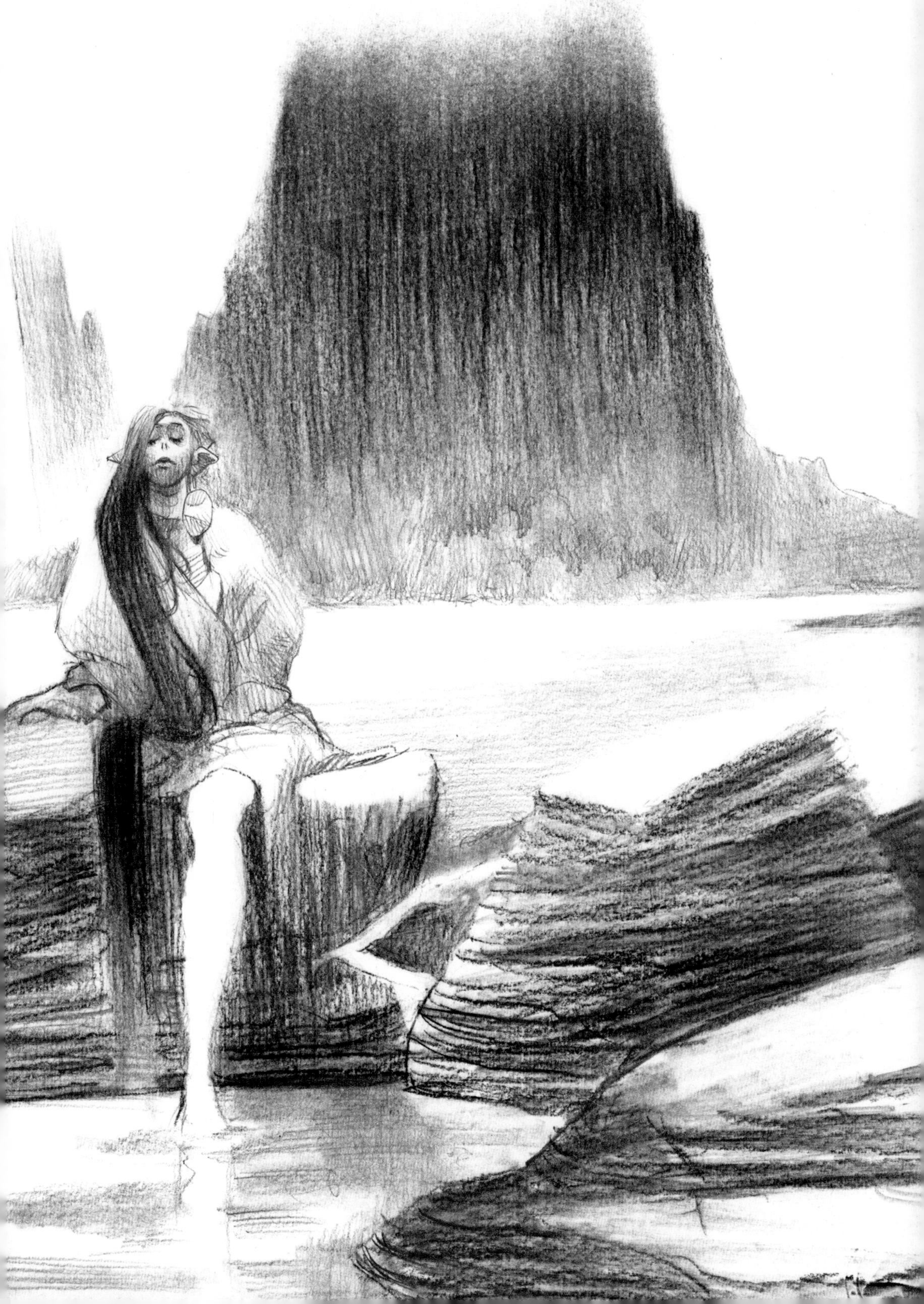

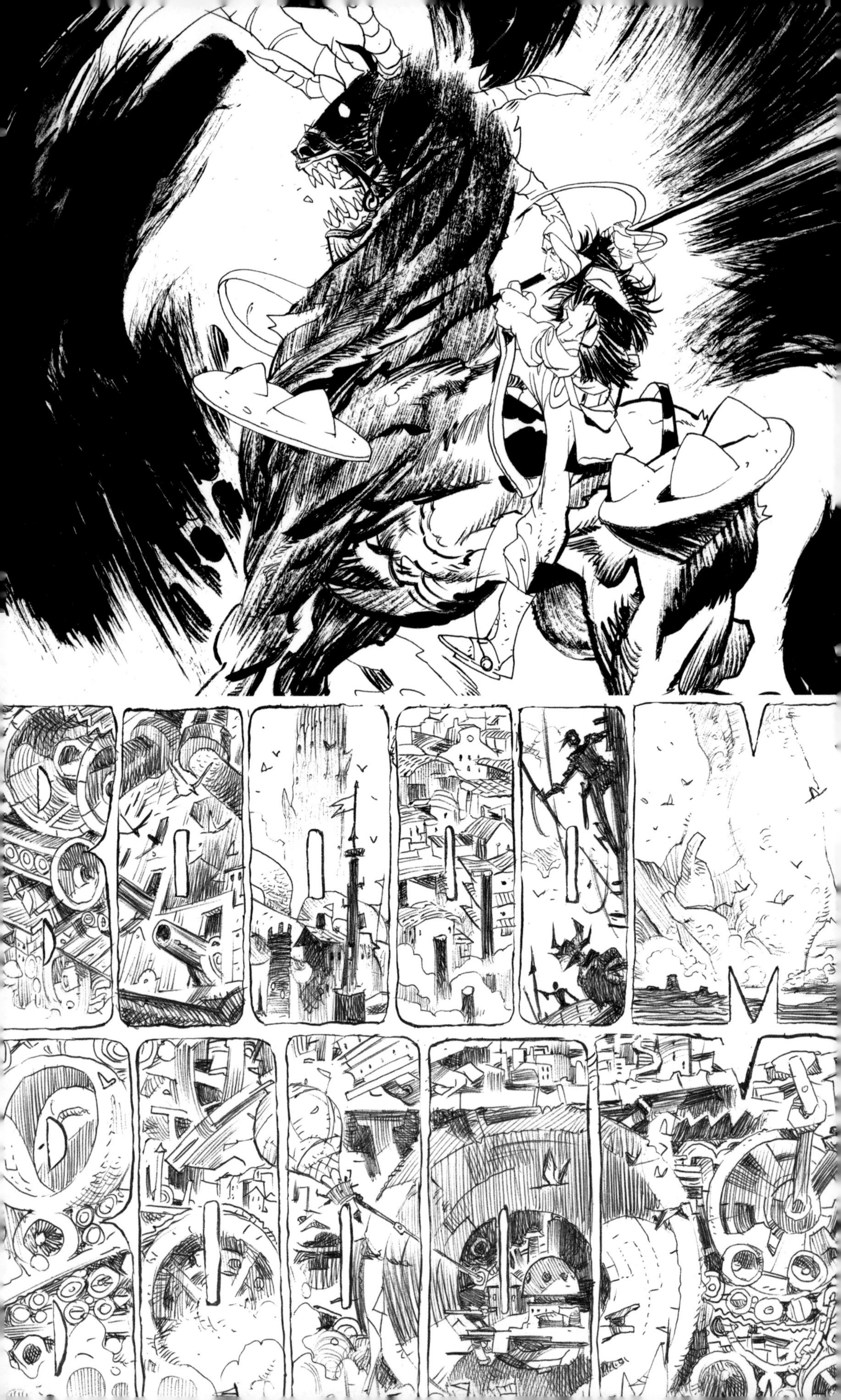

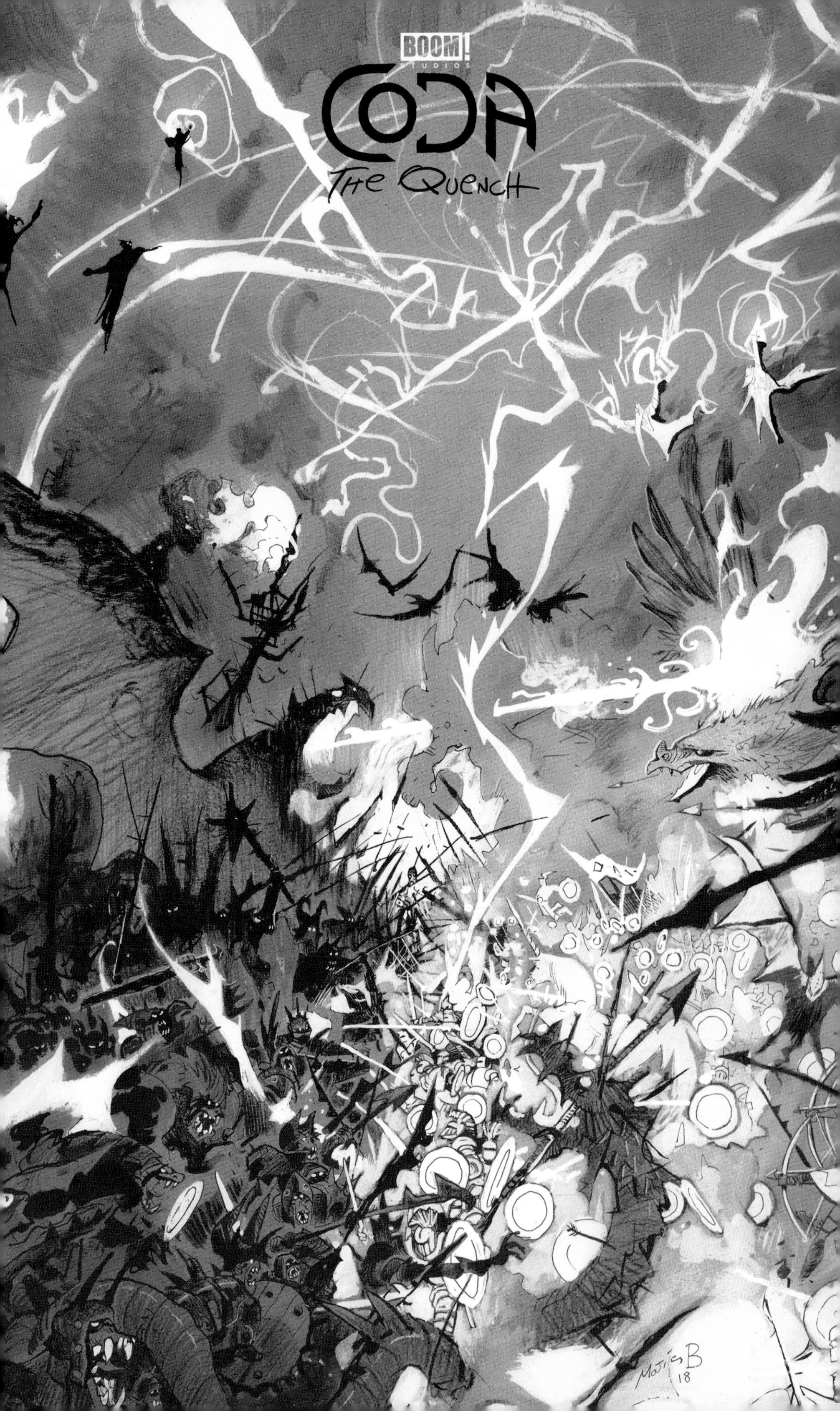
BOOM! STUDIOS
CODA
THE QUENCH
Matias B
18

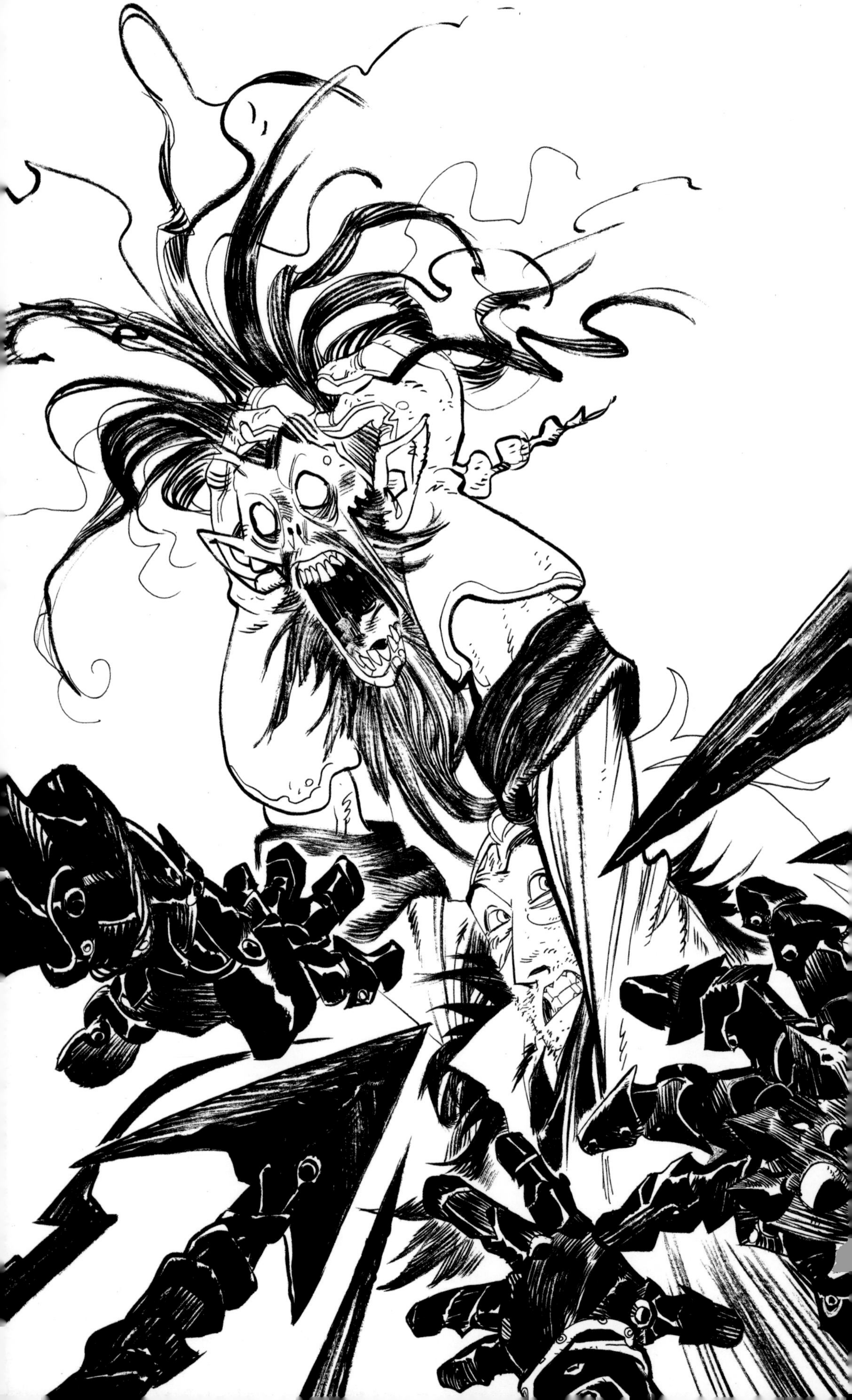

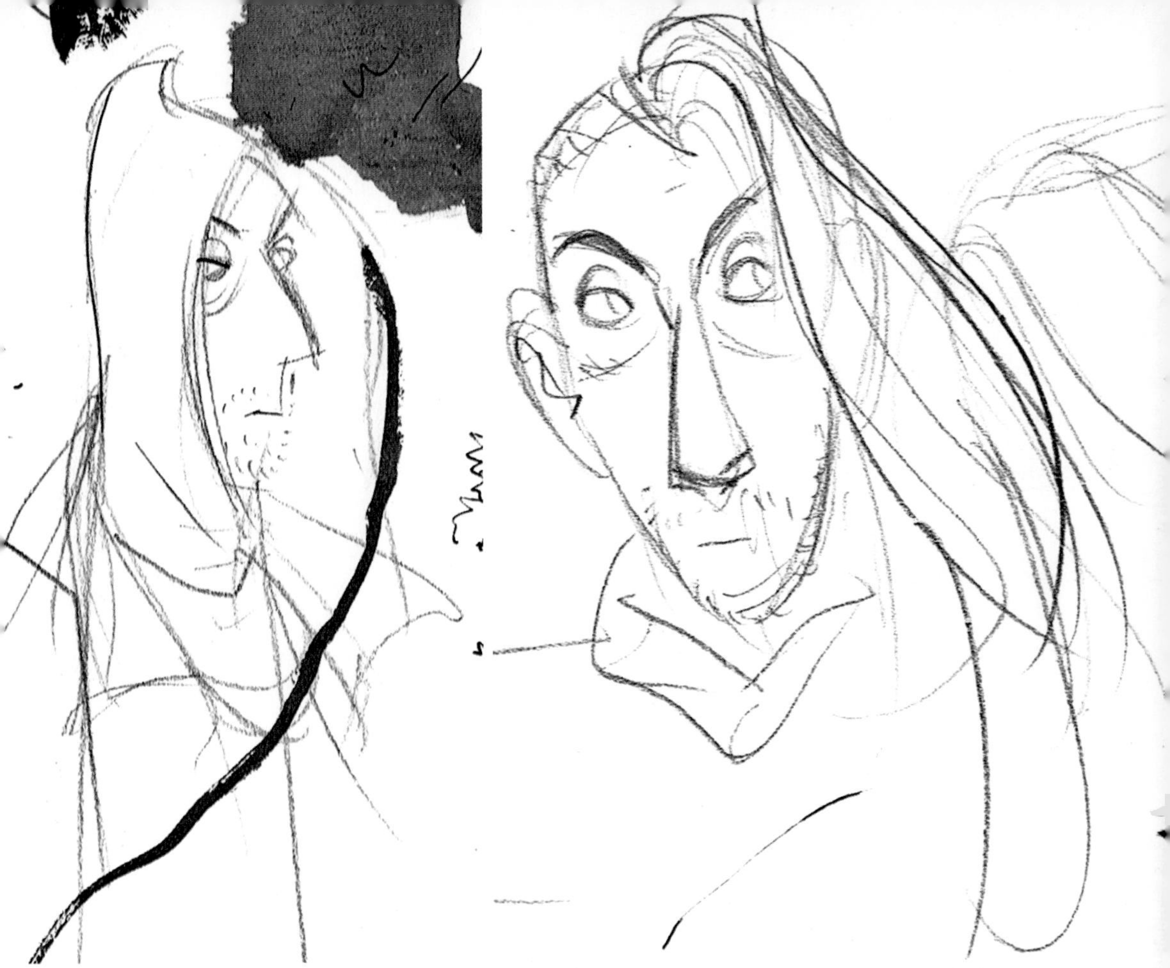

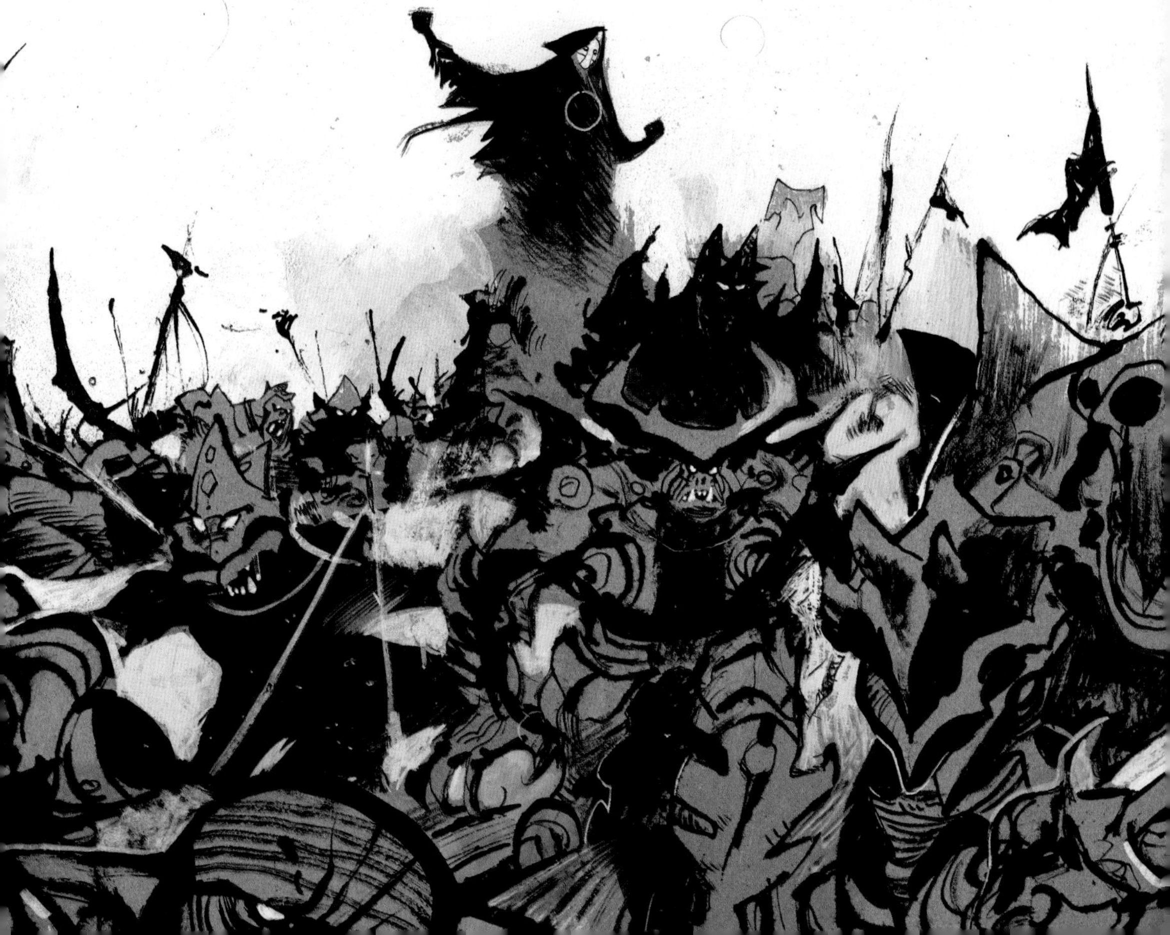

ABOUT THE AUTHORS

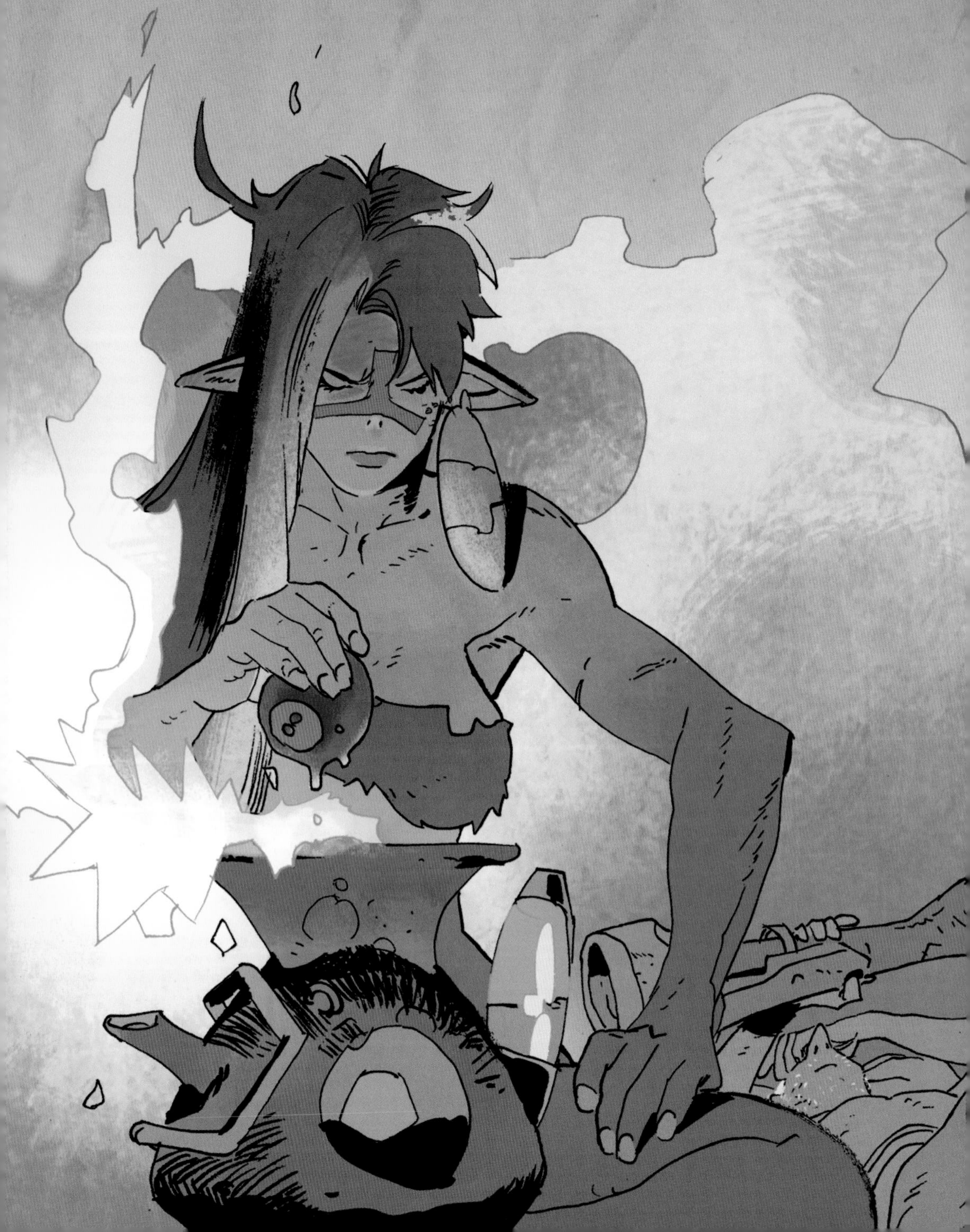

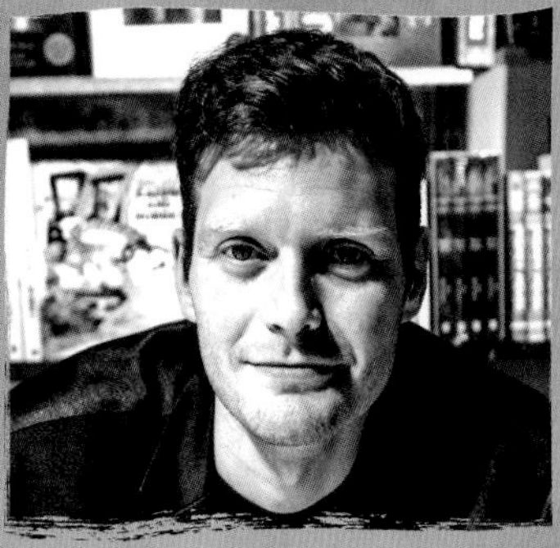

Simon Spurrier is a writer of actual words. His comic book credits stretch from *2000AD* and *Judge Dredd* to *X-Men Legacy*, *Suicide Squad*, and *Star Wars*. His creator-owned books include *Cry Havoc*, *Angelic*, and Eisner Nominee *The Spire*. He's published several prose novels, including *Contract* and *A Serpent Uncoiled*. His absurdist-noir novella *Unusual Concentrations* was shortlisted for the Shirley Jackson Award and is available online. He is currently working on new television and comic book projects. He lives in the south of Britain and normally isn't very good at writing about himself in the third person, but I think this time I'm actually doing pretty well.

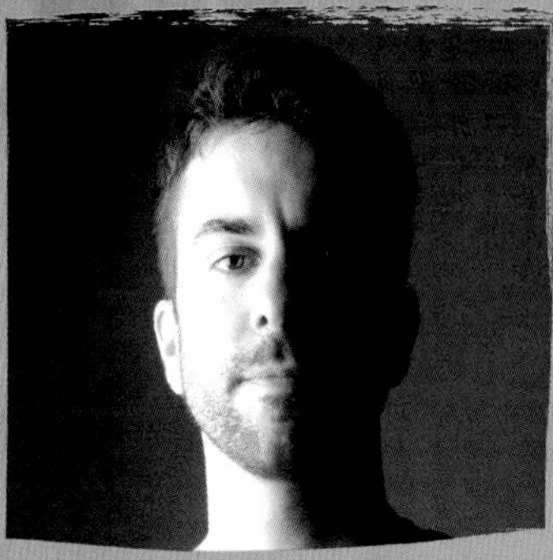

Matias Bergara was born and still lives in the curious little country of Uruguay. He's been illustrating comics, book covers, and video game art ever since leaving a college career in literature. Most of his published work was created for Latin America and Europe, so he's a recent arrival on U.S. titles such as *Sons of Anarchy* (BOOM!, 2014) and *Cannibal* (Image, 2016).

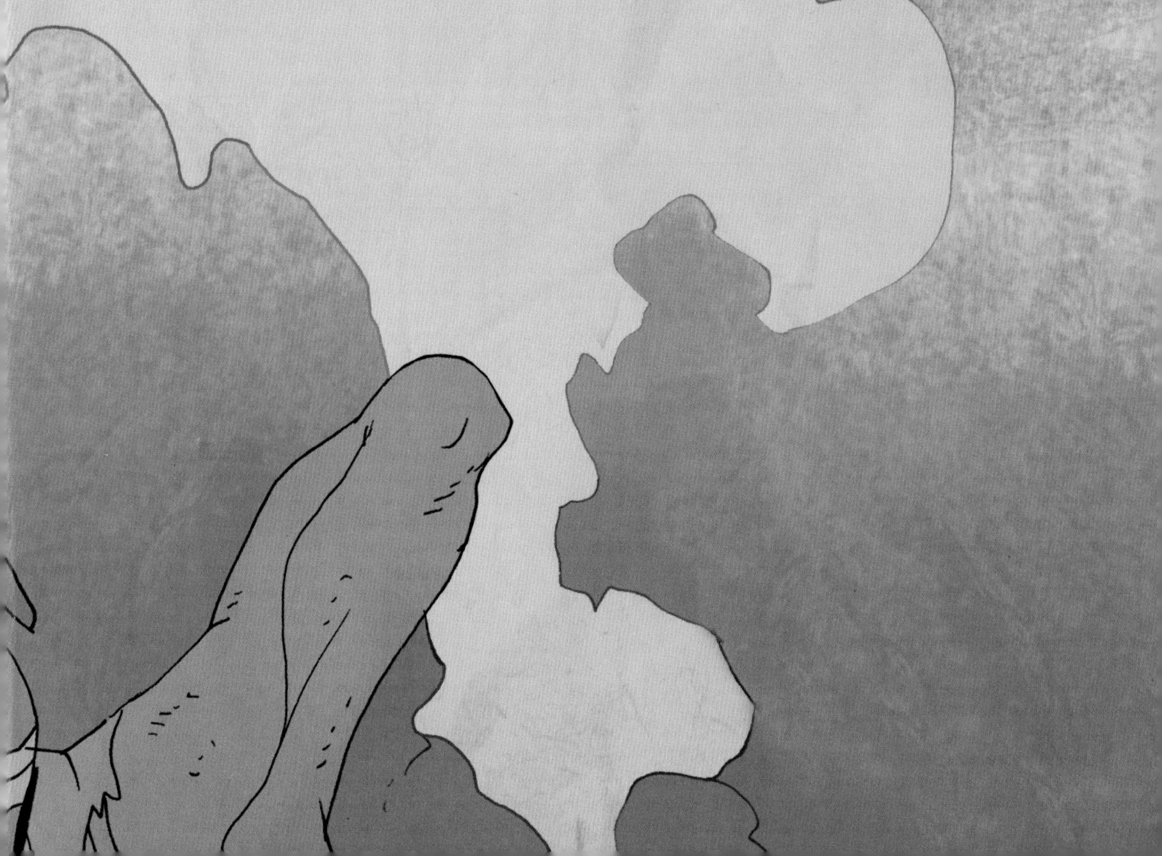

DISCOVER
EXCITING NEW WORLDS

WEAVERS.
SPURRIER
BURNETT
FARRELL

GODSHAPER
SIMON SPURRIER • JONAS GOONFACE

Jim Henson's
LABYRINTH
CORONATION
VOLUME ONE
Simon Spurrier • Daniel Bayliss • Dan Jackson

Jim Henson's
THE POWER OF THE
DARK CRYSTAL
SIMON SPURRIER
KELLY AND NICHOLE MATTHEWS
"A bold leap forward for the franchise. 10/10"
—Newsarama

SIX-GUN
GORILLA
SIMON SPURRIER JEFF STOKELY

"The Spire is fantastic! My kind of genre free-for-all."
—BRIAN K. VAUGHAN (Saga)
THE SPIRE
SIMON SPURRIER
JEFF STOKELY
ANDRÉ MAY

Coda
Simon Spurrier, Matías Bergara
Volume 1
978-1-68415-321-3 | $9.99 US
Volume 2
978-1-68415-369-5 | $14.99 US

Extermination
Simon Spurrier, Jeffrey Edwards, V Ken Marion
Volume 1
978-1-60886-296-2 | $14.99 US
Volume 2
978-1-60886-315-0 | $14.99 US

Godshaper
Simon Spurrier, Jonas Goonface
978-1-60886-939-8 | $19.99 US

Jim Henson's Labyrinth: Coronation
Simon Spurrier, Ryan Ferrier, Daniel Bayliss
Volume 1
978-1-68415-266-7 | $24.99 US
Volume 2
I978-1-68415-358-9 | $24.99 US

Jim Henson's The Power of the Dark Crystal
Simon Spurrier, Phillip Kennedy Johnson, Kelly & Nichole Matthews
Volume 1
978-1-60886-992-3 | $24.99 US
Volume 2
978-1-68415-139-4 | $24.99 US
Volume 3
978-1-68415-208-7 | $24.99 US

Six-Gun Gorilla
Simon Spurrier, Jeff Stokely
978-1-60886-390-7 | $19.99 US

The Spire
Simon Spurrier, Jeff Stokely
978-1-60886-913-8 | $29.99 US

Weavers
Simon Spurrier, Dylan Burnett
978-1-60886-963-3 | $19.99 US

BOOM! STUDIOS

AVAILABLE AT YOUR LOCAL COMICS SHOP AND BOOKSTORE
To find a comics shop in your area, visit www.comicshoplocator.com
WWW.**BOOM-STUDIOS**.COM